D1559702

Distribution and
Development

Distribution and Development
A New Look at the
Developing World

Gary S. Fields

Russell Sage Foundation
New York, New York

The MIT Press
Cambridge, Massachusetts
London, England

This book was set in Palatino by Asco Typesetters, Hong Kong, in 3B2.
Printed and bound in the United States of America.

Library of Congress Cataloging-in-Publication Data

Fields, Gary S.
   Distribution and development : a new look at the developing world / Gary S. Fields.
      p.   cm.
   Includes bibliographical references and index.
   ISBN 0-262-06215-1 (alk. paper)
   1. Income distribution—Developing countries. 2. Poverty—Developing countries.
3. Developing countries—Economic conditions. I. Title.
HC59.72.I5 F54 2001
339.2'2'091724—dc21   00-064592

Contents

Preface

In 1980 I published a book entitled *Poverty, Inequality, and Development*. That book was adopted around the world by teachers of advanced courses in economics and other social sciences and by practitioners in national and international development agencies. It is a source of great pride to me that many of the leading people in the income distribution field today studied from that book or taught from it.

Poverty, Inequality, and Development's central questions were: Who benefits how much from economic growth, and why? Those are also the central questions of *Distribution and Development*. What has changed in the last two decades is not the questions but the answers. We are fortunate that more extensive data are now available. The concepts one can cover have broadened to include not only poverty and inequality but also income mobility and economic well-being. How we conceive of each of these concepts has also changed: the enormous gain in popularity of distributionally sensitive poverty measures, the rise and fall of the Kuznets curve, the analysis of newly available panel data gauging changes over time for given individuals or families, the use of dominance methods for comparisons of economic well-being, and the general acceptance of axiomatics and rigorous formulations of once-imprecise concepts. About all that is left of the earlier book are some examples and some of the intellectual history of this field.

For years I have had a story to tell, but not enough time in which to tell it, and so I was delighted when the Russell Sage Foundation offered to finance full-time research on this project at their headquarters in 1997/98. I thank the Foundation for providing an exceptional intellectual and living environment. The manuscript was completed the following year at DELTA (Département et Laboratoire

d'Economie Théorique et Appliquée) in Paris, France, and at the
School of Industrial and Labor Relations at Cornell University. I am
grateful to these institutions for their hospitality and support.

My deepest thanks go to my family. Vivian got me into this field—
literally a life-changing experience—but then she, Jeremy, and
Daniel had to put up with "Papa's trips," and later so did Alison. In
New York, Alison was my constant companion, and Vivian com-
muted weekly to be with us. It is in recognition of their adaptability,
good cheer, and love that I dedicate this book to them.

1   The Distributional Effects of Economic Growth

1.1   An Introduction to the Issues

The world contains 1.3 billion desperately poor people who subsist on less than one U.S. dollar per person per day, and another 1.7 billion who live on between one and two U.S. dollars per person per day (United Nations 1997; World Bank 1999). With such low incomes, they are unable to attain a minimal standard of living, as gauged by access to adequate food, clothing, shelter, clean water, sanitation facilities, education, and health services. In the world's most populous country, China, the poverty-line income will buy a "basic food bundle" (in kg/person/year) consisting of grain (216.72), vegetables (112.49), pork (9.22), fruits (4.50), vegetable oil (2.56), eggs (1.87), sugar (1.62), fish (1.26), beef and mutton (.59), milk products (.25), and poultry (.06) (Ravallion 1996). The world's billions of poor live on the "margin of life"—their material well-being, their happiness, and even, in the most severe cases, their very existence hanging in the balance.[1]

Income inequality is endemic. In Brazil the income share of the richest 20 percent of the population is thirty-two times that of the poorest 20 percent—a figure that has hardly changed since 1960. This means that for every dollar of income gain received by the poor, the rich have gotten $32. Exactly the same ratio is found on Manhattan Island in New York City. Depending on where you live and what you have seen, this may help you visualize just how unequal a highly unequal economy is.[2]

---

1. *Margin of Life* is the title of an excellent photojournalistic account by Capa and Stycos (1974).
2. The Brazil data are from the World Bank's *World Development Report 1994*. The United States data are from the U.S. Bureau of the Census.

Most of the world's poor live in the "underdeveloped" or "less developed" economies.[3] A country's economy may be said to be "underdeveloped" when its people face severely constrained choices. "Economic development" may then be thought of as the relaxation of the constraints on people's material standards of living, or alternatively, as the enlargement of people's choice sets and the expansion of their capabilities.[4] Improvements in material standards of living are not all there is to development, but that is the part of development that this book is about.

Economic development is sought primarily via economic growth. Economic growth rates in the world vary enormously. In the last twenty-five years, some countries (mostly in East Asia) achieved per capita GDP growth rates as high as +7.0 percent per annum, while others (mainly in Latin America and sub-Saharan Africa) declined at 5 percent annual rates.

This book asks, to what extent and in what circumstances does economic growth bring broad-based improvements in the material standards of living of a country's people? For a long time, the development economics community simply assumed that the answer was that the larger the pie, the larger would be everybody's piece. But not everyone was so sanguine. Prime Minister Jawaharlal Nehru of India said in 1960: "National income over the First and Second Plans has gone up by 42 percent and the per capita income by 20 percent. A legitimate query is made, where has this gone?" (quoted in Parikh and Srinivasan 1993, p. 408). A heated debate was mounted on shaky statistical foundations. The evidence was read in diametrically opposed ways by the conflicting parties. The following two statements represent the range of thinking at the time:

Development of the type experienced by the majority of Third World countries in the last quarter century has meant, for very large numbers of people, increased impoverishment. (Griffin and Khan 1978, p. 295)

Rapid sustained growth has had positive effects on the living standards of all economic groups of those countries that experienced it ... Growth has not "failed"; there has simply not been enough of it in the great majority of less developed nations. (Galenson 1977, pp. 21–22)

---

3. For profiles of who these poor are, see World Bank 1997a, forthcoming, and United Nations 1997, 1998.
4. "Enlargement of choices" features prominently in the work of the United Nations' *Human Development Reports* (various). "Capabilities and functionings" are central to the work of Nobel Prize winner Amartya Sen (e.g., Sen 1984, 1985, 1992, 1997, 1999).

The debate between "trickle-down" adherents on the one hand and "immiserizing growth" advocates on the other persisted for quite some time (Adelman and Morris 1973; Lewis 1976; Griffin 1989; Morley 1994; Rodgers and van der Hoeven 1995). Now, though, the two sides, though differing in emphasis, agree on two broad conclusions. One is that economic growth has raised the incomes of poor people and lowered the percentage in poverty. The other is that some particular groups have lost out because of changes accompanying economic growth. As the United Nations now acknowledges, "Both are right" (United Nations 1997, p. 72).

How have we gotten to this point? What should be measured to see whether progress is being made? What does the evidence show? What policies and circumstances have caused some countries to do better than others? These are the major questions addressed in this book.

1.2   The Major Approaches to Distributional Analysis

Different ways of analyzing the distributional effects of economic growth may be illustrated by means of four examples.[5] First, consider two hypothetical countries A and B, which initially are identical. After a period of time, national income data reveal that Country A grew by 9 percent (in real terms, adjusting for inflation) while Country B grew by 18 percent. In the absence of distributional data, we might simply suppose that because Country B grew faster than Country A, the people in Country B came to be better off faster than those in Country A. This conclusion, however, assumes the answer to our question of whether the material standards of living of a country's people are improved by economic growth—it doesn't show it. Let us take income as our measure of economic well-being and collect data on the distribution of income in the population. (What to measure is discussed later in this chapter.) Suppose we find that the income share of the poorest 40 percent of income recipients in each country was .363, but that their share fell to .333 in Country A and to .307 in Country B. Suppose too that we calculate a commonly used measure of income inequality, the Gini coefficient, and find that it rose from .082 to .133 in Country A and from .082 to .162

---

5. The first three of these were first published in Fields 1980.

in Country B.[6] Thus in this example there are two key facts: (1) Both economies grew, but Country B grew faster than Country A; (2) Income inequality increased in both economies, but it increased by more in Country B than in Country A. At this point, I invite you to decide whether economic development has taken place by asking yourself: Which do I prefer: the initial situation, the situation of Country A, or the situation of Country B?

Consider now a second example. Two hypothetical countries, C and D, initially start out with 10 percent of their people working in relatively high-wage jobs (paying a real wage of $2 to each worker) and with 90 percent of their people working in relatively low-wage jobs (paying a real wage of $1 to each).[7] After a certain period of time, we observe that 20 percent of the workers in Country C are in $2 jobs and 80 percent in $1 jobs, while in Country D, 30 percent are in the $2 jobs and 70 percent in the $1 jobs. Ask yourself again: Which do I prefer: the initial situation, the situation of Country C, or the situation of Country D?

The third example has two hypothetical countries, E and F, in both of which the poorest 40 percent of the people receive an average income of $40 each. We observe them later and find that the average income of the poorest 40 percent has remained at $40 in both countries. There is no point in asking which is preferable, E or F, because no progress appears to have been made.

Here now is our final example. In two hypothetical countries, G and H, we have data telling us not only people's current incomes but also their previous ones. Using these data, we find that in both countries, the nonpoor gained average income share while the poor lost. Furthermore, the difference between the average change in income share of the nonpoor and the poor was .044 in Country G and .047 in Country H. So in this example, the poor lost income share in both countries, but Country H exhibited a more disparate mobility experience than did Country G. Here too, you are invited to ask yourself which of these countries' experiences you would prefer, based on the available data.

We come now to the punch line: all of these examples come from the *same* underlying data. The initial situations were the same in all

---

6. Gini coefficients measure inequality. They range from zero in the case of perfect equality (everybody having the same income) to one in the case of perfect inequality (one person having everything and everyone else having nothing).

7. For simplicity, this example assumes that there is no unemployment.

three examples; Countries A, C, E, and G are the same country, and Countries B, D, F, and H are the same country. Their respective income distributions are:

Initial: $\underbrace{(1,1,1,1,1,1,1,1,1,}_{9} \underbrace{2)}_{1}$

A-C-E-G: $\underbrace{(1,1,1,1,1,1,1,1,}_{8} \underbrace{2,2)}_{2}$

B-D-F-H: $\underbrace{(1,1,1,1,1,1,1,}_{7} \underbrace{2,2,2)}_{3}$

The growth figures are obtained by noting that the total income goes from \$11 initially to \$12 in A-C-E-G (a 9 percent increase) to \$13 in B-D-F-H (an 18 percent increase). The income share of the poorest 40 percent is $4/11 = .363$ initially, $4/12 = .333$ in A-C-E-G, and $4/13 = .307$ in B-D-F-H. The percentages in high- and low-wage jobs are apparent. The average incomes of the poorest 40 percent in example 3 are calculated assuming that \$1 is an hourly wage and that each worker works a forty-hour work week.[8] The income mobility experiences of the currently poor and the currently nonpoor are detailed in the following footnote.[9]

---

8. How the Gini coefficient is calculated is explained in chapter 2.
9. Assume that the person who initially had an income of \$2 kept that income in both economies. The income changes in country G are then given by the following table:

Number of people	Initial income share	Final income share	Difference
8	$1/11 = 0.091$	$1/12 = 0.083$	−0.008
1	$1/11 = 0.091$	$2/12 = 0.167$	0.076
1	$2/11 = 0.182$	$2/12 = 0.167$	−0.015

We see that each of the ex post poor had a final year income share of $1/12 = .083$, an initial year income share of $1/11 = .091$, and thus a decline in income share of .008. In that same country, both of the ex post nonpoor had a final year income share of $2/12$; one had a base year income share of $2/11$ and the other a base year income share of $1/11$. These two individuals' changes in share are $+.076$ and $-.015$, producing an average income share change of $+.031$. The difference between the average share change of the non-poor and of the poor is then $+.031 - (-.008) = +.039$. Similar calculations for country H produce a disparity of $+.033 - (-.014) = +.047$. It is on this basis that one might conclude that there was a more disparate income mobility experience between the poor and the nonpoor in Country H than in Country G.

I have used the first three of these examples and asked these questions of literally thousands of students and colleagues in North America, South America, Europe, Africa, and Asia and have found very few who gave the same answer in each situation. The answers that have come back are the following: About half the respondents have said they prefer A to B. The justification commonly offered for this view is that A entails some growth (a good) and some increase in inequality (a bad) rather than the maximum amount of either one. Nearly everyone has expressed a preference for D over C. The only hesitation has been to question whether other things are equal— equal freedoms, for example—in the two cases. No one (except for a few jokesters) has favored E over F or the reverse. These examples show that one's view about economic growth—going so far as to question whether economic development takes place or not— depends on what one calculates.

I would now ask you to consider one last time which you prefer: the initial situation, the situation of Country A-C-E-G, or the situation of Country B-D-F-H? Did your answer change depending on how the data were processed?

These examples illustrate the major approaches to income distribution analysis. The first is the *relative inequality approach*: the income share of the poorest 40 percent and the Gini coefficient measure how inequality in the distribution of income changes. The second example illustrates the *absolute income approach*: how many people receive how much income (in real terms). A special case of the absolute income approach is the *absolute poverty approach*, in which a poverty line is drawn and a poverty measure is calculated (e.g., the percentage of people with incomes below the poverty line). The third example illustrates the *relative poverty approach*, because a group that is relatively the poorest (the poorest 40 percent in this case) is defined and their average incomes calculated. The fourth example demonstrates the kind of *income mobility analysis* that might be conducted when data are available for the same people over time. Combining these and looking, say, at the change in absolute poverty and in relative inequality (with negative weights assigned to each) is one way of analyzing *economic well-being*.

The point is this: The same data, processed in different ways, can lead to conflicting, even opposite, conclusions. It is important to understand why these different ways of measuring changes in income distribution produce different results. It is *not* because they are alternative measures of the same underlying entity, but rather because they are gauging different things.

1.3   Income Distribution as a Multifaceted Concept

"Income distribution" is not a single phenomenon; it is a generic term including mean growth, relative inequality, absolute poverty, income mobility, and economic well-being. In much the same way that the raw data for any random variable can be processed to give information on distinct aspects of the distribution—location (mean, median, mode), dispersion (minimum, maximum, range, variance), shape (skewness, kurtosis, etc.)—the raw data on incomes can be processed to inform us about different aspects of the income distribution. In the examples of the preceding section, these different aspects change in different ways—the mean increases, inequality increases, poverty decreases, and mobility experiences become more disparate—in each case, according to the measures presented. In actual countries' experiences as well, we find not only that these different aspects *can* change in different directions but that in fact they *do* change in different directions quite often. If one is to use such data to help gauge how material conditions of living are changing, it is therefore of the utmost importance to understand what one is doing when one compares statistics such as Gini coefficients, poverty headcount ratios, and share mobility rates, or when one uses dominance methods such as Lorenz curve comparisons, Generalized Lorenz curve comparisons, and cumulative density functions. These are *not* alternative measures of the same underlying distributional phenomenon; in fact, they measure quite different aspects of the distribution.

   As used throughout this book, the term "income distribution" will be reserved for an entire vector of incomes such as (1, 1, 1, 1, 1, 1, 1, 1, 1, 2). The phrase "income distribution improved (or worsened)" will be used to mean that a particular social welfare function $W(.)$ or a broad class of such functions evaluates one vector of incomes more highly than another. Examples of such functions, detailed in chapter 8, are quasi-Pareto improvements, abbreviated social welfare functions, and direct dominance orderings. If using such functions, we find that $W(Y_1) > W(Y_2)$, then Y_1 may be said to be "better" than Y_2. It is in this sense, and only in this sense, that the phrase "income distribution improved" will be used in this book. It will never be used to mean "the income distribution became more equal" or "poverty decreased."

1.4   Some Important Methodological Preliminaries

The Role of Theory

Theory plays an important role in this volume. As the examples earlier in this chapter indicate, different distributional concepts can yield quite different pictures of the distributional effects of growth. It is essential therefore to take care in clarifying each of these underlying notions. Then, having done so, various indices (or synonymously, "measures") may be assessed to see whether they are "good" indicators of what they purport to measure. In this way, the empirical analysis is guided by careful theoretical work on what the underlying distributional concepts are and what are good measures of them.

Theory is often used in empirical economics in another way, and that is to formulate empirical predictions that are then "tested" in data. Take, for example, the case of the famed Kuznets hypothesis, according to which income inequality tends to increase in the early stages of economic development and then decrease. Many theoretical models have been formulated which generate the Kuznets curve; these are surveyed by Glomm and Ravikumar (1994, 1995) and Aghion, Caroli, and García-Peñalosa (1999). As these authors demonstrate, the Kuznets curve can be generated from short-run increasing returns to scale, capital market imperfections, human capital accumulation, occupational choice, migration, trade liberalization, technical change, or the emergence of new organizational forms. It is interesting that all of these models were formulated decades *after* Kuznets formulated the inverted-U hypothesis, and indeed these models are not needed for "testing" the shape of the relationship between economic growth and income inequality. Even if an inverted-U shape were to appear as a broad empirical regularity, such a finding would not establish the validity of any particular underlying model. Instead, we can test the Kuznets curve hypothesis as an empirical proposition and, upon finding that the data reject it empirically (which is what we do find in chapter 3), we may then turn our attention to why inequality increases with economic growth in some countries and not in others. Inductive theory is likely to be much more promising than deductive theory at this point.

From Growth to Distribution or from Distribution to Growth?

There is ample reason to believe in dual causality, running from growth to distribution as well as from distribution to growth. Most of this book is concerned with the former, but chapter 10 addresses the latter.

The empirical literatures on the effect of growth on distribution and of distribution on growth are both vast. One point of intersection between them is in the literature on vicious and virtuous circles, the highlights of which are discussed in chapter 10. Another is in the simultaneous equations model formulated by Bourguignon (1994), reviewed in chapter 3. For the most part, however, the two literatures have proceeded almost entirely independently of one another, and this book does likewise.

The Distribution of What?

No single variable can possibly serve as a fully satisfactory measure of economic well-being (or, as it is sometimes called, "standard of living"). The question then is, what would be the best thing or things to measure?

The literature offers two broad two types of answers. One is to choose certain goods and services and measure the distribution of each of those, singly or together. Basic human needs advocates have called for direct measures of people's access to food, clothing, shelter, health care, education, etc. (ILO 1976; Streeten 1981). Life expectancy, adult literacy, and real GDP per capita have been combined into a Human Development Index by the United Nations (1990 and subsequent).

The other answer is to use data on income or consumption to proxy the ability of persons to afford to be adequately nourished, clothed, and housed. The great bulk of the work on distribution by economists has used this latter approach. Consumption is regarded as the best available proxy for long-term standard of living, but consumption data are often not available, so income measures are used instead. In either case, it is desirable to have as comprehensive a measure as possible, including not only earned income or what can be consumed from it but also nonlabor income, goods and services provided by the state, and imputed values for food and other goods and services produced and consumed at home. The World Bank's Living Standards Measurement Surveys, which have been conducted in many countries, provide relatively comprehensive measures, but in other countries, the information is far from ideal: "What was your income in pesos last month?" is a common type of question, but it is subject to recall error, rounding, and other types of misstatement. In such cases, we have little choice but to utilize the limited data available.

Additional choices need to be made. Because of income pooling within families, the family (or household) would be the better recipient unit. Total income or consumption should be adjusted on a per-capita or an adult-equivalent basis whenever possible. Systematic cost-of-living differences (rural/urban, for example) should be allowed for.

The literature on "distribution of what" is enormous. For more on these issues, see Anand and Ravallion 1993, Ravallion 1994, Fields 1994, Atkinson et al. 1995, Gottschalk and Smeeding 1997, and Sen 1997.

Data Concerns

The income distribution literature has walked a fine line between breadth of data coverage on the one hand and quality of data on the other. The compromise that has been reached in the literature is to use "minimally consistent data," that is, observations which are based on actual household surveys or censuses with national coverage and consistent definitions over time within a country (Fields 1991; Anand and Kanbur 1993a; Deininger and Squire 1996). Nonetheless, problems remain. It has been said, "There are many limitations to the data presented. They tell us nothing about expenditure, only about income; they omit important sources of income such as fringe benefits or capital gains or undisclosed earnings from the informal economy; they omit the benefits of government spending other than cash or near-cash transfers; they relate to the household and do not explore what happens within the family." These words come from the presidential address to the Royal Economic Society by A. B. Atkinson (1997, p. 299) who, for more than a quarter-century, has been one of the world's leading income distribution authorities and users of empirical data. Like Atkinson, I believe it is better to use what information we have than not to. Too much hinges on the answers to remain silent.

1.5   Plan for the Volume

In what follows, we will look in turn at inequality, poverty, income mobility, and economic well-being. To analyze and understand each, we must decide what each of these distributional concepts means and then make the necessary calculations from the available data. The rest of this book is structured accordingly.

The next eight chapters are organized in pairs, the first chapter in each pair dealing with theory and conceptual issues and the second with empirical evidence. Inequality is addressed in chapters 2 and 3, poverty in chapters 4 and 5, income mobility in chapters 6 and 7, and economic well-being in chapters 8 and 9. Chapter 10 turns to policy and discusses a range of policies for broad-based growth.

2   The Meaning and Measurement of Income Inequality

Occasionally in our field, a single piece of work changes the course of an entire research program. Such was the case with Simon Kuznets's 1954 Presidential Address to the American Economic Association on "Economic Growth and Income Inequality." Kuznets began his address by saying: "The central theme of this paper is the character and causes of long-term changes in the personal distribution of income. Does inequality in the distribution of income increase or decrease in the course of a country's economic growth? What factors determine the secular level and trends of income inequalities?" (Kuznets 1955, p. 1).

He concluded:

The excuse for building an elaborate structure on such a shaky foundation is a deep interest in the subject and the wish to share it with members of the Association. The formal and no less genuine excuse is that the subject is central to much of economic analysis and thinking; that our knowledge of it is inadequate; that a more cogent view of the whole field may help channel our interests and work in intellectually profitable directions; that speculation is an effective way of presenting a broad view of the field; and that so long as it is recognized as a collection of hunches calling for further investigation rather than a set of fully tested conclusions, little harm and much good may result. (Kuznets 1955, p. 26)

As a direct result of Kuznets's efforts, for the last forty years, economists and other social scientists have dealt with the effect of economic growth on income inequality.[1]

---

1. Because of Kuznets's focus on inequality as opposed to poverty, it was not until twenty years later that poverty moved to center stage in mainstream development economics. However, elsewhere, the concern with poverty as opposed to inequality came much sooner. The government of India's early concern for poverty alleviation, as expressed in the 1962 Fifteen Year Development Plan, is recounted in Srinivasan and Bardhan 1974.

In chapter 3, we will review the empirical evidence on this issue. But before doing so, it is necessary to be clear about the meaning of inequality, the ways of measuring how much of it there is, and ways of determining whether it is larger or smaller in one time period or country than another. Those are the tasks of this chapter.

2.1   The Meaning of Inequality

"Inequality" has been likened to an elephant: You can't define it, but you know it when you see it. Unfortunately, such vague notions of inequality cannot be quantified or taken to data, so we must push ahead, relying primarily on introspection. By asking ourselves how the inequality (or later, the poverty or income mobility or social welfare) in one situation compares with that of another, we impose properties (or "axioms") which define the very meaning of "inequality." Taken together, these properties lead to specific analytical tools of measurement, including both numerical measures for cardinalizing inequality and a graphical method for making ordinal inequality comparisons.

We will need the following notation and concepts in what follows. Let y_i be the "income" (or more generally, the measure of economic well-being) of income recipient i. An "income distribution" is a vector of the form $Y = (y_1, \ldots, y_n)$. The set of all income distributions under consideration is represented by $\Omega := \{Y | Y \in \mathfrak{R}^n\}$. These distributions are expressed in units of the same real currency so that they are directly comparable to each other. Given two vectors $X, Y \in \Omega$ the relation $\succeq$ (read "at least as equal as") provides a basis for comparing their inequalities. Suppose both $X \succeq Y$ and $Y \succeq X$. In that case, we shall say that X and Y are "equally unequal" and write this relation as $\sim$, that is, $X \sim Y \Leftrightarrow X \succeq Y$ and $Y \succeq X$. The binary relations $\succeq$ and $\sim$ are assumed to satisfy reflexivity $\mathbf{R}$ ($X \succeq X$ and $X \sim X$ for all $X \in \Omega$) and transitivity $\mathbf{Tr}$ (if $X \succeq X'$ and $X' \succeq X''$, then $X \succeq X''$ and likewise for $\sim$). If $X \succeq Y$ but not $X \sim Y$, we shall say that X is "more equal than" Y and denote this relation as $\succ$.

Let us now begin our introspection. Consider a population consisting of four persons named α, β, γ, and δ, having incomes \$1, \$2, \$3, and \$4, respectively. We write this as the named vector

$$Y_1 = (1, \quad 2, \quad 3, \quad 4).$$
$$\quad\quad \alpha, \quad \beta, \quad \gamma, \quad \delta$$

Now consider a second population in which the incomes are also $1, $2, $3, and $4, but these amounts accrue to different recipients; for instance:

$$Y_2 = (1, \quad 2, \quad 3, \quad 4).$$
$$\quad\;\; \delta, \quad \gamma, \quad \beta, \quad \alpha$$

How do the inequalities of Y_1 and Y_2 compare?

Unless there is something different about the income recipients in the two cases, it is appealing to say that Y_1 and Y_2 have the same inequality.[2] The idea that it suffices to look only at the income amounts received (when possible, adjusted for family size and family composition) without having to pay attention to the names of the particular individuals receiving those income amounts is the property of *anonymity*. Thus, if one income distribution is a permutation of another, then the two are equally unequal. More formally:

A1—ANONYMITY (**A**): If $X \in \Omega$ is obtained from $Y \in \Omega$ by a permutation of Y, then $X \sim Y$.

Anonymity enables us to look just at the income amounts themselves, which we will do from now on.

A second issue is how to compare inequalities in economies with different total income amounts. How, for instance, does the inequality of

$$Y_3 = (2, 4, 6, 8)$$

compare with that of

$$Y_1 = (1, 2, 3, 4)?$$

Two kinds of answers are typically given.

One answer is that Y_3 is manifestly more unequal that Y_1. The income difference between the richest person and the poorest person in Y_3 is twice what it is in Y_1. The variance of incomes in Y_3 is four times the variance in Y_1. And so on.

---

2. If, in fact, there *are* important differences in the two situations, these differences should be reflected in the base itself. Suppose, for instance, that the recipient unit is the family and that high-income families in one situation are systematically larger than those in another, and therefore have greater needs. We would do better to gauge economic well-being using a per capita adjustment or some other equivalence scale rather than by using total family income, and we should adjust the underlying data accordingly before making inequality comparisons.

A second answer is that the inequalities of Y_3 and Y_1 are the same. In each case, the richest person is four times as rich as the poorest person. In both Y_3 and Y_1, the richest person receives 40 percent of total income and the poorest person 10 percent. The coefficients of variation are .447 in both cases.

Which is it? Are the inequalities the same or different? The distinction here is between two fundamentally different concepts of inequality. *Absolute inequality*, which is what is being measured in the first answer, relies on dollar *differences* in real incomes. By contrast, in the second answer, what is being measured is *relative inequality*, which is measured in terms of income *ratios*. Absolute inequality and relative inequality are not alternative measures of the same underlying concept; they measure fundamentally different concepts.

There are three reasons why you might want to choose to use relative inequality measures. One is pure conceptual appeal, based on what you "see" when you compare the inequality of Y_3 with that of Y_1. If these two distributions "look" equally unequal to you, your judgment is a relative inequality one.

The other two reasons are practical. Virtually the entire literature on distribution and development, from Kuznets 1955 onward, uses such measures, and to use anything else would be to present one's measure of apples against everyone else's measure of oranges.[3] But leaving this aside, if absolute inequality measures were to be used, we would have to conclude as a practical matter that economic growth *always* raises income inequality and economic recession always lowers it, because empirically the dollar differences in real incomes between rich and poor and the variance of incomes *always* increase with economic growth and decline with economic recession.[4] So if you choose an absolute inequality measure, you will get an answer, but if you choose a relative inequality measure, you will as often as not get a different one. Which you choose depends on what you think the right answer is in comparing Y_3 with Y_1. I join the vast majority of inequality analysts in favoring relative inequality measures over absolute inequality ones and therefore accept the following general axiom:

---

3. Of course, there are times when being contrarian advances scientific understanding, but one has to be careful about it.
4. More precisely, I have yet to see a place where this relationship does not hold.

A2—INCOME HOMOGENEITY (ALSO CALLED SCALE INDEPENDENCE) (**H**): If $X \in \Omega$ is obtained from $Y \in Z$ by multiplying everyone's income by the same positive scalar multiple λ, then $X \sim Y$.

A third issue is how to compare populations of different sizes. Suppose that one population is a scale replica of another; for instance,

$$Y_4 = (2, 2, 4, 4, 6, 6, 8, 8)$$

is obtained from

$$Y_3 = (2, 4, 6, 8)$$

by replicating each income a second time. How do the inequalities of Y_3 and Y_4 compare?

It would probably not be a good idea to judge Y_4 to be more unequal than Y_3 simply because Y_4 has more people, and therefore more income differences, than Y_3. This means that we need some criterion for comparing inequalities in populations of different sizes. Many people find it appealing to regard the inequalities of Y_3 and Y_4 as the same. More generally, when one income distribution is an n-fold replication of another, you may want to regard the two distributions as equally unequal. This idea can be formalized as:

A3—POPULATION HOMOGENEITY (ALSO CALLED POPULATION INDE- PENDENCE) (**P**): If $X \in \Omega$ is obtained from $Y \in \Omega$ by replicating each income an integral number of times, then $X \sim Y$.

Finally, we have a property that goes back to the beginning of this century in the work of Pigou (1912) and Dalton (1920), and that is the question of what happens when a transfer of income is made from someone who is relatively rich to someone who is relatively poor, holding their ranks in the income distribution the same. Suppose, for example, that the richest person in Y_3 transfers a dollar of income to the poorest person, producing the new income distribution

$$Y_5 = (3, 4, 6, 7).$$

The judgment that such a transfer reduces inequality, and therefore Y_5 is more equal (less unequal) than Y_3, commands widespread, though not universal, support.[5] This idea can be expressed as follows:

---

5. For experimental evidence on this point, see Amiel and Cowell 1994.

A4—TRANSFER PRINCIPLE (ALSO CALLED THE PIGOU-DALTON CONDI-
TION) (**T**):   If, holding all other incomes the same, $X \in \Omega$ is obtained
from $Y \in \Omega$ by transferring a positive amount of income from a relatively rich person α to a relatively poor person β while keeping α's
and β's ranks in the income distribution the same, then $X \succ Y$.

These four ideas—anonymity (**A**), income homogeneity (**H**),
population homogeneity (**P**), and the transfer principle (**T**)—are
powerful ones that receive a great deal of support in the inequality
literature. We shall denote the class of inequality relations that
satisfy these four properties, along with reflexivity (**R**) and transitivity (**Tr**), by $\succeq_I$.

If you accept the properties in relation $\succeq_I$, what should you do (or
not do)? We will answer this question shortly. First, though, we need
to consider another important tool in inequality analysis, that of
Lorenz curves.

2.2   Lorenz Curves and Lorenz Curve Comparisons

Lorenz curves were first suggested by Lorenz (1905). The Lorenz
curve is a graphical depiction of an income distribution, constructed
as follows. The population (of size n) is ordered from lowest income
to highest. On the horizontal axis, plot the cumulative percentage of
population: poorest $1/n$th, poorest $2/n$th, etc. On the vertical axis,
plot the cumulative percentage of income received by each cumulative percentage of population. The graph of cumulative percentage of
income against cumulative percentage of (ordered) population is the
Lorenz curve. In the case of the income distribution

$Y_1 = (1, 2, 3, 4),$

the points on the Lorenz curve are

Cumulative percentage of population	Cumulative percentage of income
0	0
25	10
50	30
75	60
100	100

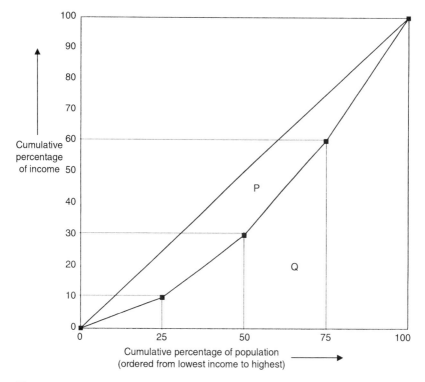

Figure 2.1
Lorenz curve for $Y = (1, 2, 3, 4)$

and the graph is as shown in figure 2.1, the points being connected by straight lines.

Because the population of income recipients is ordered from lowest income to highest, the change in the cumulative percentage of income is always (weakly) larger for income recipient i than it is for recipient $i-1$, and therefore Lorenz curves always have the convex shape shown in figure 2.1. The two limiting values are of particular interest. If the income distribution were *perfectly equal*, with each income recipient receiving $1/n$th of total income, the poorest $1/n$th of the population would receive $1/n$th of the income, the poorest $2/n$ths would receive $2/n$ths of the income, and so on, in which case the Lorenz curve would lie along the 45-degree line. At the other extreme, if the income distribution were *perfectly unequal*, with one person receiving all the income and everyone else receiving nothing, the poorest $1/n$th, $2/n$ths, ... $(n-1)/n$ths would receive nothing, but the poorest 100 percent would receive 100 percent of the income, and

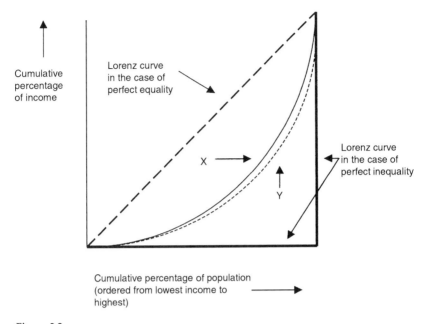

Figure 2.2
Lorenz curve when distribution X Lorenz dominates distribution Y

therefore the Lorenz curve would lie along the bottom and right-vertical axes.

These considerations lead to the intuition that the closer is the Lorenz curve to the 45-degree line, the more equal (less unequal) is the underlying distribution of income. By the same logic, we are also led to the following intuition for inequality comparisons of two income distributions $X, Y \in \Omega$: If the Lorenz curve for distribution X lies somewhere above and never below the Lorenz curve for distribution Y, then X is said to *Lorenz-dominate* Y, denoted $L_X > L_Y$. When one distribution Lorenz-dominates another, then the one that dominates is more equal than the one that is dominated. Lorenz-domination is illustrated in figure 2.2. This idea may be formalized as:

L.1—INEQUALITY COMPARISONS IN THE CASE OF LORENZ-DOMINANCE: For two distributions $X, Y \in \Omega$, if distribution X Lorenz-dominates distribution Y (which we write as $L_X > L_Y$), then X is more equal than Y by the Lorenz criterion ($\succ_L$), that is, $L_X > L_Y \Rightarrow X \succ_L Y$.

Although the Lorenz curve for one income distribution *may* dominate that of another, it is not necessary that this happen. Two cases may be distinguished. On the one hand, compare the Lorenz curve for

$$Y_3 = (2, 4, 6, 8)$$

with that of

$$Y_1 = (1, 2, 3, 4).$$

Because the cumulative income shares for each cumulative population share are the same for the two distributions, their Lorenz curves are identical. Therefore, the Lorenz curves for Y_1 and Y_3 lie equally close to the line of perfect equality (or perfect inequality), and for this reason, it is reasonable to say that two distributions with the same Lorenz curve have the same degree of inequality. This property may be generalized as:

L.2—INEQUALITY COMPARISONS IN THE CASE OF LORENZ-COINCIDENCE: For two distributions $X, Y \in \Omega$, if distribution X has the same Lorenz curve as distribution Y (which we write as $L_X = L_Y$), then X and Y are equally unequal by the Lorenz criterion ($=_L$), that is, $L_X = L_Y \Rightarrow X =_L Y$.

There is a third possibility: that when Lorenz curves are plotted, they cross. For instance, the Lorenz curves for

$$M = (10, 20, 30, 40)$$

and

$$N = (10, 22, 25, 43)$$

are given by

Cumulative percentage of population	Cumulative percentage of income in distribution M	Cumulative percentage of income in distribution N
0	0	0
25	10	10
50	30	32
75	60	57
100	100	100

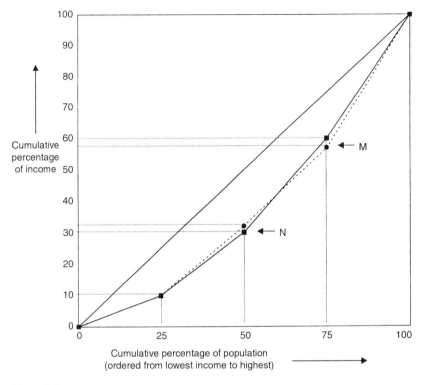

Figure 2.3
The Lorenz curve for $M = (10, 20, 30, 40)$ crosses the Lorenz curve for $N = (10, 22, 25, 43)$

The crossing of the Lorenz curves for M and N is displayed in figure 2.3.

How can inequalities be compared when Lorenz curves cross? The simple answer is that they can't using Lorenz comparisons alone. Furthermore, different relative inequality measures will give different answers. In the preceding example, if we measure inequality by the income share of the poorest 50 percent of the population (with higher values signifying greater equality, because we are comparing income shares of the poorest), we would judge N to be *more equal* than M. But if we instead choose as our measure the income share of the richest 25 percent, we would find that this share is larger in N than in M, and would accordingly judge N to be *more unequal* than M. Indeed, when Lorenz curves cross, we can *always* find different relative inequality measures that will disagree, which is why a comparison of Lorenz curves alone does not enable inequality comparisons to be made in such cases. Specifically, we have:

L.3—INEQUALITY COMPARISONS IN THE CASE OF LORENZ-CROSSINGS: If the Lorenz curves of two income distributions X and Y cross, then the inequality of the two distributions cannot be compared using the Lorenz criterion alone.

Together, the three Lorenz criteria L.1–L.3 define the *Lorenz ordering* and are denoted by $\succeq_L$. The Lorenz ordering gives us a practical way of deciding when one income distribution is more or less equal than another. See which holds: Lorenz-dominance, Lorenz-coincidence, or Lorenz-crossing. Rankings can be made in cases of Lorenz-dominance and Lorenz-coincidence but not Lorenz-crossing. It bears repeating that the ordering produced by Lorenz curve comparisons is incomplete, in the sense that certain pairs of income distributions cannot be ranked.[6]

2.3   Lorenz Curves and Inequality Comparisons

In section 2.1, we considered four aspects of "inequality" which many observers regard as desirable. Likewise in section 2.2, we considered three criteria for Lorenz comparisons of inequality. How do these four aspects of "inequality" and the three Lorenz criteria relate to each other? The relation is given by the following theorem:

THEOREM: The inequality ranking $\succeq_I$ and the Lorenz ranking $\succeq_L$ are equivalent.[7]

The practical import of this theorem is the following: When you rank the inequalities of two income distributions according to their Lorenz curves, you are accepting reflexivity ($\mathbf{R}$), transitivity ($\mathbf{Tr}$), anonymity ($\mathbf{A}$), income homogeneity ($\mathbf{H}$), population homogeneity ($\mathbf{P}$), and the transfer principle ($\mathbf{T}$)—which, in view of the equivalence of $\succeq_I$ and $\succeq_L$, may be termed collectively the *Lorenz-properties* ($\mathbf{L}$).[8] If you don't

---

6. If we were willing to commit to a particular inequality measure and abide by the results of the calculation, inequality comparisons could always be made. But absent that, this is as far as Lorenz comparisons can take us. More will be said about inequality measures below.
7. See Foster 1985 for a proof and a review of the relevant literature.
8. They are also called the "relative inequality properties."

want to accept one or another of these properties, you shouldn't rank inequalities according to Lorenz curves. The advantage of ranking inequalities according to Lorenz curves is that most observers accept the Lorenz rankings when rankings are provided. The disadvantage is that the Lorenz criterion is incomplete, namely, when Lorenz curves cross, nothing can be said. Actually, the measures that satisfy the axioms may render different rankings because, from the corollary, if there is no unambiguous Lorenz ranking then there is no unanimous ranking among measures. These features are explored in further depth in the next two sections.

2.4   A Note on Dominance Analysis in Theory and Practice

What we have just done in comparing Lorenz curves is to use a methodology known as *dominance analysis*. That is, we have seen that when a certain condition holds (in this case, Lorenz-dominance or Lorenz-coincidence), ordinal rankings of inequality can be gotten not only for a particular inequality measure but for a *broad class* of inequality measures. The preceding theorem tells us exactly what that class is: the class of inequality measures satisfying the Lorenz-properties (**L**). (Which measures these are will be discussed below.) These are called the "Lorenz-consistent inequality measures." So if you want to use a particular Lorenz-consistent inequality measure $I_1(.)$ and someone else wants to use a different Lorenz-consistent inequality measure $I_2(.)$, or if you are not sure *which* inequality measure $I_1(.), I_2(.), \ldots, I_K(.)$ you prefer but you know that you definitely want the measure you use to be Lorenz-consistent, we know that your ordinal rankings will *always agree* in cases of Lorenz-dominance or Lorenz-coincidence but that they *will not necessarily agree* in cases of Lorenz-crossing.

Lorenz-dominance is one type of dominance analysis. What we have in dominance analysis in general is a conditional statement of the form: When certain conditions are fulfilled, all who accept a specified set of properties will agree on the same ordinal ranking. Specifically, in the context of Lorenz curve comparisons for inequality orderings, we have: When the Lorenz curve for distribution X dominates that for distribution Y, all who accept the Lorenz-properties **L** would rank distribution X as more equal than distribution Y.

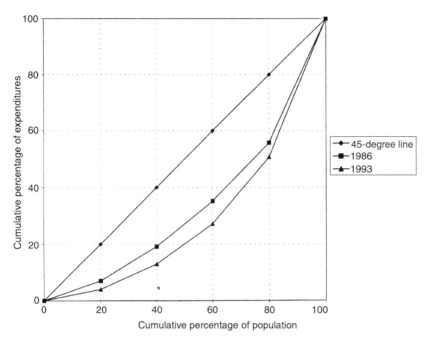

Figure 2.4
Nigeria: Lorenz curves of expenditures, 1986 and 1993

How useful is Lorenz-dominance in actual practice? Lorenz-dominance arises quite often. The following table gives the data on the distribution of expenditure for two different years in Nigeria:

Cumulative percentage of population	Cumulative share of expenditure in Nigeria, 1986	Cumulative share of expenditure in Nigeria, 1993
0	0.00	0.00
20	.0696	.0399
40	.1916	.1292
60	.3523	.2729
80	.5580	.5070
100	1.00	1.00

These data are plotted in figure 2.4, where we see that the 1986 Lorenz curve dominates the 1993 one. Using criterion L.1, this means

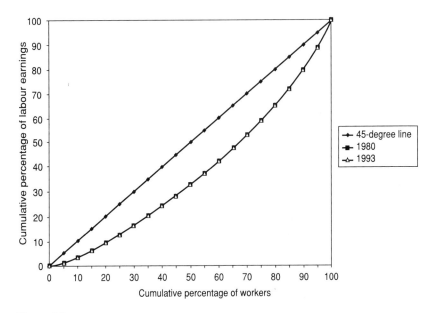

Figure 2.5
Taiwan: Lorenz curves of labor earnings, 1980 and 1993
Source: Fields and O'Hara Mitchell 1999, figure 5.2.

that that country's distribution of expenditures became more unequal over that seven year period. It also means, using the theorem of section 2.3, that all inequality measures that accept the properties of section 2.1 would rank the 1993 distribution as more unequal than the 1986 one.

A second possibility that we have considered is that two Lorenz curves may coincide. Coincidence of Lorenz curves does not happen often in empirical research, but it does happen occasionally. Such a case is shown in figure 2.5, where the Lorenz curves for income-earners in Taiwan in 1980 and 1993 are plotted. Taiwan's real per capita income increased by 121 percent in those thirteen years. The coincidence of Lorenz curves means that for every vingtile (each 5 percent grouping), real income increased by almost exactly 121 percent. By criterion L.2, given that these two Lorenz curves coincide, we may conclude that relative inequality among income earners in Taiwan was unchanged.

There is a third possibility: that when Lorenz curves are plotted, they cross. For instance, this happens when the Lorenz curves for Nepal in 1995 and for Estonia in 1995 are plotted:

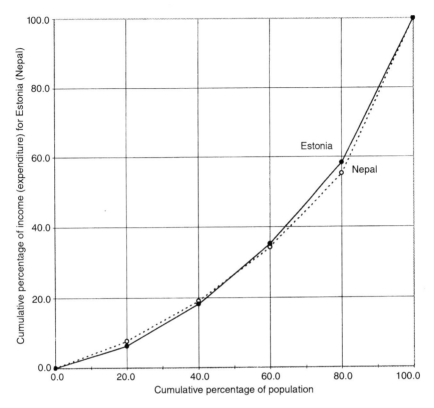

Figure 2.6
Lorenz curves for Nepal and Estonia, 1995
Source: World Bank 1999, World Development Indicators, pp. 70–71.

Cumulative percentage of population	Cumulative percentage of expenditures in Nepal, 1995	Cumulative percentage of income in Estonia, 1995
0	0	0
20	7.6	6.2
40	19.1	18.2
60	34.2	35.2
80	55.2	58.3
100	100	100

Source: World Bank 1999, World Development Indicators, pp. 70–71.

In this case, they cross between the fortieth and the sixtieth percentiles of the income distribution. The crossing of these Lorenz curves is displayed in figure 2.6.

How can inequalities be compared when Lorenz curves cross? The simple answer is that they can't using Lorenz comparisons alone; an inequality measure must be used to get an answer. In the preceding example, if we measure inequality by the income share of the poorest 40 percent of the population (with higher values signifying greater equality, because we are comparing income shares of the poorest), we will judge Nepal to be *more equal* than Estonia. But if we instead choose as our measure the income share of the richest 20 percent, we will find that this share is larger in Nepal than in Estonia, and will accordingly judge Nepal to be *more unequal* than Estonia.

To repeat a point made earlier, when Lorenz curves cross, we can always find different relative inequality measures that will give opposite answers. This is why a comparison of Lorenz curves alone does not enable inequality comparisons to be made in such cases and why those analysts who wish to make rankings in cases of Lorenz crossings must adopt specific inequality measures. It is to this topic that we now turn.[9]

2.5   Inequality Measures and Lorenz Comparisons

Continuing with our analysis of the question of which of two income distributions is more equal than another, you need to decide how you will treat cases of Lorenz-crossing. If you are willing to accept properties A.1–A.4 of section 2.1 *and only those properties*, then when Lorenz curves cross, you will have nothing to say about which income distribution is more or less equal than another. All you can say in that case is, "I cannot say." But if you *do* want to make inequality comparisons even when Lorenz curves cross, you must impose additional properties, which would reduce (but not necessarily eliminate) the extent of incompleteness. Although some authors (e.g., Shorrocks and Foster 1987; Fields 1993) have proposed such additional properties, most of the literature has gone in a different direction, which is to choose inequality measures that are consistent with the Lorenz

9. The topic of dominance analysis will come up again for poverty rankings in chapter 4, for mobility comparisons in chapter 6, and for rankings of economic well-being in chapter 8.

ordering whenever Lorenz comparisons can be made but which go beyond the Lorenz ordering to give rankings even in cases of Lorenz crossings. We turn now to these inequality measures.

A number of inequality measures are defined in table 2.1.[10] Formally, an *inequality measure* (also termed a "numerical inequality measure" or an "inequality index") is defined to be a function $I(.) : \mathfrak{R}^n \to \mathfrak{R}$ determining how much inequality there is for a given vector of incomes $X = (x_1 x_2 \ldots x_n)$. An inequality measure is a *relative inequality measure* if it satisfies income homogeneity, that is, if $I(\lambda X) = I(X)$ for all $\lambda > 0$. We will work primarily with relative inequality measures in what follows.

Earlier, we compared the inequalities of the distributions

$$M = (10, 20, 30, 40)$$

and

$$N = (10, 22, 25, 43),$$

for which the Lorenz curves cross (figure 2.3), and saw that (i) using the income share of the poorest 50 percent of the population, N is *more equal* than M, but (ii) using the income share of the richest 25 percent, N is *more unequal* than M. The use of a particular inequality measure embodies a judgment. In this case, the judgment is whether we are more concerned about the income share of the rich or of the poor, and that judgment is implicit in the very choice of whether to use the income share of the richest x percent or poorest y percent. For other inequality indices (in particular, for the Atkinson index, discussed below), a subjective element enters explicitly: in the case of the Atkinson index, it is the inequality-aversion parameter ε. Some people think that when no such subjective element appears explicitly, the inequality measure is ipso facto objective. This reasoning is wrong: *all* inequality measures have subjective elements.[11] Sometimes those elements are explicit, sometimes not. Our task, at this

---

10. In addition, there are other familiar inequality measures including the variance and the standard deviation. Good introductions to inequality measures can be found in Sen 1973, Allison 1978, Atkinson 1983a, Jenkins 1991, Cowell 1995, 1999, Foster and Sen 1997, Wolff 1997, and Ray 1998.

11. This point is discussed carefully by Atkinson (1970) and Sen (1973). Some inequality measures are more sensitive to income changes at the top of the income distribution, some at the middle of the distribution, and some at the bottom. The classic analysis of this particular issue is by Champernowne (1974).

Table 2.1
Income inequality measures

Measure	Definition
Income share of the richest $R\%$	$S_R = \dfrac{\sum_{i=n^{(1-R)}+1}^{n^{100}} x_i}{n\mu_x}$
Income share of the poorest $P\%$	$S_P = \dfrac{\sum_{i=1}^{n^P} x_i}{n\mu_x}$
90–10 ratio	$R_{90-10} = x_{n^{90}}/x_{n^{10}}$
$R\% - P\%$ ratio	$R_{R-P} = x_{n^R}/x_{n^P}$
Gini	$G = \dfrac{-(n+1)}{n} + \dfrac{2}{n^2\mu_x}\sum_{i=1}^{n} i x_i$
Theil's first measure	$T = \dfrac{1}{n}\sum_{i=1}^{n}\dfrac{x_i}{\mu_x}\ln\left(\dfrac{x_i}{\mu_x}\right)$
Atkinson	$A_\varepsilon = \begin{cases} 1 - \left[\dfrac{1}{n}\sum_{i=1}^{n}\left(\dfrac{x_i}{\mu_x}\right)^\varepsilon\right]^{1/\varepsilon} & \text{for } \varepsilon \leq 1 \text{ and } \varepsilon \neq 0 \\ 1 - \prod_{i=1}^{n}\left(\dfrac{x_i}{\mu_x}\right)^{1/n} & \text{for } \varepsilon = 0 \end{cases}$
Generalized entropy	$I_\alpha = \begin{cases} \dfrac{1}{\alpha(1-\alpha)}\dfrac{1}{n}\sum_{i=1}^{n}\left[1 - \left(\dfrac{x_i}{\mu_x}\right)^\alpha\right] & \text{for } \alpha \neq 0,1 \\ \dfrac{1}{n}\sum_{i=1}^{n}\dfrac{x_i}{\mu_x}\ln\left(\dfrac{x_i}{\mu_x}\right) & \text{for } \alpha = 1 \\ \dfrac{1}{n}\sum_{i=1}^{n}\ln\left(\dfrac{\mu_x}{x_i}\right) & \text{for } \alpha = 0 \end{cases}$

Source: Author's derivations and Sen 1997.
Notes:
Recipients are ordered from lowest income to highest
x_i = income of recipient i
μ_x = average income
n^Q = cumulative Q'th percentile
n = total number of recipients

point, is to search for good inequality measures, where "good" means that it represents what we want it to.[12]

Three sets of inequality measures may be distinguished based on how they treat situations of Lorenz-dominance:

1. An inequality measure $I(.)$ is *strongly Lorenz-consistent* if (i) whenever one Lorenz curve $L(X)$ dominates another $L(Y)$, $I(X) > I(Y)$, and (ii) whenever two Lorenz curves coincide, $I(X) = I(Y)$. (Note the strict inequality in 1.i.)

2. An inequality measure is *weakly Lorenz-consistent* if (i) whenever one Lorenz curve $L(X)$ dominates another $L(Y)$, $I(X) \geq I(Y)$, and (ii) whenever two Lorenz curves coincide, $I(X) = I(Y)$. (Note the weak inequality in 2.i.)

3. An inequality measure is *Lorenz-inconsistent* if ever, when one Lorenz curve dominates another, $I(X) < I(Y)$.

Inequality measures fall into these three categories as follows:

1. Among the inequality measures that are *strongly-Lorenz-consistent* are the Gini coefficient, Theil's two measures, the Atkinson index, and the coefficient of variation.

2. Among the inequality measures that are *weakly but not strongly Lorenz-consistent* are the income shares of the richest x percent and poorest y percent, the m percent/n percent ratio (e.g., the 90/10 ratio), and the relative mean deviation.

3. Among the inequality measures that are *Lorenz-inconsistent* are the variance, the standard deviation, and the log variance.[13]

---

12. The task here parallels that of constructing a utility function that adequately represents consumer preferences in standard consumer theory. The word "represents" is used here in the following technical sense. Let S and T be two preordered sets, and denote by $\preceq_S$ (respectively $\preceq_T$) the preordering on S (respectively on T). A function f from S to T is said to be a *representation* of S in T if

$X \sim_S Y$ implies $f(X) \sim_T f(Y)$

and

$X \prec_S Y$ implies $f(X) \prec_T f(Y)$.

13. The variance and standard deviation are not Lorenz-consistent because they violate income homogeneity (**H**). The log-variance is not Lorenz-consistent, because certain transfers from someone relatively rich to someone relatively poor may *increase* the log-variance. The problems with the log-variance are discussed thoroughly by Foster and Ok (1999).

Several remarks may be made:

• The measures that are only weakly but not strongly Lorenz-consistent generally use some but not all of the data.

• Given two Lorenz-consistent inequality measures $I_1(.)$ and $I_2(.)$, if ever $I_1(X) > I_1(Y)$ and $I_2(X) < I_2(Y)$, then the Lorenz curves of X and Y necessarily cross.[14]

• The income share of the poorest person is *not* Lorenz-consistent.[15]

2.6 About the Gini Coefficient

Of the strongly Lorenz-consistent inequality measures, the one that is used most often in empirical work is the Gini coefficient. Although the formula in table 2.1 provides an exact definition, you may find it easier to understand what the Gini coefficient is by turning back to figure 2.1. There, you see that the area between the Lorenz curve and the 45-degree line is denoted by P, and the area between the Lorenz curve and the horizontal and right-vertical axes is denoted by Q. By definition, the Gini coefficient $G \equiv P/(P+Q)$.

The Lorenz-consistency of the Gini coefficient is readily verified. *Anonymity* holds, because if we permute the income distribution, we get the same Lorenz curve and hence the same Gini coefficient. *Income homogeneity* holds, because if everyone's income is multiplied by the same positive scalar multiple λ, the Lorenz curve is unchanged, and therefore the Gini coefficient is unchanged as well. *Population homogeneity* holds, because if we replicate the population an integral number of times, the new points will lie along the straight lines connecting the original points, and therefore the Lorenz curve will be the same and the Gini coefficient will be unchanged.[16] Finally, the *transfer principle* holds, because when a rank-preserving transfer is made from a relatively rich individual j to a relatively poorer

14. In particular, if, for some $a, b > 0$, the income share of the richest a percent of the population is found to be higher in X than in Y and if the income share of the poorest b percent is also found to be higher in X than in Y, then the Lorenz curves of X and Y must cross somewhere between a and b.

15. This is because the income share of the poorest person violates population homogeneity (**P**), and thus Rawlsians (see chapter 8 for a definition) would not want to accept this axiom. However, in no way does this rule out the use of the income of the poorest person as an indicator of poverty or economic well-being.

16. This is true if and only if the points on the Lorenz curve are connected by straight lines, which is why we have done so: population homogeneity requires it.

individual i, the Lorenz curve will shift upward between i and j, causing the Gini coefficient to decline, thereby signifying less inequality.[17] We have thus demonstrated that the four Lorenz properties are satisfied by the Gini coefficient, and therefore the Gini coefficient is strongly Lorenz-consistent.

Because the Gini coefficient can always be calculated, we know that we can rank the inequalities of two income distributions even when Lorenz curves cross. Therefore, the Gini coefficient completes the ordinal ranking which the Lorenz-ordering leaves incomplete. Note too that the answer it gives is a cardinal answer.[18]

Finally, there is the question of whether, when Lorenz curves cross, the answer given by comparisons of Gini coefficients is "better" or "worse" than the answer given by other Lorenz-consistent inequality measures. Specialists tend to regard the Gini coefficient as about as good as any other measure.[19] This careful examination of the Gini coefficient's properties, combined with its familiarity, is why the Gini is used so much empirically.

2.7 Summary

In this chapter, we have considered the meaning of "inequality" and have regarded four properties as desirable: anonymity, income homogeneity, population homogeneity, and the transfer principle. We also considered the three Lorenz criteria for making inequality comparisons and observed that the Lorenz criteria are exactly equivalent to the preceding four properties. In cases of Lorenz-dominance and Lorenz-coincidence, we can get an inequality ranking using the

---

17. The amount of the shift is the amount transferred, expressed as a percentage of total income in the economy.

18. And thus, in a very meaningful sense, a distribution with a Gini coefficient of 0.6 (e.g., Brazil) can be said to have twice as much inequality as one with a Gini coefficient of 0.3 (Taiwan).

19. With one important exception: The Gini coefficient is not decomposable in the sense of Bourguignon (1979), who defines an inequality measure as decomposable when the total inequality of a population can be broken down into a weighted average of (1) the inequality existing within subgroups of the population using that same inequality measure and (2) the inequality existing between the subgroups. However, the Gini coefficient *is* decomposable in the sense of Pyatt, Chen, and Fei (1980), who showed that when each household's total income is expressed as the sum of its income from each of a number of sources (e.g., income from labor, income from capital, and income from transfers), the Gini coefficient is expressible as a weighted average of the Gini coefficients of each income source.

Lorenz criteria, but in cases of Lorenz-crossing, we cannot. Analysts wishing a ranking when Lorenz curves cross must turn to numerical inequality measures. We noted which numerical inequality measures are strongly Lorenz-consistent, which are weakly but not strongly Lorenz-consistent, and which are Lorenz-inconsistent.

Let us now use these tools to see how income inequality changes with economic growth.

3   Economic Growth and Inequality: A Review of the Empirical Evidence

3.1   The Kuznets Curve

The Kuznets Curve in Economic Thought

One of the most famous hypotheses in all of economics was formulated by Simon Kuznets. He wrote:

> One might thus assume a long swing in the inequality characterizing the secular income structure: widening in the early phases of economic growth when the transition from the pre-industrial to the industrial civilization was most rapid; becoming stabilized for a while; and then narrowing in the later phases. (Kuznets 1955, p. 18)

It was not the empirical information presented by Kuznets that made this work a classic—he had data for only five countries at a single point in time. It is, rather, that he first articulated what he thought was the primary mechanism by which growth affects income inequality, namely intersectoral shifts. Economic growth brings about the gradual reallocation of economic activity from relatively low inequality "traditional" activities to relatively high inequality "modern" ones. If we hold the within-sector income distributions the same, it follows that inequality will necessarily be higher once this process is completed than when it began. Kuznets produced some numerical examples showing that inequality would at first increase in the process of intersectoral shifts and then decrease. This result was derived mathematically in subsequent work by Robinson (1976), Knight (1976), Fields (1979a), and Anand and Kanbur (1993b).

Additional empirical evidence presented in a follow-up paper (Kuznets 1963) led him to the following explicit formulation:

It seems plausible to assume that in the process of growth, the earlier periods are characterized by a balance of counteracting forces that may have widened the inequality in the size distribution of total income for a while ... It is even more plausible to argue that [there was a] recent narrowing in income inequality observed in the developed countries. (Kuznets 1963, p. 67)

The pattern of inequality first rising and then falling with economic growth is what has come to be called "the Kuznets curve" or "the inverted-U hypothesis."

The Kuznets curve idea acquired enormous weight among economists and others. For example, Adelman and Robinson (1989), in their chapter on income distribution and economic development in the *Handbook of Development Economics*, wrote: "All these studies agree on one descriptive result: the initial phase of the development process, during which a mostly agrarian economy starts industrialization, is *necessarily* marked by substantial increases in the inequality of the distribution of income" (p. 958; emphasis added).

In short, the Kuznets curve was regarded as more than a central tendency; it was seen, rather, as a "law" of economic development.

Following Kuznets's 1963 paper, the literature went in two directions. One was to develop theoretical models that would generate an inverted-U.[1] The second was to add to the empirical base. The balance of this section reviews what we have learned from the data.

Findings from Traditional Cross-Sectional Studies

The first studies of how economic growth affects income inequality (including Kuznets 1955) were cross-sectional in nature. That is, they looked across different countries at approximately the same point in time and examined how the pattern of income inequality varied in moving from lower-income to successively higher-income countries.

These studies can be interpreted in either of two ways. At first, the dominant way of viewing them was in causal terms, reflecting the Harvard "patterns of growth" approach (Kuznets 1966; Adelman and Morris 1973; Ahluwalia 1974, 1976; Chenery and Syrquin 1975; and others.) Those working in this tradition understood that time

---

1. These models are surveyed by Glomm and Ravikumar (1994, 1995) and Aghion, Caroli, and García-Peñalosa (1999).

series data would have been better for making causal statements about growth processes, but felt that in the meantime, analysis of cross-sectional patterns was better than nothing.[2]

The other way in which the cross-sectional studies can be viewed is simply as establishing cross-sectional patterns in a correlative sense. Taken in this way, the question is whether middle-income countries have higher inequality than lower-income or higher-income countries do, with no causality implied.

By now, there is a vast cross-sectional empirical literature on the Kuznets curve, including studies by Kravis (1960), Paukert (1973), Adelman and Morris (1973), Ahluwalia (1974, 1976a, 1976b), Chenery and Syrquin (1975), Cline (1975), Lydall (1977), Ahluwalia, Carter, and Chenery (1979), Saith (1983), Bigsten (1984), Lecaillon et al. (1984), Lindert and Williamson (1985), Papanek and Kyn (1986), Ram (1988), Campano and Salvatore (1988), Bourguignon and Morrisson (1989, 1998), Anand and Kanbur (1984, 1993a), Oshima (1991, 1994), Gradstein and Justman (1993), Randolph and Lott (1993) Nielsen (1994), Nielsen and Alderson (1995), Fishlow (1995), Jha (1996), Glomm (1997), Deininger and Squire (1998), Inter-American Development Bank (1998), Barro (1999), and Deutsch and Silber (1999). Surveys of the cross-sectional literature may be found in works by Fields (1980), Bigsten (1987), Adelman and Robinson (1989), Williamson (1991), and Kanbur (1999).

The first cross-section studies presented only tabular evidence on the Kuznets curve. Typical of this genre is the work of Paukert (1973). Countries were grouped according to GDP per head, and inequality was measured by the Gini coefficient. His data are reproduced in figure 3.1, in which individual country data are represented by light dots and group averages by heavy dots. These group averages exhibit a clear inverted-U pattern.

Later cross-sectional studies beginning with those of Cline (1975) and Ahluwalia (1976b) estimated regressions of income inequality on

---

2. One of the most famous papers on the Kuznets curve observed: "The use of cross country data for the analysis of what are essentially dynamic processes raises a number of familiar problems. Ideally, such processes should be examined in an explicitly historical context for particular countries. Unfortunately, time series data on the distribution of income, over any substantial period, are simply not available for most developing countries. For the present, therefore, empirical investigation in this field must perforce draw heavily on cross country experience." (Ahluwalia 1976b, p. 307)

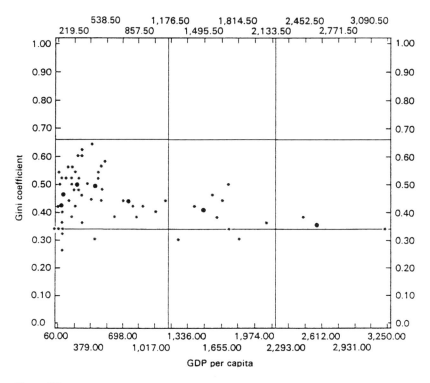

Figure 3.1
Gini coefficient and gross domestic product per capita, 56 countries
Source: Fields 1980 (figure 4.2), computed from data in Paukert 1973.

per capita national income, entered nonlinearly.[3] To give a flavor of
the usual results, figure 3.2 plots the best "central" curve applying
the standard Ordinary Least Squares (OLS) methods. The inverted-U
pattern is confirmed both for the income share of the richest 20
percent (a measure of inequality) and for the income share of the

3. Two functional forms have been used. One is to include per capita national income
and its square (or the logarithms thereof) as explanatory variables. In order for the
inverted-U to be found, the coefficient on national income must be positive, the coefficient on national income squared must be negative, and the derivative must change
sign from positive to negative within the range of the data. The other functional form
includes per capita national income and its inverse. In this case, an inverted-U arises if
both coefficients are negative and a maximum is reached within the range of the data.
    The studies by Ahluwalia, Cline, and many others use single-equation models in
which income inequality is regressed nonlinearly on per capita national income. A
more recent empirical literature has examined the effect of inequality on subsequent
economic growth. To the best of my knowledge, a Kuznets *curve* has not yet been
estimated as part of a simultaneous equations system with a growth-inequality equation also included.

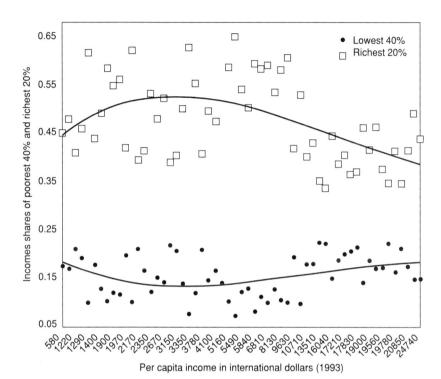

Figure 3.2
The inverted-U hypothesis in the Deininger-Squire data
Source: Ray 1998 (figure 2.6).

poorest 40 percent (which, because it applies to the poorest group, is an inverse measure of inequality). The inverted-U arises in nearly all cross-sectional studies.[4]

Together, the tabular and regression studies were thought to give strong support for the Kuznets hypothesis, taken as an indication of central tendency in a cross-section of countries. However, we also see in both figures 3.1 and 3.2 that the individual country observations are widely scattered, and accordingly in the regression studies, the R^2 for national income alone is low, on the order of 0.2 or less.[5]

---

4. See, however, Anand and Kanbur 1993a, as discussed below.

5. For instance, Cline (1975) took as his measure of inequality the ratio of the income share of the top quintile to the share of the bottom quintile, regressed this inequality measure on real per capita GNP and its square, and found

$$INEQ = 7.23 + .0258\ GNP - .000014\ GNP^2, \quad R^2 = .12.$$
$$(.0096) (.000005)$$

(Standard errors in parentheses.)

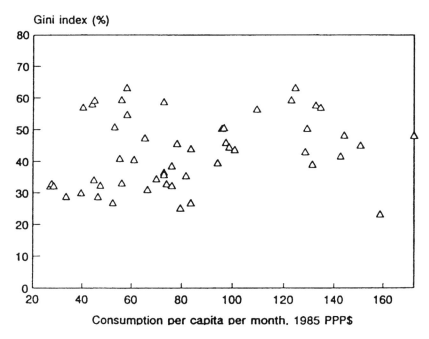

Figure 3.3
Gini index against mean consumption
Source: Ravallion 1995.

Thus, the cross-sectional relationship is not at all tight, and there is wide scope for individual country variations. The Kuznets curve is not a law.

Even so, what might be called the Kuznets "tendency" has itself been called into question. There are two critiques. The first is that recent cross-sectional evidence does not support the inverted-U shape. Figure 3.3, taken from Ravallion 1995, plots the Gini coefficient against mean per capita consumption in fifty-two surveys covering thirty-six countries.[6] The Gini coefficient and mean per capita consumption are not significantly correlated with each other, and no inverted-U appears either. Nothing is being found, because nothing appears to be there.

A quite different objection arises, which returns us to where we started this subsection. The cross-sectional methodology is not the preferred one. If we are interested in the effects of growth on inequality, we would really like to be looking at changes in inequality

---

6. Two surveys are included for sixteen of the countries.

within countries as they grow over time. The cross-sectional method-ology may have been justified when all that was available was cross-sectional data. Now, though, we can and should use intertemporal data. When we do, the results turn out to be strikingly different.

A Revisionist View of the Cross-Sectional Patterns

More recent research (Fields and Jakubson 1994; Ravallion 1995; Deininger and Squire 1998; Bruno, Ravallion, and Squire 1998) calls the findings from the traditional studies into question. The Fields-Jakubson data includes 35 developing countries with anywhere from one to nine observations per country. The Deininger-Squire data set is even larger: 108 countries, both developed and developing, of which 32 offer eight or more observations.[7] With multiple observa-tions, it is possible to fit not one but rather a *family* of parallel curves. By doing this, one would allow for highly unequal countries such as Brazil to be on higher-than-average Kuznets curves and others such as Taiwan to be on lower-than-average curves. The "central" curve—that is, the curve that would be predicted for an "average" country—can be estimated using the fixed effects methodology described in the appendix to this chapter.

When this is done, Fields and Jakubson find that the shape of the Kuznets curve *flips*.[8] Figure 3.4 and table 3.1 show the results of one such specification, in which the curve goes from a statistically sig-nificant *inverted-U* estimated by OLS to a statistically significant *U* with fixed effects estimation. Robustness tests using alternative functional forms, sample restrictions, and econometric procedures indicate that the initial phase of rising inequality is *always* reversed—that is, inequality *declines* in the early stages of economic develop-ment, up to the income levels of Korea and Taiwan. Then, for some particular specifications, we find an inverted-U as shown in figure 3.4, and other times we obtain a monotonically declining pattern (not pictured).

Panel data methods were subsequently used by other authors. Ravallion (1995), Deininger and Squire (1998), Schultz (1998), and Bruno, Ravallion, and Squire (1998) all found that when country fixed effects are included and the model is estimated using first differences

---

7. The data set itself is described in Deininger and Squire (1996). It is available online at http://www.worldbank.org/html/prdmg/grthweb/dddeisqu.htm.
8. This was first reported in a 1990 version of the Fields-Jakubson paper.

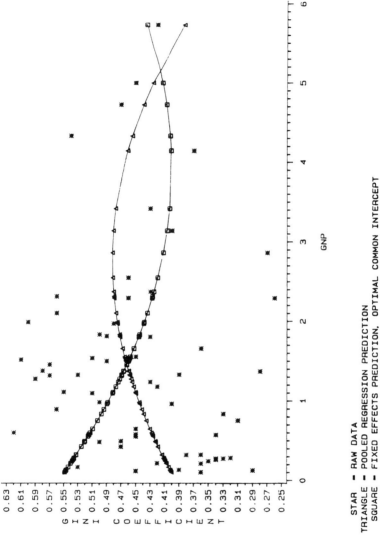

STAR   = RAW DATA
TRIANGLE = POOLED REGRESSION PREDICTION
SQUARE   = FIXED EFFECTS PREDICTION, OPTIMAL COMMON INTERCEPT

Figure 3.4
Comparison of pooled and fixed-effect models
Source: Fields and Jakubson 1994.

Table 3.1
Comparison of OLS and fixed effects models. Dependent variable = Gini. 20 countries with both GNP and ICP data and comparable income concept and recipient unit, 62 observations. (standard errors in parentheses)

Variable	(1) OLS	(2) Fixed effects
GNP	.030	−.050
	(.013)	(.015)
GNP^2	−.011	.010
	(.005)	(.004)
Constant	.462	
	(.014)	
Optimal average		.462
		(.006)
Simple average		.448
		(.009)
Optimal average minus simple average		.014
		(.006)
R^2	.089	.888

Source: Fields and Jakubson 1994.

(which Fields and Jakubson also did), the coefficients on income and income squared (or income inverse in some cases) are not statistically significantly different from zero at conventional levels.[9] In Ravallion's words: "The rejection of the inverted U hypothesis could hardly be more convincing ... These data do not suggest that growth *tends to* either increase or decrease inequality" [emphasis in the original].

Nielsen and Alderson (1995) used a random effects model, and they too found no tendency for inequality to increase with level of development.

The reason the econometric procedure makes such a difference is that what is going on *within* countries is different from what is going on *across* countries. Figure 3.5 shows what happens over time *within* a number of the countries covered by Fields and Jakubson. Only for Brazil do the data trace out an inverted-U as per capita GNP rises. For the others, the data either are U-shaped (Hong Kong and Singapore) or something else (Costa Rica, Pakistan). Yet, looking *across* countries and treating the data in figure 3.5 anonymously as OLS estimation does, it becomes clear why the inverted-U must be found:

9. List and Gallet (1999) included an income-cubed term, which they found to be statistically significant. Income and income-squared both were statistically insignificant, however.

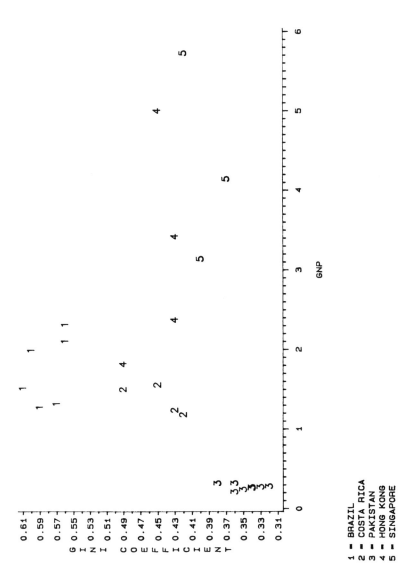

Figure 3.5
Plot of the data for selected countries
Source: Fields and Jakubson 1994.

1 = BRAZIL
2 = COSTA RICA
3 = PAKISTAN
4 = HONG KONG
5 = SINGAPORE

the curve must start with the low inequality points in the lower left, rise to pass through the high inequality points in the middle, and fall to pass through the low inequality points in the lower right.

When we look again at the data for all thirty-five countries in the Fields-Jakubson data and see which countries are which, we see in figure 3.6 that *all* of the high inequality developing countries are middle-income Latin American countries. Thus, the inverted-U pattern in the cross-section has nothing to do with growth per se; what it has to do with is the fact that for particular historical, political, and cultural reasons, Latin American countries have higher inequality than do other developing countries. As a result, when Latin America dummy variables have been added to the cross-country regressions, often these terms are found to have a significant positive association with inequality, driving the national income variables to be statistically insignificant (Fishlow 1996; Deininger and Squire 1998) or to have the wrong signs (Fishlow 1995)—"wrong" in the sense that they are opposite to what the Kuznets hypothesis would predict.[10]

These doubts about the inverted-U shape are reinforced by the results of intertemporal studies, to which we now turn.

Findings from Time Series Studies

The most direct evidence on whether inequality tends to rise in the early stages of economic development and then fall would be a time series on inequality. To be consistent with Kuznets's idea that it is growth that is the primary determining factor, the data would more appropriately be ordered according to per capita income level rather than by calendar time in those unfortunate cases (primarily Latin American and sub-Saharan African) where national income did not grow monotonically over time.

Figure 3.5 above depicted such data for a number of developing countries, only one of which (Brazil) exhibited the inverted-U pattern. Additional country-by-country data for developing countries reveal a similarly mixed picture. An inverted-U was found for Colombia (Londoño 1990), but an ordinary U appears for Taiwan (Republic of China 1999). No particular pattern arises for a number of Asian countries (Oshima 1991). Thus, data for the developing countries simply do not support the inverted-U as a general pattern.

---

10. Though, for a study in which the inverted-U shape appears even when Latin America and Africa dummy variables are included, see Barro 1999.

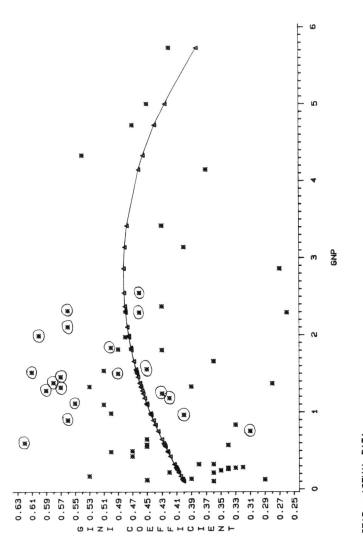

STAR – ACTUAL DATA
TRIANGLE – PREDICTED RELATIONSHIP
CIRCLED – LATIN AMERICAN

Figure 3.6
Latin American countries identified
Source: Fields and Jakubson 1994.

The same is true of data for the developed countries. In studies of individual countries, Williamson and Lindert (1980) and Williamson (1985) found support for the inverted-U in the United States and Great Britain respectively over many decades.[11] However, the inverted-U does *not* fit the cases of Germany (Dumke 1991) or Australia (Thomas 1991).

Multicountry tabulations are similarly unsupportive of the inverted-U. Although the two early studies by Kuznets (1955 and 1963) are widely cited as providing evidence in favor of the Kuznets curve, the actual data he presents do not support this. His key table, reproduced here as table 3.2, reveals only two countries (Prussia and Saxony) in which the inverted-U pattern held; in the other seven (United Kingdom, Germany, Netherlands, Denmark, Norway, Sweden, and the United States), inequality fell.

Similar results appear in the comparative studies by Lindert and Williamson (1985) and by Kaelble and Thomas (1991). The Lindert-Williamson data, reproduced in figure 3.7, exhibit what Williamson (1991, p. 14) termed "the twentieth century downswing" in inequality. The Kaelble-Thomas data, presented here in table 3.3, show that of thirteen developed countries analyzed, only Sweden exhibits an inverted-U.[12] For Austria, Canada, Denmark, Finland, France, Germany, Japan, the Netherlands, Norway, Switzerland, the United Kingdom, and the United States, Kaelble and Thomas find that inequality is constant or falling.

Finally, this issue has received systematic treatment in the work of Deininger and Squire (1998). They had time series data on inequality and per capita national income for forty-eight countries, developing and developed. As table 3.4 shows, in only 10 percent of these was the inverted-U pattern found; in another 10 percent, an ordinary U was found; and in the remaining 80 percent, no statistically significant quadratic was found in almost every country of this group.

In sum, in only a small minority of countries do the time series data we have confirm the inverted-U hypothesis.[13]

---

11. But see Feinstein 1988 for a critique of the methodology used in Williamson's study of Great Britain.

12. And even there, the pattern is open to doubt (Soderberg 1991).

13. It might be argued that the twentieth century data used by most authors do not provide a fair test of the Kuznets hypothesis, since these data do not start until after the industrialization process was well under way. The conclusion stated in the text does not deny the possibility that the inverted-U hypothesis might be an apt description if nineteenth century data were to be included. The point, simply, is that the data we have do not support the initially increasing phase.

Table 3.2
Long-term estimates of shares of ordinal groups in selected countries

Successive dates and entries

United Kingdom — Changes in inequality over time: Decline

	Bowley		Clark	Seers		Lydall		
Dates	1880	1913	1929	1938	1947	1938	1949	1957
Income before tax:								
Richest 5%	48	43	33	31	24	29	23.5	18
Richest 20%	58	59	51	52	46	50	47.5	41.5
Income after tax:								
Richest 5%				26	17	24	17	14
Richest 20%		34		48	39	46	42	38

Prussia — Changes in inequality over time: Rising inequality at first, possible decline later

	Procopovitch				Reich Statistical Office	
Dates	1854	1875	1896	1913	1913	1928
Richest 5%	21	26	27	30	31	26
Richest 20%		48	45	50	50	49
Poorest 60%		34		33	32	31

	Mueller				
Dates	1873–1880	1881–1890	1891–1900	1901–1910	1911–1913
Richest 5%	28	30	32	32	31

Saxony — Changes in inequality over time: Slight increase at first, then decline

	Procopovitch			Reich Statistical Office	
Dates	1880	1896	1912	1913	1928
Richest 5%	34	36	33	33	28
Richest 20%	56	57	55	54	50
Poorest 60%	27	26.5	27	28	31

Germany–West Germany — Decline

	Reich Statistical Office			Mueller		United Nations		Wochenbericht	
Dates	1913	1928	1928 (adj.)	1928	1936	1936	1950	1955	1959
Richest 5%	31	27	21	20	23	28	24	18	18
Richest 20%	50	49	45			53	48	43	43
Poorest 60%	32	31	34			26.5	29	34	34

Netherlands — Decline

Dates	1938	1949	1954
Richest 5%	19	17	13
Richest 20%	49	45.5	38.5
Poorest 60%	31	34	40

Denmark — Decline

	Zeuthen I			Zeuthen II		Bjerke		
Dates	1870	1903	1925	1903	1925	1939	1949	1955
Richest 5%	36.5	28	26	30	26	24.5	19	17.5
Richest 10%				39	37	35	29.5	27.4
Richest 20%	50	38	36	55	53	51	45	44
Poorest 60%				31	25	27	32	32

Norway — Decline

Dates	1907	1938	1948
Richest 5%, country districts	27	20	14
Richest 5%, cities	28–32	22	19

Sweden — Decline (Bentzel)

Earned income before tax

Dates	1930	1935	1945
Richest 5%	30	28	24
Richest 20%	59	58	52
Poorest 60%	19	19	23

Table 3.2 (continued)

Country	Changes in inequality over time		Successive dates and entries						
			United Nations						
		Dates	1935	1945	1948	1948	1954		
		Total income before tax							
		Richest 5%	28	23.5	20	20	17		
		Richest 20%	56	51	47	45	43		
		Poorest 60%	23	26	29	32	34		
		Total income after tax							
		Richest 5%	25.5	21	17				
		Richest 20%	54	48	43				
		Poorest 60%	23	28	32				
			Kuznets						
United States	Decline	Dates	1913–1919	1919–1928	1929–1938	1939–1943	1944–1948		
		Income before tax							
		Richest 1%	14	14	13	11	9		
		Richest 5%	24[a]	25	25	21	17		
		Income after federal tax							
		Richest 1%	13	13	12	9	6		
		Richest 5%	22[a]	24	24	18	14		

Department of Commerce

Dates	1929	1935–1936	1941	1944–1947	1950–1954	1955–1959
Income before tax						
Richest 5%	30	26.5	24	21	21	20
Richest 20%	54	52	49	46	45	45
Poorest 60%	26	27	29	32	33	32
Income after federal tax						
Richest 5%	29.5		21.5		18	18
Richest 20%	54		47		43	44
Poorest 60%	26.5		30		34	34

Source: Kuznets 1963 (table 6), reproduced in Fields 1980 (table 4.4).
a. 1917–1919.

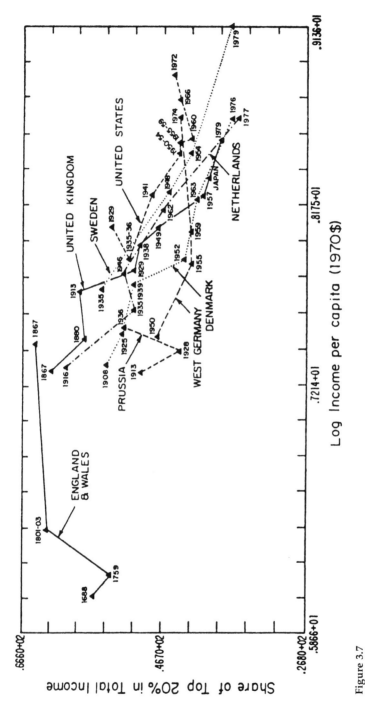

Figure 3.7
The Kuznets curve: Historical time series from five European countries and the United States.
Source: Lindert and Williamson 1985 (p. 345).

Table 3.3
Shares of the top and bottom income-earners in Western Europe, North America, Japan, and Australia, 1880–1970 (income before tax)

(a) Top 10 percent

	1880	1890	1900	1910	1920	1930	1940	1950	1960	1970
Western Europe										
Austria						24.8		22.6	24.9	24.7
Denmark					39.0	37.8	36.8	28.6	27.3	32.0[b]
Finland					50.9	48.3		32.8	30.5	30.2
France								36.2	34.0	29.3
Germany				40.5		35.1		36.0	39.4	34.4
Prussia		32.3	32.9	31.1						
Saxony	42.8	43.9	43.8	42.6						
Netherlands								36.1	31.6	29.5
Norway		42.1		29.8		38.2		28.6	27.2	24.7
Sweden					39.2	44.5	33.7	28.8	25.9	24.0
Switzerland								37.1	38.1	32.5
United Kingdom							38.8	33.2	29.2	27.5
Non-European countries										
Canada								27.4	24.9	26.5
Japan									25.2	23.2
United States								28.9	27.0	28.4

Table 3.3 (continued)

(b) Bottom 20 percent

	1880	1890	1900	1910	1920	1930	1940	1950	1960	1970
Western Europe										
Austria						10.5[a]		5.4	4.7	4.7
Denmark					0.1	0.2		4.6	4.2	0.2[b]
Finland							0.1	0.1	3.6	2.1
France									2.8	3.8
Germany									1.8	3.8
Netherlands								0.8	5.9	6.5
Norway		1.8		3.8(0.1)		3.1		0.6	2.0	4.8
Sweden					1.7			4.6	6.3	8.4
Switzerland							3.2	0.3	2.6	9.3
United Kingdom									5.3	5.6
Non-European countries										
Canada								4.7	3.7	3.8
Japan									7.8	8.7
United States							4.1	3.7	3.7	3.8

Source: Kaelble and Thomas 1991 (table 1.2).
Notes:
a. 1930 to 1950: break in comparability.
b. Break in comparability.
Austria: 1930: average 1928, 1933; 1930 to 1950: break in comparability; 1950: 1953; 1960: 1964.
Denmark: 1920: population census after exclusion of economically inactive income recipients; 1970 not comparable to former years.
Finland: 1920: 1922; 1930: 1929.

France: 1950: 1956; 1960: 1965; 1970.

Germany: 1913: 1913; 1930: average 1928, 1932; 1960: 1961; 1970: average 1968, 1971.

  Prussia: 1890: 1891.

  Saxony: 1880: average 1879, 1881; 1890: average 1889, 1891; 1900: average 1899, 1901; 1910 average 1909, 1912.

Netherlands: 1960: average 1959, 1962, 1970.

Norway: 1890: 1891 (representative sample for active males); 1910: 1910 (unadjusted tax data, covering recipients with taxed income of 1 kr. and over), second number population census 1911; 1930: 1929 (unadjusted); 1950: 1952.

Sweden: 1920: 1920 (population census); 1940: 1943.

Switzerland: 1950: average 1949, 1951; 1960: average 1959, 1961; 1970: average 1969, 1971.

United Kingdom: 1940: 1938 and 1950: 1949; 1960: average 1959, 1961.

Canada: 1950: 1951; 1960: 1959; 1970: 1972.

Japan: 1960: 1962; 1970: 1972.

United States: 1950: average 1947, 1952; 1960: average 1957, 1962; 1970: 1972.

Table 3.4
Results from estimation of the Kuznets curve with country specific dummies

	Hypothesis III							
	Coefficient on income	t-value	Coefficient on 1/income	t-value	Predicted turning point	No. obs.	GDP difference	Years difference
Countries with a significant 'Kuznets curve' (inverted U-shaped relationship)								
Brazil	$-5.76E-03$	(1.96)	$-5.59E+04$	(2.29)	3117	15	2533	29
Hungary	$-1.97E-02$	(2.01)	$-4.23E+05$	(2.06)	4628	8	1925	29
Mexico	$-5.19E-03$	(2.13)	$-6.39E+04$	(2.01)	3511	8	3368	39
Philippines	$-6.60E-02$	(2.30)	$-1.10E+05$	(2.18)	1292	6	629	31
Trinidad	$-4.14E-03$	(2.83)	$-1.97E+05$	(2.37)	6905	4	6798	23
Countries with a significant U-shaped relationship contrary to Kuznets' prediction								
Costa Rica	$2.59E-02$	(2.45)	$2.07E+05$	(2.60)	2822	7	1534	28
India	$1.75E-02$	(1.94)	$1.83E+04$	(2.49)	1022	31	674	41
United States	$1.79E-03$	(3.10)	$2.39E+05$	(2.63)	11558	45	9323	44
United Kingdom	$5.01E-03$	(5.03)	$3.79E+05$	(4.08)	8696	31	6270	30
Countries with no statistically significant association between inequality and income								
Australia	$-4.93E-03$	(1.39)	$-9.86E+05$	(1.83)	14143	9	4767	22
Belgium	$-4.34E-03$	(0.31)	$-7.20E+05$	(0.35)	12882	4	2805	13
Bangladesh	$1.99E-02$	(0.58)	$1.54E+04$	(0.49)	879	8	460	22
Bulgaria	$-1.12E-03$	(0.27)	$8.97E+02$	(0.01)		27	2942	31
Canada	$-5.69E-04$	(1.23)	$-5.06E+04$	(0.89)	9432	23	11013	40
Chile	$1.00E-03$	(0.11)	$3.69E+04$	(0.26)	6070	5	1690	24
China	$7.14E-02$	(2.43)	$7.40E+04$	(1.83)	1018	12	530	12
Côte d'Ivoire	$-7.14E-01$	(0.72)	$-1.62E+06$	(0.74)	1506	4	139	3

Colombia	8.15E − 03	(0.52)	6.00E + 04	(0.53)	2713	7	1157	21
Czechoslovakia	−6.56E − 04	(0.17)	2.35E + 03	(0.08)		10	2310	30
Germany	−3.17E − 03	(0.38)	−4.21E + 05	(0.45)	11532	6	3328	15
Denmark	−5.28E − 03	(0.26)	−1.01E + 06	(0.33)	13813	4	3170	16
Egypt	−1.40E − 02	(1.19)	−2.45E + 03	(0.19)	418	4	1133	32
Spain	−3.29E − 03	(1.35)	−1.42E + 05	(1.42)	6582	8	4658	24
Finland	−1.62E − 03	(0.28)	−2.19E + 05	(0.32)	11640	10	3343	14
France	−3.25E − 03	(2.53)	−9.82E + 04	(1.20)	5499	7	6951	28
Hong Kong	8.35E − 04	(1.31)	3.19E + 04	(0.68)	6176	7	10757	20
Indonesia	−5.66E − 03	(0.50)	−2.13E + 03	(0.10)	614	7	996	14
Iran	−1.96E − 02	(0.65)	−4.21E + 05	(0.68)	4635	5	1153	15
Italy	3.98E − 03	(1.24)	5.71E + 05	(1.71)	11975	15	4320	17
Jamaica	2.12E − 02	(1.59)	1.17E + 05	(1.88)	2347	8	1230	35
Japan	5.62E − 04	(1.53)	3.38E + 04	(1.85)	7756	23	10777	28
Korea	−1.45E − 03	(1.43)	−1.22E + 04	(2.15)	2898	11	4549	23
Sri Lanka	9.29E − 03	(0.85)	2.34E + 04	(0.91)	1588	9	991	37
Malaysia	−6.99E − 03	(1.68)	−6.00E + 04	(1.38)	2930	6	2520	19
Netherlands	1.57E − 02	(1.74)	1.88E + 06	(1.53)	10949	12	2941	16
Norway	−7.53E − 04	(0.87)	−6.84E + 03	(0.08)	3014	9	8969	29
New Zealand	3.50E − 02	(1.45)	3.82E + 06	(1.32)	10437	12	1717	17
Taiwan	8.15E − 04	(1.67)	1.41E + 04	(2.21)	4165	26	6521	29
Pakistan	−2.73E − 02	(0.56)	−3.88E + 04	(0.60)	1192	9	448	22
Panama	3.31E − 03	(0.08)	1.47E + 05	(0.41)	6667	4	808	19
Poland	2.57E − 02	(1.02)	5.09E + 05	(1.11)	4453	9	1076	16
Puerto Rico	1.01E − 02	(1.07)	3.84E + 05	(1.18)	6177	4	3019	17
Singapore	1.53E − 04	(0.11)	5.94E + 03	(0.08)	6233	6	6302	16

Table 3.4 (continued)

	Hypothesis III				Predicted turning point	No. obs.	GDP difference	Years difference
	Coefficient on income	t-value	Coefficient on 1/income	t-value				
Soviet Union	9.07E – 03	(0.34)	3.52E + 05	(0.28)	6225	5	1622	13
Sweden	2.47E – 03	(0.21)	4.38E + 05	(0.21)	13324	13	2741	16
Thailand	4.40E – 03	(2.38)	4.17E + 03	(0.55)	974	8	2947	30
Tunisia	–6.92E – 03	(1.00)	–2.34E + 04	(0.97)	1841	5	1674	25
Venezuela	–1.68E – 02	(1.74)	–7.60E + 05	(1.61)	6732	9	2350	19
Yugoslavia	–3.49E – 02	(1.90)	–4.11E + 05	(1.97)	3429	4	3069	26

$DW = 1.875$

$Adj. R2 = 0.9481$

Source: Deininger and Squire 1998 (table 7).
No information on income for the Bahamas was available.
Differences refer to the difference between the first and last observation.

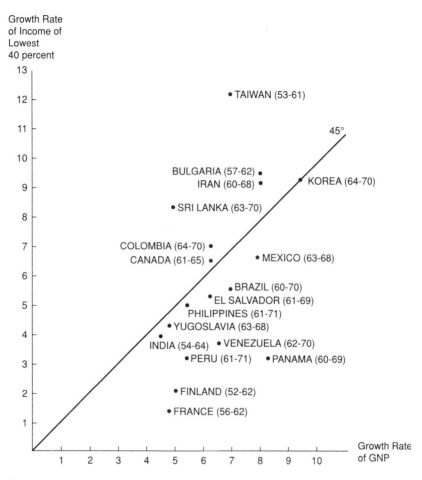

Figure 3.8
GNP growth and income growth of the lowest 40 percent
Source: Ahluwalia 1974 (p. 14).

Findings from Spell Analysis

A final test of the Kuznets hypothesis involves examining spells (a "spell" is defined as the period between one survey year and a later one) and analyzing how the change in inequality relates to the rate of economic growth or level of national income. The first such test was performed by Ahluwalia (1974); the results are reproduced in figure 3.8. In his words:

The scatter suggests considerable diversity of country experience in terms of changes in relative equality. Several countries show a deterioration in relative equality but there are others showing improvement ... *There is no strong pattern relating changes in the distribution of income to the rate of growth of GNP.* In both high-growth and low-growth countries there are some which have experienced improvements and others that have experienced deteriorations in relative equality. (Ahluwalia 1974, p. 13; emphasis added)

Fields (1980) compiled data on economic growth and changing inequality in thirteen developing countries. In seven of these, inequality rose; in five, inequality fell; and in one, the evidence was mixed. No relationship was found between the change in inequality and the rate of economic growth. This led to the following conclusion:

The most impressive feature of [the data] is the lack of any pronounced pattern. It is sometimes thought that the increase or decrease in inequality would be associated with such economic conditions as the initial level of inequality, the level of economic development, or the rate of economic growth. The absence of systematic relationships among these variables suggests otherwise. (Fields 1980, p. 94)

A similar finding was reached by Morawetz (1977).

This conclusion is reinforced by a number of regional studies. Let us begin with *Asia*. In the rapidly growing countries of East Asia, Oshima (1991) found that inequality was generally falling in the 1970s and rising in the 1980s, which is the exact opposite of Kuznets's inverted-U. The patterns differed across countries—falling inequality in Japan, U-shaped paths in Hong Kong, Singapore and Taiwan, and an inverted-U path in Korea—reflecting "diverse factors and mechanisms" at work in the different countries. A more recent World Bank study found that inequality rose with economic growth in Hong Kong, Taiwan, Thailand, and China, fell with economic growth in Singapore and Malaysia, and was effectively unchanged in Korea and Indonesia (Ahuja et al. 1997). In India, inequality fell in the 1960s and was essentially unchanged thereafter (Bruno, Ravallion, and Squire 1998).

In *Latin America*, Psacharopoulos, et al. (1993) reported income distribution becoming more equal during growth spells and becoming less equal during recessionary ones (table 3.5). This finding suggests the hopeful conclusion that economic growth is good for inequality as well as for poverty. However, their finding on inequality has been called into question by two studies of Latin American countries. Fields and Newton Kraus (1996) used only those countries for which the data were national in coverage and found that inequality had changed monotonically in all three (Brazil, Costa Rica,

Table 3.5
Income inequality and the economic cycle

Change in income distribution	Recession		Recovery	
More equal	Argentina	(1980–1982)	Brazil	(1983–1986)
	Argentina	(1982–1985)	Chile	(1983–1987)
			Chile	(1987–1990)
			Colombia	(1980–1989)
			Costa Rica	(1983–1986)
			Costa Rica	(1981–1989)
			Venezuela	(1989–1991)
			Uruguay	(1981–1989)
Less equal	Argentina	(1985–1988)	Guatemala	(1986–1989)
	Argentina	(1980–1989)		
	Bolivia	(1986–1989)		
	Brazil	(1979–1983)		
	Brazil	(1986–1989)		
	Brazil	(1979–1989)		
	Chile	(1980–1983)		
	Costa Rica	(1980–1982)		
	Guatemala	(1981–1986)		
	Mexico	(1977–1984)		
	Mexico	(1984–1989)		
	Peru	(1981–1984)		
	Peru	(1984–1989)		
	Panama	(1979–1989)		
	Venezuela	(1981–1989)		

Source: Psacharopoulos et al. 1993.

and Venezuela), which implies that there can be no correlation between the rise or fall in inequality and the rate of economic growth. Similarly, Londoño and Szekely (1998) found that in most Latin American countries, income inequality rose both in the 1980s and in the 1990s. Because economic growth was negative in most Latin American countries in the 1980s and positive in the 1990s, these data also imply the absence of an association between growth and the direction of inequality change in Latin America.

In *Africa*, where the data are most limited, the Deininger-Squire data set (1996) includes six African countries with data on changes in inequality over time, often for very short periods. Three of these countries had national income growth and three did not. Inequality fell in two of those with income growth (Ghana and Mauritius) and

rose in one (Morocco). As for those which either stagnated or con-
tracted, inequality rose in two (Nigeria and Uganda) and fell in one
(Côte d'Ivoire). Based on this limited body of information, we do not
find any tendency for inequality to change differently in the growing
economies of Africa as compared with the nongrowing ones.

In the *transition economies* of Eastern Europe and the countries of
the former Soviet Union, the evidence has been summed up by
Milanovic (1999), Flemming and Micklewright (1999), and Kanbur
and Lustig (1999). In all of these countries, there has been a dramatic
rise in inequality. Kanbur and Lustig (1999) report that within a
decade in the transition economies: "In eleven countries ... the Gini
coefficient has increased between five and nine percentage points; in
seven countries, between ten and nineteen percentage points; and in
two countries, by more than twenty (!) percentage points" [excla-
mation point in the original]. The collapse of the socialist system
resulted in massive economic contractions in the late 1980s and
early 1990s. Since then some countries, such as Poland, have seen
some economic growth, while others, notably Russia, have seen their
economies continue to decline. It seems clear that the increase in
inequality is attributable to the change in the structure of these
economies rather than economic growth or contraction per se.

Summing up, income inequality is no more likely to rise or fall
when economic growth is high than when economic growth is low or
negative.

Turning now to a comparison of higher-income and lower-income
developing countries, look again at figure 3.1, which comes from
Paukert 1973. This shows an inverted-U pattern in the average inequality among countries grouped by per capita income: in the cross
section, inequality (measured by the Gini coefficient) rose until a per
capita annual income of US$300 (in 1965 prices) and fell thereafter.
The data set reported in Fields 1991 contains forty-three "growth
spells" for developing countries.[14] Half of these growth spells were
in "high-income developing countries" (i.e., above Paukert's turning
point) and the other half in "low-income developing countries" (i.e.,
below Paukert's turning point). If inequality tends to increase in the
early stages of economic development and decrease in the later
stages, we would expect to find a higher proportion of inequality

---

14. A "growth spell" is a comparison of inequality in two successive surveys, over
which time economic growth took place. Indonesia, 1970–1976 is one growth spell;
Indonesia, 1976–1978 another; etc. Most "spells" are "growth spells," because most
economies had growth.

increases when national income is below the $300 turning point (in 1965 dollars) than when it is above that point.

The evidence does not come out that way. As shown in table 3.6, in both the "high-income developing countries" and the "low-income developing countries," inequality increased in half the growth spells and decreased in the other half. There is no evidence here of an inverted-U.

The same idea was tested by Deininger and Squire (1998), using a somewhat different methodology. They split their sample of countries into two groups—those below and those above a national income of US$3,000 per capita in 1995 dollars—and estimated Kuznets curves for each group. The Kuznets hypothesis predicts a disproportionately large number of positive effects in the lower-income countries and a disproportionately small number in the higher-income countries. But the findings are nearly all statistically insignificant. In Deininger and Squire's words: "Together, these results offer virtually no support for an increase of inequality at low levels of income and a decrease at higher income levels as suggests by Kuznets' inverted-U relationship."

In addition, Ravallion and Chen (1997) examined changes in the late 1980s and early 1990s for 64 spells in 42 developing countries. Of these, 29 were growth spells, in which the mean income or consumption grew between surveys. In half of these growth spells, inequality rose, and in half, inequality fell.

Summing up, there is no indication that income inequality is any more likely to rise or fall in the higher-income developing countries than in the lower-income ones.

The Kuznets Curve: A Good Idea, But ...

This section has reviewed the available evidence on the Kuznets hypothesis, namely, the idea that income inequality tends to increase in the early stages of economic development and decrease in the later stages. In cross-section work, researchers have generally found higher inequality in the middle-income countries than in either richer or poorer countries; this produces a cross-country inverted-U. But although the inverted-U fits the cross-sectional data better than any other shaped curve does, variation in national income explains only a small fraction of the variation in income inequality. Furthermore, the cross-section inverted-U arises because of the particular econometric method used (ordinary least squares) and because the highest-

Table 3.6
Change in Gini coefficient in high-income and low-income countries, growth spell analysis

Part A Low-income countries	Part B High-income countries
Growth spells in which Gini coefficient increased (n = 10)	*Growth spells in which Gini coefficient increased (n = 9)*
Bangladesh, 1973/74–1976/77	Bahamas, 1977–1979
Indonesia, 1970–1976	Brazil, 1970–1972
Indonesia, 1976–1978	Costa Rica, 1971–1977
Pakistan, 1971/72–1979	Hong Kong, 1976–1981
Pakistan, 1979–1984	Jamaica, 1968–1973
Sri Lanka, 1973–1978/79	Korea, 1970–1976
Sri Lanka, 1978/79–1981/82	Malaysia, 1970–1976
Thailand, 1962/63–1968/69	Mexico, 1958–1963
Thailand, 1968/69–1975/76	Mexico, 1963–1969
Thailand, 1975/76–1981	*Growth spells in which Gini coefficient decreased (n = 10)*
Growth spells in which Gini coefficient decreased (n = 11)	Bahamas, 1975–1977
Bangladesh, 1976/77–1981/82	Brazil, 1976–1978
Egypt, 1964/65–1974/75	Costa Rica, 1977–1979
Indonesia, 1967–1970	Hong Kong, 1966–1971
Indonesia, 1978–1980	Korea, 1976–1982
Pakistan, 1963/64–1966/67	Malaysia, 1976–1979
Pakistan, 1966/67–1968/69	Mexico, 1969–1977
Pakistan, 1968/69–1969/70	Singapore, 1972/73–1977/78
Pakistan, 1969/70–1970/71	Trinidad and Tobago, 1971/72–1975/76
Philippines, 1965–1971	Turkey, 1968–1973
Philippines, 1971–1975	*Growth spells in which Gini coefficient was unchanged (n = 3)*
Sri Lanka, 1963–1973	Brazil, 1978–80
	Chile, 1968–1971
	Hong Kong, 1971–1976

Source: Fields 1991 (table 9).

inequality countries are all middle-income Latin American ones. When fixed effects estimation is used instead, the inverted-U pattern disappears and inequality is shown to fall over a long range of incomes in the developing countries. Looking over time, the inverted-U has been found in the economic history of some countries, both developed and developing, but this happens in only a small minority of cases. Most of the evidence is to the contrary, the dominant pattern being a *fall* in inequality over time during the twentieth century. Finally, the Kuznets hypothesis leads to the prediction that inequality would decrease more often in the "high-income developing countries" (i.e., those richer than the cross-sectional turning point) than in the "low-income developing countries." But the evidence shows that inequality rises half the time and falls half the time in both groups of countries. Nor is any empirical tendency found for the rise or fall in inequality to be linked to the rate of economic growth in a country or to the initial level of inequality.

One view often attributed (mistakenly) to Simon Kuznets is that inequality *must* increase before it decreases. What Kuznets in fact hypothesized is that inequality *tends* to increase before it decreases. But from the findings reached here, even this hypothesis is open to question.

3.2   Influences on Inequality

Having found that the variables thought to be important by Kuznets produced no pattern in the data, we are naturally led to ask what are the factors that *do* determine whether inequality increases or decreases. The data seem to be telling us that what matters is what particular countries do. Individual country studies, assembled through comparative analysis, are needed to gain a proper understanding of this issue.

Unfortunately, no systematic investigation of country experiences has yet been undertaken for the developing countries, so the best we can do at present is to rely on cross-country inequality comparisons.[15]

---

15. In this regard, the experiences of the developed countries are suggestive. In the OECD countries, there was a broad postwar trend toward falling inequality, followed by increasing inequality in many countries in the 1980s with continued inequality increase in most in the 1990s (OECD 1993, 1996; Atkinson, Rainwater, and Smeeding 1995; Gottschalk and Smeeding 1997, 1999; Burniaux et al. 1998). No apparent relation is observed between the change in inequality and either initial inequality or geographical patterns.

The abundant literature on the correlates of income inequality has been surveyed by Fields (1980), Bigsten (1987), Adelman and Robinson (1989), and Kanbur (1999). The methodology followed in this literature is to run cross-country regressions to isolate the "effects" of particular variables in the presence of others. For example, in the pioneering series of papers by Ahluwalia (1974, 1976a, 1976b), a measure of income inequality (income share of the top 20 percent, middle 40 percent, or lowest 40 percent) was regressed on a number of explanatory variables including the logarithm of per capita income and its square; the primary and secondary school enrollment rates; the rate of growth of population; the rate of growth of GNP; agriculture's share in GDP; and dummy variables for developed country and socialist country. After insignificant variables were dropped out, those that remained statistically significant were the income variables, school enrollment rates, and the socialist country dummy. Essentially the same methodology has been followed in all of the studies cited below.

Various aspects of the structure of economies have been found to be associated with inequality in the distribution of income. One is the *basic nature of the economic system* itself. Research has shown that income inequality is lower in socialist economies other things equal than in nonsocialist ones (Ahluwalia 1974; Anand and Kanbur 1993; Jha 1996; Deininger and Squire 1998). The patterns of asset ownership and government spending are clearly at work here. For this reason, related variables such as the importance of state employment in total employment (Milanovic 1994) and the extent of government intervention in the economy (Papanek and Kyn 1986) have also been included in regression models and have been shown to have significant effects on inequality.

Another factor is the *structure of output*. The more important is agriculture in the economy (whether measured in terms of production, employment, or the endowment of arable land), the lower is income inequality (Ahluwalia 1974; Chenery and Syrquin 1975; Nielsen and Alderson 1995; Bourguignon and Morrisson 1998; Inter-American Development Bank 1998). This reflects the fact, originally observed by Kuznets (1955), that income inequality in nonfarm sectors tends to be higher than in farm sectors.

We then have the share of *primary/mineral exports* in total output. This share is thought to reflect the unequal ownership of such resources, the rents earned on such ownership, and the relative lack of employment generated by activities of this kind. Other things equal, the higher this share, the higher income inequality has been found to be (Chenery and Syrquin 1975; Papanek and Kyn 1986; Bigsten 1987; Bourguignon and Morrisson 1989; Inter-American Development Bank 1998).

Then there are well-established *regional* patterns. Latin America and sub-Saharan Africa are the world's high inequality regions (Deininger and Squire 1996; World Bank 1999). Even when other things such as national income level are held equal, being a Latin American country raises inequality (Fishlow 1996; Schultz 1998; Barro 1999) whereas being an Asian country lowers it (Milanovic 1994). Latin America's poor distributional performance has been attributed to a variety of factors including the continued unequal distribution of land; the low level, unequal distribution, and often poor quality of education; inadequate infrastructure investments; misallocation of government spending; the failure to adopt an outward-oriented, labor-demanding development strategy (but also having engaged to a greater extent in world trade); the inability to generate sufficient productive employment; great resistance to progressive taxation; poor economic and cultural integration; and excessive populism (Fishlow 1995; Birdsall, Ross, and Sabot 1995b; Londoño and Székely 1997; Wood 1997; Iglesias 1998; Sheahan and Iglesias 1998; Inter-American Development Bank 1998). The significance of the Latin America dummy variable can thus be understood as a proxy for policy decisions and for the inequality of productive assets, to which we now turn.

Another structural feature is *economic dualism*. A dualistic labor market is one with different wages and/or labor market institutions in the various major sectors. In particular, wages in the non-agricultural sectors of the economy may be set at an exogenously high level, causing employment in those sectors to be low, whereas in agriculture employment is high and productivity and incomes are low. Research using the ratio of the productivity of labor in non-agricultural sectors of the economy to the productivity of labor in agriculture as a proxy for the extent of dualism has shown that dualism raises inequality (Bourguignon and Morrisson 1998).

Because most people in the developing world derive most if not all of their income from the work they do, the *structure of employment* plays an important role. The poorer the country, the more important is self-employment on family farms and in family businesses. In most of South Asia and sub-Saharan Africa, self-employment is the predominant form of income-earning activity (Squire 1981; ILO 1987, 1998; Turnham 1993; World Bank 1995). Consequently, a critical determinant of income inequality is inequality in the distribution of assets with which the self-employed have to work.

One such asset is *land*. Those countries with the most unequal distributions of landholdings tend to be the ones with the greatest income inequality. This appears both in simple correlations (e.g., Rodrik 1995a; Deininger and Squire 1997) and controlling for other variables in multiple regressions (e.g., Li, Squire, and Zou 1998; Bourguignon and Morrisson 1998).

Another important asset is *capital*. Capital is very unequally distributed in the developing world. In fact, the majority of households own no capital, and therefore receive no capital income whatsoever. Consequently, inequality decomposition studies for developing countries including Taiwan (Fei, Ranis, and Kuo 1978; Pyatt, Chen, and Fei 1980; Fields and Leary 1999), Pakistan (Ayub 1977; Adams and Alderman 1992), and Colombia (Fields 1979b) have concluded that capital income inequality accounts for a much smaller share of total income inequality than labor income inequality does.

An important determinant of income inequality in a country is the state of development of its *capital market*. Lack of access to credit can limit the poor's ability to make worthwhile investments in a wide variety of areas including education, farm productivity, self-employment opportunities, owner-occupied housing, and the foregoing of child labor (Banerjee and Newman 1991, 1993; Galor and Zeira 1993; Bénabou 1996; Basu 1999). Thus, present inequalities are exacerbated by underdeveloped capital markets, and inequalities are transmitted across the generations (Stiglitz 1993). When empirical studies have included variables representing capital market development, these variables have been found to be associated with lower income inequality, ceteris paribus (Li, Squire, and Zou 1998).

Another asset of great importance is *human capital*. Human capital theory predicts that the inequality of labor market earnings would reflect the mean levels of schooling and post-school experience in the economy and the inequality of each (Mincer 1970, 1974; Chiswick 1971). In theory, educational expansion could have an equalizing or a disequalizing effect on income distribution, depending on which level of education it is that is expanded. Empirically, though, the evidence is clear: controlling for other factors, higher rates of schooling and higher literacy are associated with *lower* income inequality (Adelman and Morris 1973; Ahluwalia 1974; Chenery and Syrquin 1975; Papanek and Kyn 1986; Bourguignon and Morrisson 1989; Psacharopoulos and Tilak 1991; Nielsen and Alderson 1995; Birdsall, Ross, and Sabot 1995b; Jha 1996; Fishlow 1996; Li, Squire, and Zou 1998; Barro 1999). Education has thus played a role in helping to equalize income inequality.

Finally, a potentially important asset is what the government provides to its citizens in terms of *social income*. At issue is what entitlements people have by virtue of residence or citizenship in particular nations. Some countries grant substantial benefits to their people in the form of food, housing, health care, and other publicly provided goods and services. How much is spent on these items and the particular form such expenditures take (e.g., whether on primary health care clinics for the masses or hospital care for a select few) can make a great deal of difference to overall inequality and economic well-being; see Jimenez 1995 and van de Walle 1995 for surveys of this literature.

All in all, what these findings suggest is that whether a country follows a high-inequality growth path or a low-inequality one is determined both by structural factors and by policy choices. While some of these can be changed only with difficulty if at all, others are choices that can be made by the country itself. In chapter 10, we will take up these policy issues at some length.

3.3   Conclusions

Overall, in this chapter, we have seen that the Kuznets curve is *not* a necessary feature in the data, nor even the best general description of changes over time. It is not the *rate* of economic growth or the *stage* of economic development that determines whether inequality increases or decreases.

This is actually a long-standing result. Two decades ago, I wrote: "Growth itself does not determine a country's inequality course. Rather, the decisive factor is the *type* of economic growth as determined by the environment in which growth occurs and the political decisions taken" (Fields 1980, p. 94). This new review of the evidence shows that that conclusion remains equally valid today.

Other variables also determine inequality. These include the basic nature of the economic system itself; the structure of output; the composition of exports; regional patterns; the structure of employment; the distributions of land and capital; the state of development of the capital market; the level and inequality in the distribution of human capital; and the distribution of social income.

Looking ahead, it would appear that there is little point to working further on cross-sectional patterns. The highest payoff, rather, would appear to be in in-depth country studies over time and comparisons of the patterns found and reasons for them.

Appendix: Summary of Econometric Methodology Used in Gary S. Fields and George H. Jakubson "New Evidence on the Kuznets Curve"

The objective is to estimate the parameters of the inequality-development relationship

$$I_{it} = f(X_{it}), \tag{3A.1}$$

where $X_{it} = [\text{GNP}, \text{GNP}^2]$ or $[\log(\text{GNP}), \log(\text{GNP})^2]$ or $[\text{ICP}, \text{ICP}^2]$ or $[\log(\text{ICP}), \log(\text{ICP})^2]$. Following the literature, we choose a linear-in-parameters form

$$I_{it} = \alpha_0 + \gamma' X_{it} + e_{it}. \tag{3A.2}$$

OLS estimation of (3A.2) is inconsistent if there are unobserved country-specific factors correlated with X_{it}. One way of allowing for country-specific factors that are correlated with X_{it} is to adopt a fixed effects specification:

$$I_{it} = \gamma' X_{it} + [\alpha_i + u_{it}], \tag{3A.3}$$

where u_{it} is assumed to be a classical disturbance, that is, i.i.d. with zero mean, uncorrelated with X_{it} and homoscedastic. Note that this allows for the α_i to be correlated with the X_{it}. OLS applied to equation (3A.3) produces consistent and efficient estimates of parameters for a family of parallel Kuznets curves.

An equivalent way of estimating γ is as follows. Let $\bar{I}_i$ be the mean over time of the I_{it} for country i. Define $\bar{X}_i$ and $\bar{u}_i$ similarly. Taking deviations from means:

$$[I_{it} - \bar{I}_i] = \gamma'[X_{it} - \bar{X}_i] + [u_{it} - \bar{u}_i]. \tag{3A.4}$$

OLS on (3A.4) gives consistent, efficient estimates of γ. This estimate is denoted $\hat{\gamma}$.

To estimate the α_is, use the fact that the fitted relationships from least squares go through each country's mean value:

$$\hat{\alpha}_i = \bar{I}_i - \hat{\gamma}'\bar{X}_{it}. \tag{3A.5}$$

The "central" Kuznets curve—that is, the inequality that would be predicted given national income for a randomly chosen country—is given by

$$E[I_{it}|X_{it}] = \alpha^* + \hat{\gamma}'X_{it}, \tag{3A.6}$$

where $\alpha^* = E[\alpha_i]$ and the γs in this equation are given by (4). The intercept, α^*, can be efficiently estimated by pooling the data, ignoring the country-specific structure, and estimating the analog of equation (3A.2) using least squares. See Fields and Jakubson 1994 for further details.

4   The Measurement of Poverty

In the present time, through the greater part of Europe, a creditable day-labourer would be ashamed to appear in public without a linen shirt.

—Adam Smith, *Wealth of Nations*, 1776

4.1   Introduction

"Poverty" has been defined as the inability of an individual or a family to command sufficient resources to satisfy basic needs. The workman who, in Adam Smith's day, could not appear in public wearing a proper linen shirt, was ipso facto poor, not only to Smith but to Amartya Sen who, commenting on Smith's observation, wrote: "On the space of the capabilities themselves—the direct constituent of the standard of living—escape from poverty has an absolute requirement, to wit, avoidance of this type of shame. Not so much having equal shame as others, but just not being ashamed, absolutely" (Sen 1984, p. 335).

Nowadays, an income recipient is classified as poor on the basis of more than a single item of clothing. A basket of "basic needs" is defined and costed out. Given this figure in dollars, pesos, or rupees, we classify a recipient unit as poor if its income (or consumption, if that is the chosen measure of economic well-being) is below the cutoff amount. Throughout this book, this cutoff amount will be called the "poverty line" and be denoted by z.

Over time, the poverty line needs to be adjusted for changes in the cost of acquiring the basket of basic needs. When the poverty line is adjusted for inflation and only for inflation, the line defines "absolute poverty."[1]

---

1. This is contrast to "relative poverty," which is taken up in section 4.6.

Often it is of interest to concentrate our attention on the poor to the exclusion of the rest of the income distribution—for instance, in gauging how much economic misery there is in an economy or in determining whether economic misery is increasing or decreasing. For such purposes, we may be justified in focusing our attention on the economic condition of poor people while ignoring the incomes of those who are demonstrably nonpoor. The idea that the extent of poverty in a population is independent of the incomes of those above the poverty line is sometimes called the "focus axiom," and it justifies gauging poverty solely with reference to the incomes of persons below the poverty line.

The rest of this chapter deals with four topics: setting a poverty line, clarifying the concept of poverty, constructing a poverty measure, and testing for poverty dominance. For detailed results on these topics, see inter alia Foster 1984, Atkinson 1987, Seidl 1988, Ravallion 1994, Zheng 1997, and Foster and Sen 1997.

4.2   Setting a Poverty Line

In some countries, the poverty line has already been set and the best thing to do is to speak of poverty in the same way that others in the country do. In other countries, though, one may be able to define a single poverty line or an entire range of poverty lines, and will therefore have to make some choices about how to do it. In such instances, a number of decisions will need to be made:

1. *Is the basis income or consumption, and how comprehensively will the chosen concept be measured?* Consumption is regarded as the better indicator of living standards, provided it can be accurately measured. The best measure is a comperehensive one, including imputations for food and other goods produced and consumed at home, basic goods provided free or at subsidized rates by the government, and nonwage benefits such as "free" housing provided by the employer.

2. *What is the recipient unit: individual, family, per capita, or adult equivalent?* Adjustments for family size are needed. One method to adjust for family size is to set different poverty lines for families of different sizes (which enables adjustments for economies of scale). Another method is to set a poverty line on a per capita or an adult-

equivalent basis, then adjust income or consumption accordingly.[2] The number of families in poverty should be used only as a last resort.

3. *Will there be a single poverty line or will there be separate ones for urban and rural areas or different regions of the country?* Typically, the cost of the basic basket of necessities is significantly higher in urban than in rural areas, which is why the South Asian countries have been using separate poverty lines for urban and rural areas for decades.

4. *Is the poverty line income determined scientifically, politically, subjectively, or as a matter of convenience?* Governments of individual countries such as India and the United States as well as international organizations such as the Inter-American Development Bank (IDB) and the Economic Commission for Latin America and the Caribbean (ECLAC) have determined their poverty lines "scientifically" by figuring the cost of purchasing nutritional necessities consistent with local dietary habits and adding to that the cost of housing, clothing, and other nonfood necessities.[3] In other countries, the poverty line is determined politically—for example, in Brazil, "poverty" denotes those persons with incomes less than the national minimum wage.[4] Yet another approach is to define poverty subjectively, in answer to a question such as, "What income level do you personally consider to be absolutely minimal? That is to say that with less you could not make ends meet?" There is a long tradition of analyzing poverty subjectively, especially in the Netherlands but elsewhere in Europe as well (Jenkins et al. 1998). And in some cases, there is no poverty line at all, and "poverty" is defined as a matter of convenience in round numbers: below 100,000 New Taiwan dollars or 100,000

---

2. The setting of equivalence scales is complex and requires detailed technical analysis. Despite the existence of the topic in the literature for more than a century no consensus has been reached. Two good surveys of the main issues are those by Ravallion (1994, pp. 17–25) and Deaton (1997, pp. 241–270).

3. What is defined as a necessity varies from country to country. Contrast, for instance, Council of Economic Advisers 1964 and Orshansky 1965 for the United States, with Dandekar and Rath 1971, Minhas et al. 1987 and Srinivasan and Bardhan 1988 for India. Because of these variations, we can think of countries having "absolute poverty lines, set relatively." For a recent overview, see Lipton and Ravallion 1995.

4. About which two things should be said: (1) Because the minimum wage is revised regularly by the Brazilian government and therefore is not constant in real terms over time, it is not a good measure of absolute poverty. (2) Sadly, in published income distributions, the category "less than one minimum wage" has more income recipients than any other.

Korean won or one U.S. dollar per person per day.[5] Clearly, the more scientific the basis for setting the poverty line, the better.

5. *What use should be made of indicators other than consumption or income?* The United Nations, through its *Human Development Reports*, and Nobel Price winner Amartya Sen are among those who have been forceful and consistent voices in favor of broad indices of human development and human capabilities.[6] Although one may quarrel with the specific form of the United Nations's human development index, there is little disagreement about the desirability of moving beyond consumption- and income-based measures when possible. Meanwhile, it is often the case that data are not available on consumption, income, functionings, or capabilities, so other measures are used instead including social indicators (e.g., school attendance, adult literacy rate, per capita food consumption, percentage of dwelling units with running water, extent of electrification, population per physician) and labor market indicators (e.g., unemployment rates, minimum wages, industrial and occupational composition of employment, extent of wage and salary employment).

Finally, it bears repeating that in setting absolute poverty lines, there are two essentials. First, the poverty line must be adjusted for inflation, so that it remains constant in real currency units; when inflation is running at triple-digit rates, such adjustments may have to be made monthly or even weekly.[7] Second, the *only* adjustment to be made to the poverty line is for inflation; the poverty line must *not* be adjusted for economic growth, for then it ceases to be an absolute poverty line.

The answers just given have been very brief. For further discussion of these issues, see Atkinson 1987; Ravallion 1994; Gottschalk and Smeeding 1997; Anand and Sen 1997; and Foster and Sen 1997.

4.3 The Concept of Poverty

The next steps in measuring poverty in an economy are to gauge the poverty of each recipient unit and then to aggregate them. For con-

---

5. The latter is a figure often used by the World Bank.

6. Sen's work is summarized in Foster and Sen (1997, chapter A.7) and in Sen (1997).

7. It should be noticed that adjusting the poverty line by using a general price index entails a potential problem. The basket of goods of the price index may be different from the basket of goods used to define the poverty line. In this case, the poverty line may be over/under adjusted.

creteness, let us suppose that poverty is to be determined by comparing the "income" of an "individual" (y_i) with the poverty line (z).
The individual poverty function $p(y_i, z)$ tells us how much poverty is
associated with individual income y_i when the poverty line is z. The
aggregator function then gives us a measure of poverty in the population as a whole. At issue is what properties the individual poverty
function $p(y_i, z)$ and the aggregator function should have in order to
produce a "good" poverty measure.

Three commonly used individual poverty functions are the indicator function

$$p_1(y_i, z) = 1 \text{ if } y_i < z,$$

$$= 0 \text{ otherwise,}$$

the poverty gap function

$$p_2(y_i, z) = z - y_i \text{ if } y_i < z,$$

$$= 0 \text{ otherwise,}$$

and the normalized gap function

$$p_3(y_i, z) = (z - y_i)/z \text{ if } y_i < z,$$

$$= 0 \text{ otherwise.}$$

It is useful to think of these individual poverty functions as loss
functions $L(y_i, z)$, indicating the loss from having income y_i when the
poverty line is z. These three particular loss functions—the indicator
function, the poverty gap function, and the normalized gap function
—are depicted in panels (a)–(c) of figure 4.1.

To get a poverty measure for the economy as a whole, these individual poverty functions are then aggregated. Denote the number of
poor people by q and the total population by n. Aggregation might
perhaps be by summing

$$P = \sum_i p(y_i, z),$$

by averaging over the poor population

$$P = \frac{1}{q} \sum_i p(y_i, z),$$

or by averaging over the entire population

$$P = \frac{1}{n} \sum_i p(y_i, z).$$

In view of these possibilities, what would be a "good" poverty measure? We shall proceed as in chapter 2 by considering a number of examples, except now we are trying to compare the amount of poverty in different situations, not the amount of inequality.

As before, we will suppose that we are given a set Ω of income vectors. Given two vectors $X, Y \in \Omega$, the relation $\succeq_P$ (read "at least as much poverty as") provides a basis for comparing their relative degrees of poverty. When both $X \succeq_P Y$ and $Y \succeq_P X$, we shall say that X and Y "have equal poverty" and write this relation as $\sim_P$, for example, $X \sim_P Y \Leftrightarrow X \succeq_P Y$ and $Y \succeq_P X$. The binary relations $\succeq_P$ and $\sim_P$ are assumed to satisfy reflexivity **R** ($X \succeq_P X$ and $X \sim_P X$ for all $X \in \Omega$) and transitivity **Tr** (if $X \succeq_P X'$ and $X' \succeq_P X''$, then $X \succeq_P X''$ and likewise for $\sim_P$).

Let us work with a number of the same examples used in chapter 2. In all of these examples, the poverty line z is taken to be $2.50 per unit of time.

Consider two income distribution vectors

$$Y_1 = (1, \quad 2, \quad 3, \quad 4)$$
$$\quad\;\; \alpha, \quad \beta, \quad \gamma, \quad \delta$$

and

$$Y_2 = (1, \quad 2, \quad 3, \quad 4)$$
$$\quad\;\; \delta, \quad \gamma, \quad \beta, \quad \alpha$$

which are identical except that one is a permutation of the other. As with inequality comparisons, unless there is something different about the income recipients in the two cases, it is appealing to say that Y_1 and Y_2 have the same degree of poverty.[8] Accepting this idea as an axiom, anonymity in poverty comparisons is defined as the following property:

---

8. And, as with income inequality, if there were such differences, we would have wanted to have adjusted the base accordingly, for example, by basing our poverty comparisons on per-capita incomes or per-adult-equivalent incomes rather than total incomes.

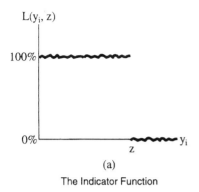

(a)

The Indicator Function

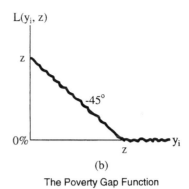

(b)

The Poverty Gap Function

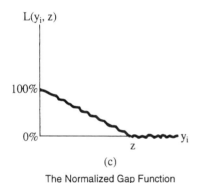

(c)

The Normalized Gap Function

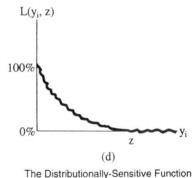

(d)

The Distributionally-Sensitive Function

Figure 4.1
Four loss-from-poverty functions

ANONYMITY (**A**): If $X \in \Omega$ is obtained from $Y \in \Omega$ by a permutation of Y, $X \sim_P Y$.

Our next question is how to compare the degrees of poverty in two economies with different total income amounts. Suppose that everyone's real income doubles, producing the new income distribution vector

$$Y_3 = (2, 4, 6, 8).$$

How does the poverty of Y_3 compare with that of Y_1 and Y_2?

This is where the decision to look at absolute poverty is crucial. For as long as the poverty line z is set as a *constant* real income figure, when everyone's real income rises, poverty must fall (or at least not increase). Continuing with our example, when the poverty line is $2.50, in Y_1 and Y_2, two people are poor and their average income shortfall is $1, whereas in Y_3, one person is poor and his/her shortfall is $.50. This demonstrates why it is that we do *not* want to have an income-homogeneity axiom for a *poverty* measure, and for this reason, no such axiom is proposed.

Consider now how to compare poverties in populations of different sizes, for example,

$$Y_3 = (2,4,6,8)$$

and

$$Y_4 = (2,2,4,4,6,6,8,8),$$

again using a poverty line of $2.50. Two answers are reasonable, though they convey different information. On the one hand, it could be said that Y_4 has *twice as much* poverty as Y_3, because Y_4 has two poor people whereas Y_3 only has one, Y_4 has a total poverty gap of $1.00 (= $.50 per poor person × 2 poor persons) whereas Y_3 has a gap of only $.50, and so on. On the other hand, Y_3 and Y_4 both have 25 percent of the population in poverty and the average poverty gap is $.50 in both, so in this sense, Y_3 and Y_4 have *the same* poverty as each other.

When populations of different sizes are being compared, the per capita comparison may convey a better sense of the magnitude of the problem. In most circumstances, we would probably not want to say that India has more poverty than Singapore simply because there are more than three hundred times as many Indians as Singaporeans. So the following axiom may be appealing:

POPULATION HOMOGENEITY. (ALSO CALLED POPULATION INDEPENDENCE) (**P**): If $X \in \Omega$ is obtained from $Y \in \Omega$ by replicating each income an integral number of times, then $X \sim_P Y$.

Thus far, we have no basis for making poverty comparisons when income amounts differ. An axiom which has been used by Sen (1976) and others enables such comparisons to be made in some circumstances:

MONOTONICITY AND STRONG MONOTONICITY (**M** AND **SM**): 1. Monotonicity: If $X \in \Omega$ is obtained from $Y \in \Omega$ by adding a positive amount of income to someone who was below the poverty line, holding all other incomes the same, then $Y \succeq_P X$.
2. Strong monotonicity: Replace $\succeq_P$ by $\succ_P$.

Finally, we have a transfer principle for poverty measurement, also introduced by Sen (1976). If a transfer of income is made from a poor person to any person who is richer, then poverty must increase. For example, take the income distribution

$Y_1 = (1, 2, 3, 4)$,

and let the poverty line be $2.50. Now let the person with an initial income of $1 transfer $.25 to the individual with an initial income of $2, producing the new income distribution

$Y_5 = (.75, 2.25, 3, 4)$.

It might be argued that poverty *increases* when such a transfer is made, because although there are the same number of poor and the same average income shortfall among the poor in the two situations, the transfer of income from a very poor person to a not-so-poor poor person may be said to raise the economic well-being of the recipient by less than it lowers the economic well-being of the donor.[9] By this argument, the loss-from-poverty function is strictly convex on $[0, z]$, as shown in panel (d) of figure 4.1. In the poverty literature, such functions are said to be "distributionally sensitive." Accordingly, we have the following axiom:

DISTRIBUTIONAL SENSITIVITY (**DS**): If, holding all other incomes the same, $X \in \Omega$ is obtained from $Y \in \Omega$ by transferring a positive amount of income from a poor person α to a richer person β, then $X \succ_P Y$. (The strict poverty relation $\succ_P$ is defined as $\succeq_P$ but not $\sim_P$.)

We have defined reflexivity (**R**), transitivity (**Tr**), anonymity (**A**), population homogeneity (**P**), monotonicity (**M**) and strong monotonicity (**SM**), and distributional sensitivity (**DS**). Let us now see how a number of commonly used poverty measures stack up against these axioms.

---

9. One justification for this would be diminishing marginal utility of income using interpersonally comparable social evaluation functions.

4.4 Four Groups of Poverty Measures

In this section, we shall consider four groups of poverty measures. These are the poverty headcount and headcount ratio; the Sen index and generalizations; the P_α class; and other miscellaneous poverty measures. Throughout this section, z will be used to denote the poverty line, n the total number of income recipients ("persons"), and q the number who are adjudged to be poor using poverty line z.

The Poverty Headcount and Headcount Ratio

The poverty headcount (H) is defined as the *number* of people in a population who are poor, while the poverty headcount ratio (H) is the *fraction* who are poor:

$$H = q$$

and

$$H = q/n.$$

Both of these measures use the individual poverty function

$$p(y_i, z) = 1 \text{ if } y_i < z,$$
$$= 0 \text{ otherwise.}$$

Their aggregator functions are, respectively,

$$P = \sum_i p(y_i, z)$$

and

$$P = \frac{1}{n} \sum_i p(y_i, z).$$

Which of the preceding properties are satisfied by H and H? As with all the other poverty measures to be considered in this section, H and H satisfy reflexivity (**R**), transitivity (**Tr**), and anonymity (**A**). The income distribution $(1, 1, 2, 2, 3, 3, 4, 4)$ has a higher poverty headcount H than does the income distribution $(1, 2, 3, 4)$, therefore H does not satisfy population-homogeneity (**P**). Population-homogeneity is, however, satisfied by the headcount ratio H. Because both the poverty headcount H and the headcount ratio H are concerned only with the number of people with incomes below the poverty line but not with their incomes, neither satisfies strong monotonicity (**SM**) nor distributional sensitivity (**DS**).[10]

If you find **SM** and **DS** appealing, then the poverty headcount H and the poverty headcount ratio H are not good poverty measures for you. Why, then, are these measures used so often? There are three main reasons. One is that poverty headcounts and headcount ratios are straightforward conceptually: when we read that 1.3 billion persons in the world are poor using a poverty line of US$1 per person per day (World Bank 1999; United Nations 1999), the extent of poverty is easily grasped. Second, some researchers and statistical bureaus have not fully considered the desirability of using measures with the **SM** and **DS** properties or, in some cases, acted on that understanding. And third, even in cases where the analyst is fully aware that other poverty measures are preferable to H and H, there may simply be no data enabling poverty comparisons to be made using measures with the **SM** and **DS** properties.[11] For these reasons, the poverty headcount and headcount ratio continue to be used in empirical work, as indeed they are in chapter 5 below.

When micro data are available, as they are increasingly coming to be, one can calculate a variety of other poverty measures even when they are not published by national statistical offices.[12] The two classes of measures that follow are increasingly being calculated by individual researchers.

The Sen Index of Poverty

Let us adopt the following notation:

$\bar{y}_p$ = the average income of the poor,

$\bar{I}$ = $(z - \bar{y}_p)/z$ the average (normalized) income shortfall among the poor,

and

G_p = Gini coefficient of income inequality among the poor.

---

10. Suppose that a poor person transfers enough money to a richer poor person so that the recipient is lifted above the poverty line. The poverty headcount falls—exactly the opposite of what distributional-sensitivity requires

11. For example, the U.S. government regularly publishes poverty headcount ratios going back to 1959 and updates these annually. But if you want a time series on measures using the **SM** or **DS** properties, you will have to make the calculations yourself, because no such table is published by the government.

12. One helpful computer program is POVCAL, available from the World Bank at http://www.worldbank.org/lsms/tools/povcal/.

The Sen poverty index, P_{Sen}, is defined as

$$P_{Sen} = H[\bar{I} + (1 - \bar{I})G_p].$$

It is apparent from this formula that the Sen index has the following three characteristics:

s.1. Other things equal, the larger is the fraction of income recipients who fall below the poverty line, the larger is P_{Sen};

s.2. Other things equal, the higher is the average income of those below the poverty line, the lower is P_{Sen};[13] and

s.3. Other things equal, the greater is income inequality among the poor, the greater is P_{Sen}.[14]

The Sen index has been generalized by a number of authors; see Foster and Sen 1997 (p. 173) for a summary.

The P_α Class

This class of measures was devised by Foster, Greer, and Thorbecke (1984). It is best understood by considering the ith individual's normalized gap function

$$p_3(y_i, z) = (z - y_i)/z \text{ if } y_i < z,$$

$$= 0 \text{ otherwise.}$$

Consider a poverty measure which weights each individual's normalized gap function by itself—thus, the income of an individual whose income is 10 percent below the poverty line is weighted by 10 percent, the income of an individual whose income is 50 percent below the poverty line is weighted by 50 percent, and so on. Average these squared percentage shortfalls over the entire population.[15] The

---

13. For instance, using a poverty line of $2.5, compare the amount of poverty in $Y_1 = (1, 2, 3, 4)$ with that in $Y_6 = (1.2, 2.4, 3, 4)$. These two distributions have the same poverty headcount ratio and the same Gini coefficient among the poor. By (s.2), Y_6 has less poverty by P_{Sen} than does Y_1.

14. Again, using a poverty line of $2.5, compare the amount of poverty in $Y_1 = (1, 2, 3, 4)$ with that in $Y_7 = (1.5, 1.5, 3, 4)$. These two distributions have the same poverty headcount ratio and the same average income shortfall among the poor, but Y_1 has positive income inequality among the poor whereas Y_7 does not. By (iii), Y_7 has less poverty gauged by P_{Sen} than does Y_1.

15. For individuals with incomes at or above the poverty line, the shortfall is zero, and the weight is zero.

resultant poverty measure is

$$P_2 \equiv \frac{1}{n} \sum_{i=1}^{q} [(z - y_i)/z]^2.$$

The P_α class generalizes this measure by replacing the exponent 2 by whatever value of α the researcher cares to specify:

$$P_\alpha \equiv \frac{1}{n} \sum_{i=1}^{q} [(z - y_i)/z]^\alpha.$$

Other members of the P_α class besides the P_2 measure also have intuitive meaning. For $\alpha = 1$, we have

$$P_1 = \frac{1}{n} \sum_{i=1}^{q} [(z - y_i)/z] = \frac{q}{n} \frac{1}{q} \sum_{i=1}^{q} [(z - y_i)/z] = H\bar{I},$$

that is, P_1 is the "per capita income gap" or the "normalized poverty deficit."[16] And for $\alpha = 0$, we have that $P_0 = q/n = H$, the poverty headcount ratio. We see too that as we progress from P_0 to P_1 to P_2, the P_α measure gets more and more sensitive to extremely low incomes.

In the empirical literature, the P_2 measure is being calculated increasingly often.

Other Poverty Measures
Before leaving this presentation of poverty measures, let us briefly note some other measures that one sometimes finds in use. One is *the average (normalized) income shortfall among the poor*, $\bar{I} = (z - \bar{y}_p)/z$, taken by itself. The problem with this measure is that if an individual just below the poverty line receives a large enough income gain to escape poverty, the average income among the remaining poor $\bar{y}_p$ falls, and therefore $\bar{I}$ rises. That is, making a poor person richer has *raised* poverty, violating the monotonicity axiom (**M**). This is why, if one finds monotonicity appealing, $\bar{I}$ is not a good poverty measure to use.[17]

Another poverty measure that has been suggested—actually, the first poverty measure that was sensitive not only to the number of

---

16. The per-capita income gap $H\bar{I}$ arises also for the Sen index when there is no inequality among the poor. In this case, $G_p = 0$ and $P_{sen} = H\bar{I}$.
17. It would be much better to combine $\bar{I}$ with H and G_p and use the Sen index.

poor but also to the severity of their poverty—is attributable to Watts (1968):

$$P_{\text{Watts}} = \sum_{i=1}^{q} \log(z/y_i)/n.$$

Another early poverty measure that is also sensitive to the severity of poverty is the second measure of Clark, Hemming, and Ulph (1981)

$$P_{C\text{-}H\text{-}U} = \frac{1}{c} \sum_{i=1}^{q} [1 - (y_i/z)^c]/n, \text{ where } c \leq 1.$$

One finds these measures used only occasionally in empirical work.

4.5   Poverty Dominance

All of the poverty measures presented in section 4.4 permit complete binary comparisons for any two income distribution vectors $X, Y \in \Omega$. That is, given a particular poverty measure $P(.)$ and a particular poverty line z, the poverty measure $P(.)$ is able to say which distribution has more poverty than the other.

Uncertainty arises in poverty comparisons from two sources: We may not be sure where exactly to draw the poverty line z, and we may not be prepared to commit to a particular poverty measure to the exclusion of others. We could, of course, make numerical calculations for a wide range of poverty lines and poverty measures and see if they all rank X as having more (or less) poverty than Y. But even this would not be conclusive proof; it could be that one of the other poverty measure/poverty line combinations that we didn't try would give the opposite ranking.

Fortunately, dominance methods are now available to test whether one income distribution has more poverty than another for a broad class of poverty measures and a wide range of poverty lines. Unlike inequality measurement, in which dominance theory has a long tradition, dominance analysis in poverty measurement is still a new field. Important contributions have been made by Atkinson (1987), Foster and Shorrocks (1988), Ravallion (1994), and Jenkins and Lambert (1998). Poverty dominance may be nested within the broader concept of "deprivation dominance" (Jenkins and Lambert 1997; Xu and Osberg 1998; Shorrocks 1998).

We begin by noting that most of the poverty measures considered in this chapter—including the headcount ratio, the P_α measure, the Watts index, and the Clark-Hemming-Ulph measure, among others—are members of the general additive class

$$P = \sum_{i=1}^{n} p(z, y_i)/n \text{ such that}$$

1. $p(z, y_i) = 0$ if $y_i \geq z$, and $\qquad\qquad\qquad$ (4.1)

2. $p(z, y_i) > 0$ if $y_i \leq z$

The fact that many poverty measures belong to this general class (but not all do—in particular, the Sen index does not) leads us to consider whether there are dominance criteria for these measures. One may pose three related questions:

1. Are there circumstances under which *all* members of the class of poverty measures (4.1) would rank one income distribution as having more poverty than another for a *given* poverty line z?

2. Given the controversy that usually goes with setting a poverty line, dominance criteria encompassing many poverty lines would be very desirable. In particular, are there circumstances under which a *given* poverty measure belonging to class (4.1) would rank one income distribution as having more poverty than another for a *range* of poverty lines $\underline{z} < z < \bar{z}$?

3. Are there circumstances under which *all* poverty measures belonging to class (4.1) would rank one income distribution as having more poverty than another for a *range* of poverty lines $\underline{z} < z < \bar{z}$?

This section shows that the answers to all three questions are affirmative. The following notation will be used:

z = poverty line,

y_{min} = lowest income in population,

y_{max} = highest income in population,

z_{max} = highest possible poverty line,

$F_X(z)$ = cumulative density function for distribution X when the poverty line is z, also called the "poverty incidence curve."

For the class of poverty measures given by (4.1), we now consider three levels of poverty dominance.

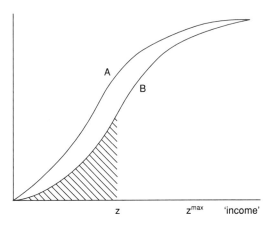

(a) Poverty Incidence Curves for two Distributions A and B

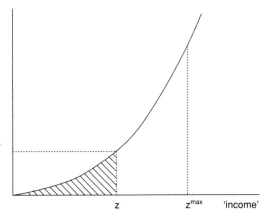

(b) Poverty Deficit Curve for Distribution B

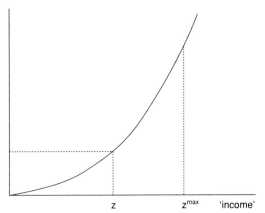

(c) Poverty Severity Curve for Distribution B

First-Order Dominance (FOD)

First-order dominance in poverty measurement is defined as follows: If the cumulative density function for distribution A (F_A) is everywhere at least as high as that for distribution B (F_B) for all z between y_{min} and z_{max}, *A first-order-dominates B*, written *A FOD B*. (See figure 4.2.a.) An increase in some poor person's income, holding other poor persons' incomes constant, is sufficient but not necessary for first-order dominance.

The relationship between *FOD* and poverty dominance using measures belonging to the class (4.1) is given by the following theorem:

THEOREM 4.1 (ATKINSON 1987; FOSTER AND SHORROCKS 1988): *A FOD B* $\Leftrightarrow pov_A > pov_B$ for all poverty measures belonging to the class (4.1), or for any monotonic transformation thereof, and for all poverty lines between y_{min} and z_{max}.

As applied to the P_α class, theorem 4.1 tells us that *A FOD B* $\Rightarrow$ $pov_A > pov_B$ for all P_α, $\alpha \geq 0$ and for all poverty lines between y_{min} and z_{max}.

Theorem 4.1 gives a condition for ranking two income distributions when their poverty incidence curves do not cross. If they do cross, rankings may be still be possible using the results of:

Second-Order Dominance

Second-order dominance in poverty measurement is defined as follows: Take the areas under the F_A and F_B curves. Call these *poverty deficit curves*, $D(z)$, as in figure 4.2.b. If the poverty deficit curve for A is somewhere above and never below the curve for B for all z between y_{min} and z_{max}, *A second-order-dominates B*, written *A SOD B*.

A subset of the measures belonging to the class (4.1) will give identical poverty rankings in cases of second-order dominance. Specifically:

THEOREM 4.2 (ATKINSON; FOSTER AND SHORROCKS): *A SOD B* $\Leftrightarrow$ $pov_A > pov_B$ for the subset of poverty measures belonging to the class (4.1) which are strictly decreasing and at least weakly convex in the incomes of the poor, or for any monotonic transformation thereof, and for all poverty lines between y_{min} and z_{max}.

Figure 4.2
Three orders of Poverty Dominance
Source: Ravallion 1994 (pp. 67–68).

For the P_α class, theorem 4.2 tells us that $A\ SOD\ B \Rightarrow pov_A > pov_B$ for all P_α, $\alpha \geq 1$ and for all poverty lines between y_{min} and z_{max}.

If poverty deficit curves do not cross, theorem 4.2 provides a criterion for ranking the poverty of different income distributions. However, the poverty deficit curves may cross, in which case poverty rankings may still be possible by turning to:

Third-Order Dominance
Third-order dominance in poverty measurement is defined analogously to second-order dominance. Take the areas under the poverty deficit curves for distributions A and B and call these *poverty severity curves*, $S(z)$. (See figure 4.2.c.) If the poverty severity curve for A is somewhere above and never below the poverty severity curve for B for all z between y_{min} and z_{max}, A *third-order dominates* B, written $A\ TOD\ B$.

Before stating the next theorem, recall the definition of distributional sensitivity given above. We then have:

THEOREM 4.3 (ATKINSON, FOSTER, AND SHORROCKS): $A\ TOD\ B \Leftrightarrow$ $pov_A > pov_B$ for the subset of poverty measures belonging to the class (4.1) which are distributionally-sensitive, or for any monotonic transformation thereof, and for all poverty lines between y_{min} and z_{max}.

For the P_α class, theorem 4.3 tells us that $A\ TOD\ B \Rightarrow pov_A > pov_B$ for all P_α, $\alpha \geq 2$ and for all poverty lines between y_{min} and z_{max}.

Comparing the Different Levels of Dominance
When we examine the definitions of the various levels of dominance, we see a hierarchical relationship among them: If $A\ FOD\ B$, then the area under the poverty incidence curve for A is necessarily greater than the area under the poverty incidence curve for B, which is the definition of second-order dominance. Likewise, given second-order dominance, the area under the poverty deficit curve for A is necessarily greater than the area under the poverty deficit curve for B, which is the definition of third-order dominance. Thus:

$$FOD \Rightarrow SOD \Rightarrow TOD. \tag{4.2}$$

Fact (4.2) makes precise exactly how far you can go in defining the variety of poverty measures and range of poverty lines for which one income distribution has more poverty than another. For instance, if neither $A\ FOD\ B$ nor $B\ FOD\ A$ but $A\ SOD\ B$, then you can conclude that A has more poverty than B only for those poverty measures in class (4.1) which are strictly decreasing and at least weakly convex in the incomes of the poor, or for any monotonic transformation thereof, and for all poverty lines between y_{min} and z_{max}. You would know too that because the poverty headcount ratio is not strictly decreasing in the incomes of the poor, that that measure would not necessarily show greater poverty in A than in B.

Suppose you have decided that you like the P_α class of poverty measures, but you are not sure how far these measures can take you in making ordinal poverty comparisons. Pulling together the preceding results, here is your answer:

1. A FOD $B \Rightarrow pov_A > pov_B$ for all P_α, $\alpha \geq 0$ and for all poverty lines between y_{min} and z_{max}.

2. A SOD $B \Rightarrow pov_A > pov_B$ for all P_α, $\alpha \geq 1$ and for all poverty lines between y_{min} and z_{max}.

3. A TOD $B \Rightarrow pov_A > pov_B$ for all P_α, $\alpha \geq 2$ and for all poverty lines between y_{min} and z_{max}.

Finally, it bears mention that your search for dominance results may be frustrated, because you have chosen a wider than necessary range for possible poverty lines. For example, you may have initially set z_{max} at a very high value (e.g., \$50,000 per capita per year) and then found that the poverty incidence curves cross at a lower income amount z^* (e.g., \$40,000), as shown in figure 4.3. In such cases, you might want to reset z_{max} to z^*, which would enable you to conclude that A FOD B for all poverty lines in the restricted range $[y_{min}, z^*]$.

4.6 The Concept of Relative Poverty

Thus far in this chapter, we have dealt only with absolute poverty. Some authors (e.g., Fuchs 1967, 1969; Ruggles 1990; Citro and Michael 1995; Ali 1997; Ali and Thorbecke 1998) take exception to this approach to determining poverty lines, preferring to measure relative poverty instead.[18] For rigorous discussions of absolute versus relative poverty, see Foster and Sen 1997 and Foster 1998.

Actually, "relative poverty" embodies two separate ideas, and the relative poverty measures therefore fall into two categories. In the first type of relative poverty measure, a group that is relatively

---

18. Other authors measure both relative and absolute poverty; for instance, Atkinson (1983a) and Blackburn (1994).

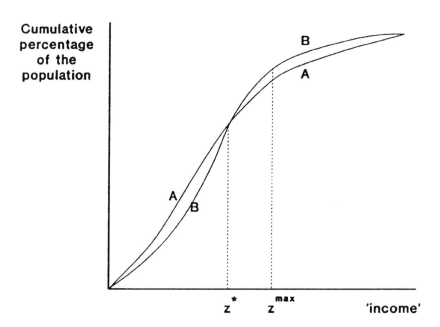

Figure 4.3
Intersecting Poverty Incidence curves
Source: Ravallion 1994 (p. 70).

the poorest (e.g., the poorest 40 percent) is defined, and the poverty measure used is then taken to be the average real income of this poorest group. Consider the example in chapter 1, in which the income distribution changes from

$$\text{Initial} = \underbrace{(1,1,1,1,1,1,1,1,1,}_{9}\underbrace{2)}_{1}$$

to

$$\text{A-C-E-G} = \underbrace{(1,1,1,1,1,1,1,1,}_{8}\underbrace{2,2)}_{2}$$

to

$$\text{B-D-F-H} = \underbrace{(1,1,1,1,1,1,1,}_{7}\underbrace{2,2,2)}_{3}.$$

The average absolute income of the poorest 40 percent of the population shows no change in this process. If you see no change in poverty in this process, this type of relative poverty measure might be a reasonable one for you. But if you judge that poverty has decreased in this process, then you are assuredly *not* a relative poverty adherent, at least in this first sense.

There is, however, a second sense in which you might wish to move in the direction of relative poverty, and that is to use a higher poverty line the richer is the country in which poverty is being measured. Ravallion, Datt, and van de Walle (1991) have found empirically that the poverty lines used in countries tend to increase with their per capita consumption levels, and Ali (1997) regards the desirability of raising the poverty line as the mean increases as "obvious to us, Africans living amidst poverty." While there are different ways of adjusting your poverty line z as a function of the mean income or consumption, μ, the easiest such adjustment is to raise z in proportion to increases in μ, producing a thoroughgoing relative poverty measure. This procedure applies either when z has been set "scientifically" to begin with (e.g., as the cost of purchasing the minimal basket of goods and services) or when z has been set relatively from the beginning. Examples of such relative poverty lines are half the median income (Fuchs 1969), two-thirds of the median income, as is done by the Luxembourg Income Study (Atkinson et al. 1995), half the mean income, as is done by the European Union (O'Higgins and Jenkins 1990; Atkinson 1998) or two-thirds of the median income, as is used on occasion by the World Bank.

Now let us examine what happens to relative poverty when the poverty line z increases proportionately with the mean μ. We may start with a given income distribution X and then increase everybody's real income by the same proportion, producing the new income distribution λX, $\lambda > 1$. When z increases proportionately with μ, the number with incomes below such a relative poverty line is unchanged. So too are the average (normalized) income shortfall of the poor $\bar{I}$ and the Gini coefficient of income inequality among the poor. This means that the poverty headcount (H), the poverty headcount ratio (H), the Sen index of poverty (P_{sen}), and the P_α class will all show *no change* in poverty when z changes in proportion to μ.

You now need to ask yourself whether this is what you want. Personally, I would want poverty in a country to *fall* when everyone experiences a given percentage increase in income. If you feel the same, then these relative poverty approaches are not for you.[19]

---

19. Be careful not to confuse poverty and inequality here. It is perfectly consistent for you to maintain that a proportionate increase in all incomes leaves relative *inequality* unchanged while reducing absolute *poverty*.

One alternative is to increase the poverty line when economic growth takes place, but by a smaller percentage than the growth rate. Because this is neither fully absolute nor fully relative, it has been termed a "hybrid" approach by Foster (1998). See Citro and Michael 1995 and Atkinson and Bourguignon 1999 for detailed proposals along these lines.

I prefer a different alternative, which is to choose an absolute poverty line, relatively defined. That is, you can set your z higher in relatively rich countries than in relatively poor ones. This is in fact done: The poverty lines used around the world (in 1985 Purchasing Power Parity [PPP] dollars, per person per day) range from $1 for developing countries as a whole to $2 in Latin America to $4 in Eastern Europe and the Commonwealth of Independence States (CIS) nations to $14.40 in the United States. Once these lines are set, they should be adjusted by the respective countries' rates of inflation and nothing more. The best problem that any country could have would be for its economy to grow so fast for so long that its current poverty line is rendered obsolete!

4.7 Summary

"Poverty" has been defined as the inability of an individual or a family to command sufficient resources to satisfy basic needs. A number of technical considerations go into setting a country's poverty line. If we can agree on where to set the poverty line, we can gauge the amount of poverty in a population by measuring the extent of poverty for each constituent individual and then totaling these using a suitable aggregator function. Among the axioms that might be desirable for poverty measures are anonymity, population-homogeneity, monotonicity or strong monotonicity, and distributional sensitivity. The poverty headcount possesses only the first of these properties and the poverty headcount ratio only the first two. However, all four properties are satisfied by the Sen poverty index and the P_α index for $\alpha > 1$. If we are uncertain which poverty measure or which poverty line to use, we may under certain conditions be able to use dominance results to obtain ordinal poverty rankings for a broad class of poverty measures and a broad range of poverty lines; see section 4.5 for details. Finally, and alternatively, if you prefer relative poverty notions to absolute poverty ones, you may prefer one of the types of measures described in section 4.6.

5

Does Economic Growth
Reduce Absolute Poverty?
A Review of the Empirical
Evidence

Most economists accept without question that economic growth reduces absolute poverty. Some of the phrases in our profession reflect this: "trickle-down," "a rising tide lifts all boats," "the flying geese," and so on. I shall refer to this view as the "shared growth" position, in that when economic growth takes place, the poor and others share the fruits of it, to a greater or lesser degree.[1]

On the other side is the distinctly less popular view that economic growth might make the poor poorer. To take just one example, Nobel Prize-winning economist Arthur Lewis (1983) gave six reasons why development of enclaves may lower incomes in the traditional sector: The development enclave may be predatory on the traditional sectors; products of the enclaves may compete with and destroy traditional trades; the wage level of the enclave may be so high that it destroys employment in other sectors; the development of the enclave may result in geographical polarization; development of the enclave may lead to generalized improvements in public health and therefore lower death rates; and development of the enclave may stimulate excessive migration from the countryside.

The most respectable present incarnation of this view is in the work of immiserizing growth theorists, who have proven rigorously that it is possible that economic growth *might* make the poor poorer.[2] Whether growth *does* make the poor poorer or not is an empirical question, to which we now turn.

---

1 Whether it is to greater or to a lesser degree is, of course, what inequality is all about. Chapter 3 reviewed the growth-inequality evidence.

The evidence reviewed in this chapter is on "absolute poverty," namely, the extent of poverty when a fixed real poverty line is used.

2. A good summary may be found in Bhagwati and Srinivasan 1983 (chapter 25). Bhagwati himself now dismisses these theoretical possibilities as the work of "ingenious economists (properly) making their mark by proving the improbable" (Bhagwati 1991).

5.1   Inferences from Cross-Section Evidence

The immiserizing growth hypothesis gained a brief bit of apparent support in the work of Adelman and Morris (1973). They wrote (p. 189): "Development is accompanied by an absolute as well as a relative decline in the average income of the very poor. Indeed, an initial spurt of dualistic growth may cause such a decline for as much as 60 percent of the population." They continued (p. 192): "The frightening implication of the present work is that hundreds of millions of desperately poor people throughout the world have been hurt rather than helped by economic development.

Their results were based on an indirect method that did not survive further scrutiny. One of the most influential subsequent studies was by Ahluwalia (1976b), who compiled data for 62 countries, both developed and developing, for roughly 1970, and regressed the income share of the poorest 20 percent, 40 percent, or 60 percent of the population against log per capita GNP, log per capita GNP squared, and other variables. These shares were then combined with GNP information to produce the average absolute incomes shown in figure 5.1. We see that as per capita national income increases in the cross section, the incomes of the poorest *rise* monotonically.

The most direct test of the poverty/national income relationship in the cross section is to be found in the recent work of Ravallion (1995), based on data from Chen, Datt, and Ravallion (1993). Using an internationally comparable poverty line ($1 of consumption per capita per day in 1985 PPP$), he calculated the poverty headcount index for each of 36 developing countries. The results, shown in figure 5.2, reveal a pronounced negative relationship between a country's poverty rate and its average level of consumption.

In follow-up work, Lipton (1998) used data for the same countries as Ravallion, but also including a second year of data where possible. His regressions showed that half the variance in poverty rates (expressed as the percentage of population below the $1 per day consumption line) could be explained by mean consumption. It may be presumed that the countries' individual circumstances and policies help explain the other half. In chapter 10, we return to a consideration of these additional factors.

In sum, twenty years of research has shown convincingly that in a cross section of countries, those with higher per capita income or con-

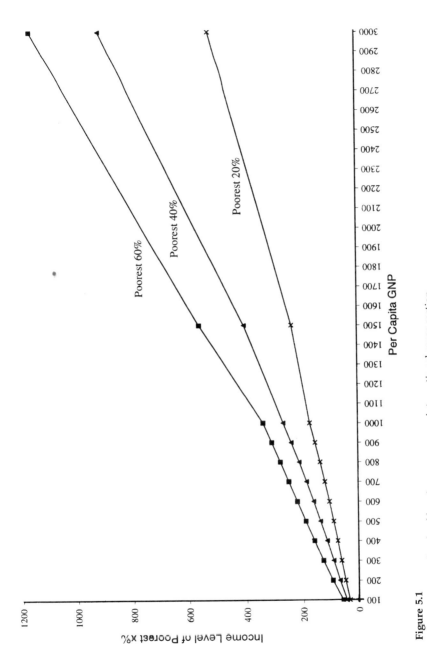

Figure 5.1

Average income levels of low-income groups, international cross section

Source: Ahluwalia 1976b.

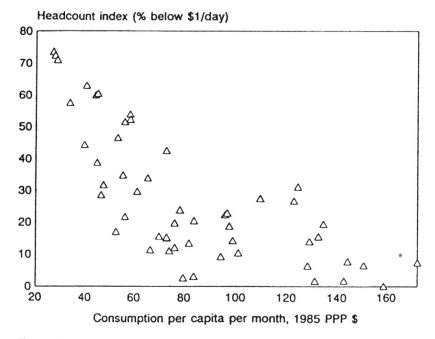

Figure 5.2
Headcount index against mean consumption
Source: Ravallion 1995 (p. 413).

sumption have less poverty. The cross-sectional version of the absolute impoverishment hypothesis has been thoroughly discredited.

5.2   Intertemporal Evidence

The results reported in the previous section described the relationship between poverty and national income growth in the cross section. What about changes in poverty over time within countries? In
the Western world, the early studies of changes in income distribution over time in individual developing countries concentrated on
inequality rather than on poverty. As described in chapters 2 and 3,
this reflected the powerful intellectual influence of Simon Kuznets
(1955, 1963) and followers.

However, in some countries of the Eastern world such as India,
the focus on poverty was there all along (Srinivasan and Bardhan
1974). What was not there for quite some time, however, was statistical information with which to measure how poverty changed with
economic growth in individual countries.

Once the data started becoming available in the 1970s, authors around the world performed studies of poverty change in individual countries. Fields (1980) synthesized thirteen of these. Poverty fell in ten of these countries and rose in three. Two of the three countries in which poverty did not fall are ones in which economic growth did not take place. The only country in which poverty rose in the course of economic growth was the Philippines. The apparent political economy explanation ("crony capitalism") is probably the right one.

In a concurrent study, Ahluwalia, Carter, and Chenery (1979) looked at changes in incomes of both the poorest 60 percent and the richest 40 percent for twelve developing countries. Their results show that in *every* case, the real incomes of the poorest 60 percent and the richest 40 percent both increased over time when the economy grew.

In the 1980s and 1990s, additional country studies were carried out, using increasingly comprehensive data sets. These include the work of Fields (1991); Chen, Datt, and Ravallion (1993); Deininger and Squire (1996); Roemer and Gugerty (1997); Timmer (1997); and Bruno, Ravallion, and Squire (1998). All of these studies used what in chapter 3 we called "spell analysis."[3] The results were always the same: It is overwhelmingly the case that growth reduces poverty and recession increases it, though in about 10 percent of the cases, poverty did not appear to fall when growth took place.

The finding that economic growth nearly always reduces poverty is sometimes misinterpreted. Of course, not every individual is made richer by economic growth, nor even every population subgroup. Early on, Fishlow (1972) wrote eloquently about the poverty that remained in Brazil despite the so-called economic miracle that had taken place there in the late 1960s and early 1970s, and Griffin and Khan (1978) demonstrated that the percentage of rural people who were poor had increased despite economic growth in a number of South and Southeast Asian economies. The reports on poverty by the World Bank (1990, forthcoming) and the United Nations (1997) remind us that even when the majority of a country's people are found to gain from economic growth, some are left out or even hurt by the growth process.

---

3. A "spell" is a period from one survey to another, for example, Malaysia 1970–1976 is one spell, Malaysia 1976–1979 another, and so on. "Spell analysis" means that individual countries can be included as many times in the growth-poverty analysis as their household censuses and surveys permit.

Economic growth would be expected to alleviate poverty, at least to some extent. How much depends on at least two factors. One is the growth rate itself. A study by Squire (1993) used an internationally comparable poverty line and regressed the rate of poverty reduction in a country against its rate of of economic growth. His results show that a one percent increase in the growth rate reduces the poverty headcount ratio by 0.24 percentage points. Similarly, Ravallion and Chen (1997) found that the larger the rate of change in log mean consumption or income in a country, the larger the decline in a country's log poverty rate. Furthermore, Roemer and Gugerty (1997) found that in the economic growth experiences of twenty-six developing countries, the rate of increase of the incomes of the poorest 20 percent was 92 percent of the rate of GDP growth, while for the poorest 40 percent, the rate of increase was essentially identical to the rate of GDP growth. Thus, in all these studies, faster economic growth has been found to lead to greater poverty reduction.

The rate of poverty reduction would also be expected to depend on the extent of economic inequality. In a very straightforward statistical sense, we would expect to find that economic growth reduces poverty by more if inequality falls than if it does not. This expectation is confirmed in cross-country analysis carried out by Bruno, Ravallion, and Squire (1998). For twenty countries during the period 1984–1993, they regressed the rate of change in the proportion of the population living on less than $1 per person per day against the rate of change in real mean income and obtained a regression coefficient of −2.12 with a t ratio of −4.67. This means that a 10 percent increase in the mean can be expected to produce a roughly 20 percent drop in the proportion of people in poverty. And when the P_2 measure is used instead, the effect is even greater: −3.46 with a t ratio of −2.98. They conclude: "Absolute poverty measures typically respond quite elastically to growth, and the benefits are certainly not confined to those near the poverty line."

To see what role inequality plays in poverty reduction, these authors also ran a multiple regression of the change in poverty (using the proportion of the population living on less than $1 per person per day) as a function of both the change in the mean and the change in inequality as measured by the Gini coefficient and found a coefficient of −2.28 (t = −6.07) on the former and 3.86 (t = 3.20) on the latter. In their words (p. 11): "Measured changes in inequality do have a strong independent explanatory power; indeed, rates of poverty reduction respond even more elastically to rates of change in the Gini index than they do to the mean."

The Bruno-Ravallion-Squire findings show that the change in poverty is related both to economic growth and to changing inequality. First, holding the dispersion of income the same, the faster is the rate of economic growth, the larger is the reduction in poverty. Second, for any given growth rate, the more dispersed the distribution is becoming, the smaller is the reduction in poverty.[4]

The relative importance of these growth and redistributive factors for poverty reduction can be gauged using the following equation devised by Ravallion and Huppi (1991); Datt and Ravallion (1992); and Kakwani (1993). Let poverty in a country at time t be denoted by

$$P_t = P(z/\mu_t, D_t),$$

where z is the poverty line, μ_t is mean expenditure per capita, and D_t is the inequality in the distribution of expenditure per capita. Then the change in poverty between a base year B and a terminal year T can be written as

$$P_T - P_B = \underbrace{P(z/\mu_T, D_B) - P(z/\mu_B, D_B)}_{\text{Growth component}}$$

$$+ \underbrace{P(z/\mu_B, D_T) - P(z/\mu_B, D_B)}_{\text{Redistribution component}} + \text{residual}.$$

Applying this methodology to developing countries in Africa, Latin America, and East and Southeast Asia, Demery, Sen, and Vishwanath (1995) came to two conclusions. First, poverty change is largely determined by economic growth. Second, changes in inequality are of secondary importance in the great majority of cases.

An important qualifier needs to be added. In countries' actual experiences, it has proved far easier to generate economic growth than to change the Gini coefficient. In the developing world, GDP per capita grew by 26 percent between 1985 and 1995 (World Bank 1997), while Gini coefficients in the world barely changed over the same period (Deininger and Squire 1998, table 5). In a similar vein, Adelman and Robinson's simulation results showed that even huge changes in policy parameters (such as a doubling of the tax rate,

---

4. In cases of economic decline, poverty rises by more the more negative is the rate of economic growth and the larger is the rate of increase of dispersion.

increasing agricultural capital stocks by 30 percent, fixing all agricultural prices at world prices, and subsidizing the consumption of
food, housing, and medical services for the poorest 60 percent of
households) would change the Gini coefficient in Korea by only one
or two Gini points in most cases. The point is that in comparing the
elasticities of poverty with respect to growth and with respect to
inequality, one should not fall into the trap of thinking that it is as
easy to lower inequality by 10 percent as it is to achieve 10 percent
growth; the former is far more difficult than the latter.

5.3 Poverty Reduction and Growth: Individual Country Experiences

The data presented in the previous section showed that the predominant tendency is for poverty to fall when economic growth
takes place. This happens in the great majority of cases. Consequently, the shared growth view is clearly a better general description of the growth/poverty relationship than is the immiserizing
growth position.

Not only does this conclusion hold in general but it holds for every
region of the world. In Asia, the "big five" countries—China, India,
Indonesia, Pakistan, and Bangladesh, which together have three-
fifths of the developing world's people and two-fifths of the poor—
have all made "impressive progress" in reducing income poverty
(United Nations 1997). Ahuja et al. (1997) report that "poverty has
been declining in every East Asian economy for which we have data
except Papua New Guinea."[5] Unfortunately, the crisis of the late
1990s in a number of East and Southeast Asian countries has demonstrated that the relationship between growth and poverty holds in
times of economic decline as well. Although direct data on poverty
are not yet available for the post-crisis period, the dramatic increase
in unemployment caused by the crisis is surely leading to an increase
in poverty (ILO 1998a; Manuelyan-Atinc and Walton 1998).

In Latin America and the Caribbean (LAC), data compiled by
Londoño and Székely (1998) show that poverty rose during the 1980s
and fell slightly during the 1990s. The 1980s was a "lost decade" for

---

5. Papua New Guinea's per capita GDP grew at about a 2 percent annual rate during
this period of time.

The countries covered in their study are China, Malaysia, Thailand, Indonesia, the
Philippines, Papua New Guinea, Lao PDR, Vietnam, and Mongolia.

Latin America, the growth rate in the region being a negative 1.2 percent (Inter-American Development Bank 1991). In the 1990s, the region experienced a modest recovery: a 6 percent increase (total, not per annum) in real GDP per capita and a 4 percent increase in private consumption. Changes in poverty within countries mirror this trend: During the negative growth decade, the poverty headcount ratio rose in ten of the thirteen countries in Latin America and the Caribbean for which we have data, whereas in the recovery, it fell in nine of the thirteen.[6]

In Africa, the experiences that have been documented also show that when growth has taken place, poverty has fallen. This was the case in Morocco and Tunisia in the latter half of the 1980s (Chen, Datt, and Ravallion 1993), in Ghana from 1987/1988 to 1991/1992 (World Bank 1995; Ghana Statistical Service 1995), in Nigeria from 1985 to 1992 (Canagarajah, Nwafon, and Thomas 1995), and in rural Ethiopia from 1989 to 1994 (Dercon, Krishnan, and Kello 1994; Dercon and Krishnan 1995). However, there were also negative results. In Kenya, lack of economic growth resulted in a constant poverty headcount ratio and continued poverty for an increasing number of people (Mukui 1994; World Bank 1996a). In Tanzania, real per capita income of the poorest 40 percent fell by 28 percent between 1983 and 1991 (Ferreira 1993, cited in Wangwe 1996)—a time during which the economy was contracting at the rate of 1 percent per year. And in Côte d'Ivoire, poverty increased during the 1985–1988 recession, using the poverty headcount ratio, the normalized poverty deficit (P_1) and the squared poverty gap (P_2) for two alternative poverty lines (Grootaert 1994). Note that in each of these cases where poverty did not fall, growth did not take place.

Finally, Eastern Europe and the countries of the former Soviet Union experienced dramatic economic contractions of the early 1990s. While there has been some growth since then in the Eastern European countries, the decline has continued in the countries of the Former Soviet Union. Along with the decline in income, the transition from socialism has also brought increasing inequality. Together,

6. Poverty rose in the 1980s and fell in the 1990s in Brazil, Guatemala, Honduras, Panama, Peru, and Venezuela, in each case reflecting the negative economic growth of the 1980s and the positive economic growth of the 1990s.

Another study that also reaches the conclusion that economic growth usually reduced poverty in Latin American countries is that by Ganuza, Morley, and Taylor (1998).

these effects have led to a massive increase in poverty: The poverty headcount ratio for the region as a whole rose from 4 percent in 1987/1988 to 32 percent in 1994 by one estimate (United Nations 1997) and from 4 percent to 45 percent in 1993/1995 by another (Milanovic 1999).

5.4   Conclusion

The lessons from the available evidence can be summed up simply. Usually but not always, economic growth reduces absolute poverty. On the other hand, when poverty has not fallen, it is generally because economic growth has not taken place.

These findings create a presumption in favor of pursuing economic growth of a type that will reduce poverty. This is hardly a new conclusion, but it is one that is supported by the latest available evidence.

6   The Meaning and Measurement of Income Mobility

People's economic positions may change for a variety of reasons. The economy in which they participate may improve or deteriorate for reasons such as macroeconomic growth or decline, employer-specific events and circumstances, expansions and downsizings, and ups and downs in local communities. Individuals themselves may experience major life course events with important economic consequences— among them, completion of schooling, promotions and other movements up the career ladder, marriage and divorce, poor health, and retirement. Economic mobility studies are concerned with quantifying the movement of given recipient units through the distribution of economic well-being over time, establishing how dependent one's current economic position is on one's past position, and relating people's mobility experiences to the various influences mentioned above.[1]

Four methodological aspects of mobility studies are worth highlighting. First, mobility analysis follows *given* economic units through time. As such, longitudinal (or panel) data are required for research on mobility, which makes mobility analysis different from the measurement of poverty, inequality, or economic well-being, which are based on data from comparable cross sections. Second, mobility analysis can be applied to a variety of recipient units. Those most commonly used are individuals and households. Third, any aspect of economic well-being can be used. Among those that are studied are the income, expenditure, labor market earnings, or occupational attainment of the individual or household. When income and expen-

---

1. Most of what follows is phrased in terms of "income mobility," but it should not be understood as being limited to the study of "incomes" per se. The concepts and methods presented here apply equally well to "economic mobility" as gauged by income, earnings, or expenditures as well as to "socioeconomic mobility" as gauged by an occupational or educational index.

ditures are used, it is often on a per capita basis. Any measure in dollars should be in real dollars, adjusted for inflation. Finally, we shall limit our attention to the recipient's economic well-being in a base year versus a final year. Other mobility studies assess mobility by looking at economic position in each of T years, but we shall not deal with those studies or measures.

Given this range of choices, it would be tedious to talk all the time about changes in income/expenditure/per capita incomes/... among individuals/households/parents and children over a period of years/across the generations. So from now on, for brevity, we will talk in terms of the "income mobility" of "persons" through "time," with the understanding that the measure of economic well-being may be something other than income, the recipient unit may be something other than persons, and "time" may be across generations rather than across years.

Notwithstanding these points of agreement about the concept of economic mobility, there are also some fundamental disagreements. This is because the term "income mobility" conjures up quite different ideas in people's minds. In much the same way that we find it helpful to reserve the term "income distribution" for a generic concept and to use "inequality," "poverty," "mobility," and "economic well-being" to distinguish among different specific aspects of the income distribution, so too is it helpful to reserve the term "income mobility" for the generic concept and to use other specific terms for particular aspects of income mobility. These five different ideas— time dependence, positional movement, share movement, symmetric income movement, and directional income movement—are presented in section 6.1. Section 6.2 then contrasts these different approaches and shows how the choice among them makes a difference in certain illustrative examples. In section 6.3, we look at various mobility measures and their axiomatic foundations.[2]

6.1 Five Mobility Concepts

It is said that Joseph Schumpeter likened an income distribution to a hotel.[3] The rooms at the top are luxurious, those on the middle levels

---

2. For a more detailed review of the technical literature on income mobility measurement, see Fields and Ok (1999).
3. This is reported in Sawhill and Condon 1992 and Danziger and Gottschalk 1995. The analogy is also used by Jarvis and Jenkins (1996).

are ordinary, and those in the basement are downright shabby. At any given time, the occupants of the hotel experience quite unequal accommodations. At a later point in time, we reexamine who is living where. We find that some have moved to higher floors, some have moved to lower floors, and some have stayed where they were. The difference in the quality of hotel rooms at each point in time is what we call inequality. The movement of hotel guests among different quality rooms is mobility. One way in which these are linked is that the more movement of guests there is among rooms, the greater is the long-term equality of accommodations.

But is the movement of guests among rooms all there is to mobility? What if the existing furnishings are redistributed from some rooms to others? Is there not mobility then? What if the hotel is refurbished so that some of the rooms are made nicer? Don't the lucky residents of the now nicer rooms enjoy upward mobility? What about those whose rooms are not upgraded? Do they suffer downward mobility?

The hotel analogy raises some fundamental questions about what economic mobility is, and by extension how it should be measured. The mobility literature is plagued by people talking past one another, because one person's "mobility" notion is not another's. Five different notions shall be distinguished.

Time dependence measures the extent to which economic well-being in the past determines individuals' economic well-being at present. *Positional movement* takes place when there is a change in individuals' economic positions (ranks, centiles, deciles, or quintiles). *Share movement* occurs when individuals' shares of total income change. Then there is *symmetric income movement*, which arises when individuals' incomes change and the analyst is concerned about the magnitude of these fluctuations but not their direction. Finally, we have *directional income movement*, in which income gains and income losses are treated separately.

Let us now look at each of these in greater detail.

Time Dependence

Time dependence is a particular form of immobility. It exists when one's current economic position is determined by one's position in the past.

Studies of time dependence arise in two contexts. In the *inter-generational* context, the question is to what extent the incomes of "sons" can be predicted by the incomes of their "fathers."[4] In the *intragenerational* context, the question is to what extent individuals' incomes at a later date can be predicted by their incomes at an earlier date. To be able to speak about both of these contexts, we can use the terminology "base income" and "final income." Again, the reader is reminded that "income" is a shorthand for whichever economic or socioeconomic variable we are interested in measuring.

Data for gauging time dependence may come either in aggregated or in disaggregated form. We take up in turn how to work with each of these two types of data.

Time Dependence in Aggregated Data

An analytical tool that facilitates measurement of time dependence is an intertemporal transition matrix. The rows of the matrix are the income classes of income recipients in the base year, and the columns are the corresponding income classes in the final year. These classes may either be income categories ($0–10,000, $10,000–20,000, etc.) or quantiles (e.g., deciles or quintiles). The entries in the transition matrix indicate what fraction of individuals with a given base year income end up with a given final year income, and thus each row sums to 100 percent. Quantile transition matrices are the type most commonly used, and so those are the ones we begin with here.

Let the population be divided into five income quintiles. One way in which there might be perfect time dependence is for each recipient's final year income quintile to be identical to his/her base year quintile. If this were the case, all entries in the transition matrix would lie along the principal diagonal running from upper left to lower right, each element on the principal diagonal would equal 100 percent, and thus the transition matrix would be an identity matrix:

$$P_1 = \begin{bmatrix} 1 & 0 & 0 & 0 & 0 \\ 0 & 1 & 0 & 0 & 0 \\ 0 & 0 & 1 & 0 & 0 \\ 0 & 0 & 0 & 1 & 0 \\ 0 & 0 & 0 & 0 & 1 \end{bmatrix} \tag{6.1}$$

---

4. Such sexist terminology is used nearly always in this literature.

The identity matrix indicates what we shall call "perfect positive time dependence." The closer is the actual transition matrix in a country to the identity matrix, the more immobility in the sense of time dependence there is said to be.

There is, however, a quite different way in which there might be perfect time dependence. Suppose that there is a complete reversal of income positions so that all of those who start out rich end up poor and all of those who start out poor end up rich. Though this is only a theoretical possibility that never arises in practice, what it would produce if it did happen is a transition matrix with all ones along the diagonal running from upper right to lower left:

$$P_2 = \begin{bmatrix} 0 & 0 & 0 & 0 & 1 \\ 0 & 0 & 0 & 1 & 0 \\ 0 & 0 & 1 & 0 & 0 \\ 0 & 1 & 0 & 0 & 0 \\ 1 & 0 & 0 & 0 & 0 \end{bmatrix} \qquad (6.2)$$

The reverse identity matrix arises in the case of so-called "perfect negative time dependence." The closer is the actual transition matrix in a country to the reverse-identity matrix, the more immobility in the sense of time dependence there is said to be.

Though these two criteria may appear to be contradictory, I assure you that they are not. This is because lying in between perfect positive time dependence and perfect negative time dependence is time independence. Time-independence arises when an individual's final year income is independent of his or her base year income. This would produce a transition matrix in which each row is the same as every other. In the special case of a quintile mobility matrix, this would mean that every entry would be equal to 0.2:

$$P_3 = \begin{bmatrix} 0.2 & 0.2 & 0.2 & 0.2 & 0.2 \\ 0.2 & 0.2 & 0.2 & 0.2 & 0.2 \\ 0.2 & 0.2 & 0.2 & 0.2 & 0.2 \\ 0.2 & 0.2 & 0.2 & 0.2 & 0.2 \\ 0.2 & 0.2 & 0.2 & 0.2 & 0.2 \end{bmatrix} \qquad (6.3)$$

In order to be able to implement the notions of positive time dependence, negative time dependence, and time independence, you need a way of measuring how close an actual transition matrix is to these various theoretical possibilities. Continuing with the illustration of what might be done if you have a quintile mobility matrix, take as your basis for comparison the number of people that would be observed in cell i, j under the null hypothesis of time independence; this would be the matrix given in (6.3) multiplied by an appropriate scaling factor such that the sum of the expected frequencies is the total sample size N:

$$P_4 = \begin{bmatrix} .04N & .04N & .04N & .04N & .04N \\ .04N & .04N & .04N & .04N & .04N \\ .04N & .04N & .04N & .04N & .04N \\ .04N & .04N & .04N & .04N & .04N \\ .04N & .04N & .04N & .04N & .04N \end{bmatrix} \qquad (6.4)$$

Denoting these expected frequencies by EXP_{ij}, you can then compare them with the observed frequencies OBS_{ij} by making a standard (Pearson) chi-squared calculation

$$\chi^2 = \sum_i \sum_j \frac{(OBS_{ij} - EXP_{ij})^2}{EXP_{ij}}.$$

The calculated chi-squared value would tell you how distant an actual transition matrix is from the one that would be observed in the case of perfect time independence. And then, in comparing the chi-squared values obtained in two different mobility situations, you would be able to say that the one with the larger chi-squared value is more time dependent, and therefore less mobile in the sense of time dependence, than the other.[5]

Table 6.1 displays two quintile mobility matrices for the United States for 1967–1979 and 1979–1991 respectively, from which chi-squared values may be calculated.[6] The chi-squared value calculated for 1967–1979 is 1.153, and for 1979–1991, it is 1.025. This indicates that the United States had less mobility in the sense of time dependence in 1967–1979 than in 1979–1991.

Consider now how you would treat aggregated data in which you are given a transition matrix among income classes that contain

---

5. For tests of statistical significance using an M × M transition matrix, compare the calculated chi-squared value with the tabulated value with $M(M - 1)$ degrees of freedom.

6. When chi-squared values are calculated from quantile transition matrices such as these, the values should be multiplied by the corresponding sample sizes before testing for statistical significance. However, because the authors (Gittleman, Horrigan, and Joyce 1997) did not report the sample sizes, this cannot be done here.

Table 6.1
Quintile mobility rates for equivalent family income

1967–79 transition matrix

	Quintile in 1979				
	Bottom	Second	Third	Fourth	Top
Quintile in 1967					
Bottom	51.3	25.0	15.3	5.9	2.4
Second	21.8	27.0	24.3	19.1	7.8
Third	12.3	21.3	22.7	24.5	19.3
Fourth	8.1	15.0	19.7	26.5	30.7
Top	6.4	11.7	17.8	24.1	40.0
N = 3,277					

1979–91 transition matrix

	Quintile in 1991				
	Bottom	Second	Third	Fourth	Top
Quintile in 1979					
Bottom	47.8	25.6	13.1	10.4	3.2
Second	22.1	26.7	24.8	18.3	8.1
Third	12.2	18.9	25.6	21.6	21.8
Fourth	12.3	19.5	18.2	23.1	26.9
Top	5.7	9.0	17.7	27.6	40.0
N = 3,322					

Source: Gittleman, Horrigan, and Joyce 1997.

unequal numbers of people. In similar fashion, you would need to calculate the distance between the observed frequency distribution and the theoretically expected one, but now the calculation would need to be made in a slightly different way. In this case, under time independence, all rows would have identical conditional probabilities, but because the marginal frequencies are different across income classes in this case (whereas they are identical in the case of quintiles or deciles), the expected frequencies would differ proportionately. Again, in comparing two mobility situations, the one with the larger calculated chi-squared statistic could be said to exhibit more mobility in the sense of time dependence than the other.

Finally, it bears mention that the chi-squared statistic is not the only statistic that might be calculated as a measure of time dependence. Standard statistical packages contain a contingency table procedure that produce quite a number of such statistics. For instance, the Stata statistical package will tell you, in addition to the standard

(Pearson) chi-squared, the likelihood ratio chi-squared, Cramér's V, gamma, and Kendall's tau-b—all of which are measures of time dependence in the sense of gauging deviations from randomness. All of these statistics show higher values for the U.S. in 1967–1979 than in 1979–1991 using the data diplayed in table 6.1, and therefore less mobility in the sense of time dependence in the seventies than in the eighties. On the other hand, Hungerford (1993) calculated the lambda asymmetric statistic, Cramer's V, and the contingency coefficient using a different extract from the Panel Study of Income Dynamics (PSID) and found that each of these produced essentially identical values in the United States in 1969–1976 as in 1979–1986. From this, he concluded that income mobility was unchanged between these two seven-year periods.

The preceding methods give practical ways of measuring time dependence in aggregated data. We turn now to the case of disaggregated data.

Time Dependence in Disaggregated Data

Increasingly nowadays, researchers are working with micro data rather than published data. Such micro data sets may contain observations on many thousands of income recipients. If you have such disaggregated data on the base year and final year incomes for each income recipient, you could if you wanted to create your own intertemporal transition matrix. However, you would lose a great deal of information by doing this, so you might prefer another option: calculating a measure of time dependence using the disaggregated data directly.

A commonly used measure of income mobility is the ordinary (Pearson) coefficient of correlation between base year income and final year income. Friedman and Kuznets (1954) were early users of this statistic. It has been used by many others; see Atkinson, Bourguignon, and Morrisson (1992, table VI) for a partial summary and the Organization for Economic Cooperation and Development (OECD 1996, chart 3.5) for more recent data.

The correlation coefficient gauges income mobility in precisely the sense of time dependence:

• The closer is the value of the correlation coefficient to +1, the more positive time dependence there is.

• The closer is the value of the correlation coefficient to −1, the more negative time dependence there is.

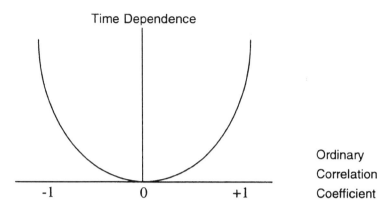

Figure 6.1.a
Time dependence as a function of the ordinary correlation coefficient

• The closer is the value of the correlation coefficient to 0, the more time independence there is.

Figure 6.1.a depicts the relationship between time dependence and the ordinary correlation coefficient.[7]

A related measure of income mobility is the rank correlation coefficient. Denote the poorest individual by 1 and the richest by N in both the base year and final year distributions and calculate the correlation among income ranks. Exactly the same three points as in the previous paragraph apply to the rank correlation coefficient, and thus the graph between time dependence and the rank correlation coefficient has the same U shape as above (figure 6.1.b).

When these measures have been used to make mobility comparisons, several patterns emerge. First, the correlation coefficient is always found to be positive, so in practice, the distinction between measures of time dependence and income movement is more a theoretical one than a practical one. Second, as would be expected, the longer the time elapsed between base year and final year, the lower the correlation between incomes in the two years.[8] And third, the variations across countries are fairly large.[9]

---

7. What matters in the present context is that time dependence needs to increase monotonically as one moves away from zero to the right or left. Whether the curve is U-shaped or V-shaped is unimportant for present purposes.
8. In a number of OECD countries, the one-year correlation coefficients are on the order of 0.8–0.9 while the five-year correlation coefficients are on the order of 0.7–0.8 (OECD 1996, table 3.8).
9. In the OECD data, the correlation coefficient between 1986 earnings and 1991 earnings ranges from 0.65 in the case of Denmark to 0.79 for Germany.

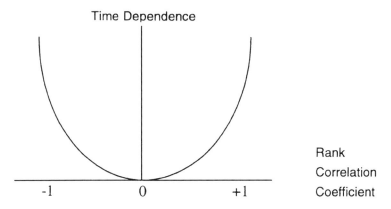

Figure 6.1.b
Time dependence as a function of the rank correlation coefficient

Let us turn now to measures that are explicitly movement measures.

Positional Movement

In the study of positional movement, the measure of economic well-being is the individual's position in the income distribution.[10] Although the most commonly-used measures of economic position are individuals' quintiles or deciles in the income distribution, there is no reason that we could not work with ventiles, centiles, or even ranks.

The main reason that positional analysis is so popular in income mobility studies is that movement among positions is the way that most analysts have gotten accustomed to thinking about mobility.[11] History plays an important role in this. In the beginning, when income mobility studies first started being done, it would have been difficult with the available technology to measure and evaluate income changes person by person. The masses of individual information had to be summarized somehow. Analyzing decile or quintile mobility matrices was a convenient and comprehensible way of

---

10. There are parallel literatures examining movement among occupations, industries, and social classes. For a recent analysis, see McMurrer and Sawhill 1998. On measurement issues, see Bartholomew 1982.
11. Most studies use positional measures. See Atkinson, Bourguignon, and Morrisson 1992 for a review of the international literature.

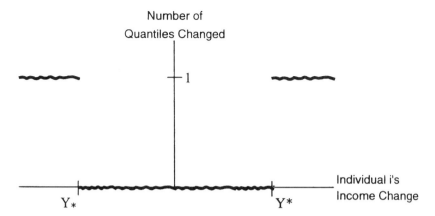

Figure 6.2
Quantiles changed as a function of income change

doing this. Researchers therefore became accustomed to working with such matrices, and simply have continued to do so for reasons of hysteresis.

Some observers give more substantive justification. To these observers, small income movements are negligible; income changes become important only when the change is large enough that the income recipient crosses a decile or quintile boundary. Figure 6.2 depicts the movement function implied by such measures. (In this figure, Y^* is the income level where the next higher quantile begins and Y_* is the corresponding amount for the next lower quantile.) If you find such a discontinuous movement function odd, then positional mobility may not be the right mobility concept for you.

But supposing that positional mobility *is* what you want to look at. How might you measure it? A natural benchmark is perfect positional immobility. In this case, everybody keeps his or her previous position. (Of course, you will need to have decided whether you are measuring positions in terms of deciles, quintiles, or whatever. The results will be sensitive to that choice.) Perfect positional immobility means that the quantile transition matrix is an identity matrix, as in (6.1), or equivalently that the normalized quantile transition matrix has entries $1/q$ (q being the number of quantiles) on the principal diagonal and zeroes elsewhere.

To gauge how far an actual quantile mobility matrix is from perfect positional immobility, some sort of metric is needed. The most commonly used is the "immobility ratio," which is the fraction of income recipients who remain in the same quantile as before.[12]

The immobility ratio varies with a number of factors. First, the longer the time period, the smaller the immobility ratio: For example, Burkhauser, Holtz-Eakin, and Rhody 1998) found immobility ratios of 67.6 percent and 69.3 percent comparing quintiles in a given year with those one year later for the United States and Germany respectively, but when the base year and final year were five years apart, the corresponding immobility ratios were 50.4 percent and 53.4 percent. Second, immobility ratios vary across countries. International comparisons across OECD countries show five-year immobility ratios that range from 0.43 in France to 0.53 in Denmark (OECD 1996). Finally, and obviously, the immobility ratio varies inversely with the number of quantiles.

The immobility ratio indicates the fraction of people who remain in or change quantiles. However, it gives no indication of how many quantiles the movers move. It seems reasonable to have a measure that is sensitive to that. One such measure is the mean number of quantiles moved, where zero is assigned to those who do not move at all. (Here too, the results may be sensitive to whether you are measuring movement across quintiles, across deciles, or across ranks.)

A great many studies have been done using positional movement measures. The reader is referred once again to Atkinson, Bourguignon, and Morrisson 1992. A set of very useful comparative analyses of developed countries is provided by OECD (1996, 1997).

In evaluating these positional movement studies, you should bear in mind that they are thoroughly relative: A person can experience relative income mobility even if his/her own income doesn't change, provided that others' incomes change by enough that the person in question experiences a change in position.[13] In positional movement analysis, what matters is one's income *position* vis-à-vis others'. But relative considerations might enter in a different kind of way, and that is by looking at one's income *share* vis-à-vis others'. We turn now to the concept and measurement of share movement.

---

12. I have classified the immobility ratio under positional movement, because that is how it is ordinarily used. It might altenatively be thought of as a measure of positive time dependence.

13. Positional movement is also relative in a different sense, which is that the usual measures of positional movement satisfy certain relative mobility axioms. More on this later.

Share Movement

People, even thoroughgoing relativists, may not care which quintile, decile, or centile of the income distribution they are in—in fact, they probably do not even know. To the extent that people are relativists in their thinking, what they are much more likely to care about is their income as it compares with others'. If your income rises by 50 percent but everyone else's rises by 100 percent, you may feel that you have lost ground. Share-movement measures would say that you have experienced downward income mobility, precisely because your share of the total has fallen.

Now that the technology permits you to make virtually instantaneous calculations of changes in income shares for samples of thousands or tens of thousands of income recipients, the practical advantage of using quantile mobility matrices rather than share movement measures is gone. So the choice among these two types of relative mobility approaches is better made on conceptual grounds. Here is a simple self-test.

Suppose you start out in a given quantile of the income distribution. (As a reader of this book, you are probably in the top income quintile unless you are a graduate student, in which case you are not yet in the top income quintile, but you probably will be.) Let's say that your income remains stationary while incomes around you are rising, but the fall in position is sufficiently small that you remain in the same quantile that you were in. (This is getting more and more personal. At my university, salaries were frozen in nominal dollars for several years. Happily for me, a program of phased salary increases recently took effect.) What is your mobility experience?

If you are a positional movement adherent, you find no income mobility: you were in the xth quantile before and you are in the xth quantile afterwards.

"Stop," you say. "That's not me. I *do* experience mobility. I have moved down." If this is your answer, then there surely is a relativist element to your concept of mobility, and it reflects your changing income *share*, not your unchanged *quantile*.

If you think in this way, what should you do to measure mobility? Your own mobility is readily gauged by the change in your income share. The population analogue is an aggregation of the changes in income shares experienced by all of the constituent individuals in the population.

What is it about these changes that you might want to measure? Of course, you would not want to measure the mean change in income shares, because this is identically zero: All of the gains in share enjoyed by some must be counterbalanced by losses of share suffered by others. Instead you might look at the standard deviation of changes in income shares, larger values signifying greater share movement. Or you might take the absolute value of the change in each person's income share and average these; here too, a larger value signifies greater share movement.

Thus far, in my review of the literature, I haven't seen anyone who has actually measured the change in income shares. However, as noted above, the correlation between base income and final income is commonly used as a measure of immobility, and it can easily be shown that the correlation between incomes is the same as the correlation between income shares. So perhaps inadvertently, share-movement *has* been measured.

Note that what share-movement measures is *flux*, that is, how much variation there is from base year to final year. Here, the aspect of flux that is being measured is income shares, whereas in the previous section, it was positions in the income distribution. If you are interested in flux but are more concerned about *incomes* than income shares or income positions, you might find the next class of measures more interesting.

Symmetric Income Movement

Imagine that you and I constitute a two-person society and that both of us experience a change in income. You experience a $1,000 income gain and I experience a $1,000 income loss. How much income movement has taken place?

If your answer is "$2,000 total" or "$1,000 per capita," you have revealed much about the concept of mobility that you are using. For one, your concept of mobility is symmetric in the sense that gains and losses are both being treated nondirectionally. For another, your concept of mobility is dollar-based, in that you regard your gain and my loss as being $1,000 regardless of our respective base incomes.

Looking at mobility in this way has been justified formally by Fields and Ok (1996). Denoting base income and final income by x_i and y_i, respectively, their measure of total dollar movement in a population of size n is the sum of the absolute values of income changes ($2,000 in the above example):

$$d^{(1)}{}_n(x, y) = \sum_{i=1}^{n} |x_i - y_i|. \tag{6.5.a}$$

Corresponding to this is a measure of per capita dollar movement in a population of size n ($1,000 in the above example):

$$m^{(1)}{}_n(x, y) = \frac{1}{n}\sum_{i=1}^{n} |x_i - y_i|. \tag{6.5.b}$$

Finally, in order to gauge whether $1,000 per capita is a large or small amount of income change, $m^{(1)}{}_n$ can be expressed as a percentage of the mean base year income:

$$p^{(1)}{}_n(x, y) = \sum_{i=1}^{n} |x_i - y_i| \Big/ \sum_{i=1}^{n} x_i. \tag{6.5.c}$$

These are measures of total symmetric dollar income movement $(d^{(1)}{}_n)$, per capita symmetric dollar income movement $(m^{(1)}{}_n)$, and percentage symmetric dollar income movement $(p^{(1)}{}_n)$ respectively. Together, these shall be denoted the F-O 1 set of measures.

To give some idea of the magnitudes involved, Fields, Leary, and Ok (1998) calculated these measures using data from the U.S. Panel Study of Income Dynamics. They found that in the United States, between 1979 and 1986, $m^{(1)}{}_n = \$16,506$ (in real 1982–1984 dollars) and the mean in that year was $33,943 (in the same real dollars). Thus, the average income change was 49 percent of the mean base year income. While this is a matter of interpretation, to me, a $p^{(1)}{}_n$ of 49 percent is a sign of considerable income flux.

Now, you may object to the perspective taken here by saying, "You haven't taken adequate account of base year income. A $1,000 income change for me is very important if my base year income is $1,000. It is much less important if my base year income is $1,000,000. What matters is by what percentage my income has changed." Fields and Ok (1999) have dealt with this concern by formulating measures of income movement which are sensitive to base year incomes. This is achieved by working with the logs of base year and final year income rather than the incomes themselves.[14] The

---

14. For small income changes, the change in log-incomes is very close to the percentage income change. The approximation gets worse and worse as the income change gets larger.

resultant measure of per capita relative income movement is

$$m^{(2)}{}_n(x, y) = \frac{1}{n} \sum_{i=1}^{n} |\log x_i - \log y_i|. \tag{6.6}$$

The total measures $d^{(2)}{}_n$ and percentage measures $p^{(2)}{}_n$ are defined analogously. Together, these are called the F-O 2 set.

When applied empirically to the same PSID data as reported above for 1979–1986, Fields, Leary, and Ok find that $m^{(2)}{}_n = .528$. That is, the mean percentage income changes between these two years in the United States was approximately 52.8 percent. Again, it is a matter of perception, but I would say that this also is indicative of a high degree of income flux.

One feature of F-O 1 and F-O 2 is that they are exactly decomposable into two parts, one that reflects income changes due to economic growth and the other that reflects income changes due to movements up and down holding the mean constant.[15] In a growing economy, the breakdown of

$$d^{(1)}{}_n(x, y) = \sum_{i=1}^{n} |x_i - y_i|$$

into a growth component and a transfer component is given by

$$d^{(1)}{}_n(x, y) = \sum_{i=1}^{n} |x_i - y_i| = G^{(1)}{}_n(x, y) + T^{(1)}{}_n(x, y), \tag{6.7.a}$$

where

$$G^{(1)}{}_n(x, y) = \sum_{i=1}^{n} y_i - \sum_{i=1}^{n} x_i \tag{6.7.b}$$

and

$$T^{(1)}{}_n(x, y) = 2 \left(\sum_{i \in L_n(x,y)} (x_i - y_i) \right), \tag{6.7.c}$$

and $L_n(x, y)$ denotes the set of people who lost income over time.[16]

---

15. No other income mobility measure has been shown to be decomposable in this way. See, for instance, Markandya 1984.
16. An analogous decomposition is available in the case of falling total income. There are also analogous decompositions of the F-O 2 measures, obtained by substituting $\log x$ in place of x and $\log y$ in place of y everywhere in (6.7). See Fields and Ok 1996, 1999 for details.

Among the panel individuals in the PSID sample, the mean growth of family income was $1,121 (3.3 percent of average base-year income) between 1979 and 1986. On the other hand, the average income change (i.e., $m^{(1)}{}_n$) was $16,506 (in absolute value) between 1979 and 1986. From these figures, it would be expected that only a small fraction of total income mobility was due to income growth in the economy, and indeed that is what the decomposition in (6.7) shows: Only 6.8 percent of symmetric income movement as gauged by $m^{(1)}{}_n$ was due to growth in the 1980s. This is because an overwhelming fraction of U.S. income mobility (in the sense of symmetric income movement) is accounted for by people moving up or down within the income distribution.

These decompositions tell us, in an accounting sense, why incomes change; they indicate to what extent change occurred because the economy grew and individuals' incomes grew along with it and to what extent it occurred because people moved up or down within a given structure. What we have measured and decomposed is income flux.

Now, it may be that you are not as interested in income flux as you are in the direction of change—in particular, how many people are experiencing income gains and losses of what magnitude and which people in the population are the gainers and the losers. Once the distinction between income gains and income losses becomes important to you, you would do better to consider directional income movements. These are taken up next.

Directional Income Movement

Subsections 6.1.B–6.1.D were concerned with different aspects of income flux: positional movement, share movement, and symmetric income movement respectively. If directional income movements are of primary concern to you, you may find the measures discussed in this section to be of interest.

Several ad hoc directional indices are in use, such as the fraction of upward or downward movers and the average amount gained by the winners or lost by the losers. Accompanying the use of these measures is a strong normative judgment, rarely stated explicitly: One income mobility situation is *better* than another when there is a larger fraction of upward movers, when the upward movers gain more on average, and when the downward movers lose less on average.

Whenever an index is used, one has (or should have) a nagging doubt about the robustness of the finding. Just as in earlier chapters, where it was shown that different poverty and inequality measures can give opposing ordinal judgments, the conclusion that one situation has better mobility than another may hinge on the choice of a particular mobility measure. In what follows, we will work solely with directional income movement. But even given that restriction, if we switch from one measure of directional income movement to another, there are conditions under which different measures will give us quite different conclusions. However, in other circumstances, we are able to determine that the same qualitative conclusion holds for a broad class of specific directional movement measures.

The technique we shall use is the familiar criterion of stochastic dominance, applied to directional income movements.[17] Let us suppose for now that our measure of income movement is the individual's income change (measured, as always, in terms of real dollars). The population is then arrayed from most negative income change to most positive. What we need for stochastic dominance analysis of income changes is the fraction of people experiencing income changes less than each possible amount. One distribution of income changes is said to stochastically dominate another if the percentage of people below any given income change amount is smaller in the first situation than in the second, or equivalently, if the income change cutoff for each given percentage grouping is higher in one distribution than another. Graphically, this means that a better distribution is one that lies everywhere below or to the right of another. (You can look at it either way.)

Figure 6.3 depicts the distribution of income changes in two provinces of China over an eleven year period.[18] Neimongu registered rapid economic growth, while Shanxi suffered an economic decline. We see that the distribution of income changes in Neimongu stochastically dominates the income changes in Shanxi. In this sense, economic growth may be said to have brought about a distribution of income changes that was *better* in Neimongu than in Shanxi.

When two directional income movement distributions are plotted, it is possible that neither dominates the other. This possibility is

---

17. On stochastic dominance, see Hadar and Russell 1969. The only application of stochastic dominance to the income mobility literature is in the work of Fields, Leary, and Ok (1998, 1999).

18. The data for these results come from the Chinese Academy of Preventive Medicine survey, described further in chapter 7.

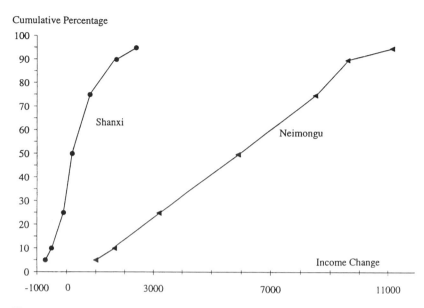

Figure 6.3
Directional Income Movement in two provinces of China, 1978–1989

shown to be a reality in the crossing curves in figure 6.4. These data pertain to directional movement distributions for the United States in the 1970s and the 1980s. The 1970s distribution dominates at the lower end of the change distribution, while the 1980s distribution dominates at the upper end. This means that in the 1980s, more people lost more dollars than in the 1970s, but those who gained gained more dollars in the 1980s than in the 1970s.

Included in the preceding calculation is the judgment that income changes are most appropriately gauged in terms of *dollars* of income movement. You may not like this practice of measuring income changes independently of base income amounts. For example, suppose that you gain $1,000 of income and I lose $1,000, but your income was twice as high as mine to start with. Your $1,000 income gain is only half as large in percentage terms as my $1,000 income loss. To assign a smaller change (in absolute value terms) to your income gain as compared with my income loss, we might do as above and measure not changes in income but rather changes in *log-income* for each person in our sample, and then test for stochastic dominance between the log-income differences.

This is done in figure 6.5. When log-dollars are used rather than dollars, it is still the case that the distribution of income changes for

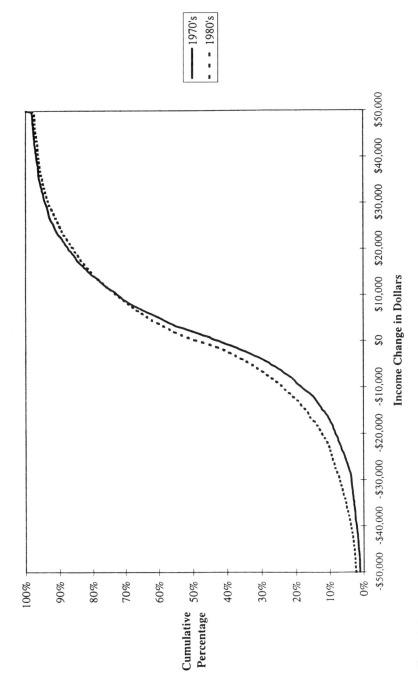

Figure 6.4
United States: Distribution of directional income movement, in dollars

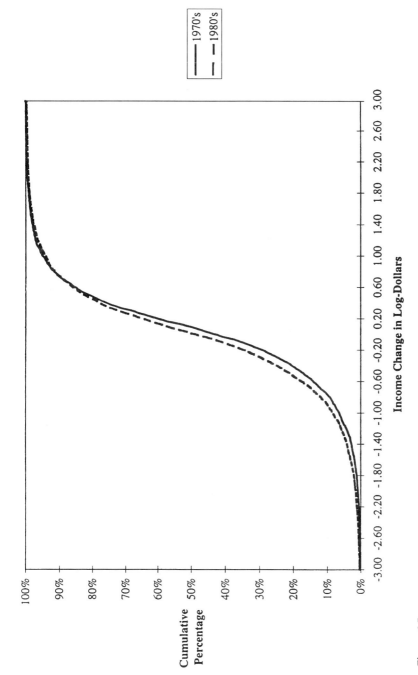

Cumulative
Percentage

Income Change in Log-Dollars

1970's
1980's

Figure 6.5
United States Distribution of directional income movement, in log-dollars

the 1970s dominates the 1980s one for the smallest ninety percent of income changes. However, for the largest 10 percent of income changes, the reverse is the case: the 1980s values are slightly above the 1970s values. Thus, in the absence of strict dominance, we might calculate a measure of changes in log-income. Such a measure, derived axiomatically by Fields and Ok (1999), is

$$m^{(3)}{}_n(x, y) = \frac{1}{n} \sum_{i=1}^{n} (\log y_i - \log x_i) \qquad (6.8)$$

that is, the mean log-dollar change in incomes. This measure shows a more positive directional mobility experience in the 1970s than in the 1980s (which is not surprising in view of figure 6.5) but it also shows more than that: the mean log-dollar change was *positive* (.036) in the 1970s and *negative* (−.038) in the 1980s. This confirms the popular perception that people did less well economically in the United States in the eighties than in the seventies.

This completes the presentation of the five different classes of mobility measures. We turn now to a comparison of them. First, we shall see how they differ in certain prototypic situations. Then, with that as base, we shall explore the axiomatic foundations of the different approaches.

6.2   The Different Mobility Concepts in Certain Stylized Examples

Does the use of different mobility concepts make a conceptual difference? At one level, the answer to this question is an obvious "yes": different measures necessarily give different results sometimes. It is more helpful to ask when they agree and when not.

This section proceeds as follows. First, we consider how different mobility approaches gauge mobility in some stylized situations. We then introduce a number of mobility measures and examine their behavior in these situations. Finally, we turn to axiomatic attributes of the different measures.

Throughout this section, we will use the following notation. Let x_i represent the base year income of the ith individual and let x be the vector of x_is arrayed in an arbitrary order. Let y_i be the final year income of the ith individual and y the vector of y_is arrayed in the same order as the xs. We shall then let $x \to y$ denote x_1 becoming y_1, x_2 becoming y_2, and so on.

Example 1.   Constant Incomes

Suppose that over time, income remains constant for every single person in society. All of the mobility notions considered above agree on one thing: when $x \to x$, there is no mobility.

Actually, this is the *only* case in which all of the different approaches agree. The differences between them in other cases can be elucidated by means of some very simple examples.

Example 2.   A Rank Preserving Equalization

Starting with a given income distribution x, let all incomes but two remain the same between base year and final year. For the two that change, let one person transfer a given sum of money to the other, such that their positions remain the same. (Whichever aspect of position it is that interests you—rank, decile, or quintile—hold that constant when the transfer is made.) What can we say about mobility?

• By the *positional movement approach, there is no mobility*, because nobody's position has changed.

• By the *share movement approach, there is mobility*, because the donor's income share went down and the recipient's income share went up.

• For the *time dependence approach, it matters what you measure*. If you measure the correlation coefficient on disaggregated data, you will get a less-than-perfect correlation between base year income and final year income, and therefore mobility takes place. However, using a quantile mobility matrix, both the donor and the recipient experience no change in quantile, and therefore no mobility takes place.

• By the *income movement approach*, whether directional or non-directional, *there is mobility* because two individuals' incomes have changed.

These differing judgments rendered in this example show two things. One, the positional movement approach and the share movement approach differ from each other. Two, the time dependence approach implemented on aggregated data may give a different answer from the time dependence approach implemented on disaggregated data.

Example 3.   A Change in Ranks within Given Quantiles

In both of the previous examples, the positional movement approach and the aggregate time dependence approach gave the same answer. Can these ever disagree? The following example shows that the answer is yes.

As in example 2, suppose that everyone's income remains the same except for two individuals, one of whom transfers a given sum of money to another. But now, unlike example 2, suppose that the amount transferred is large enough that the donor and/or the recipient change ranks in the income distribution (and of course, those whom they overtake change ranks as well). However, let these changes be small enough so that both donor and recipient remain in the same quantile (e.g., decile, quintile) of the income distribution.

Because the ranks have changed, there is positive positional movement. Yet, since everyone remains in the same quantile as before, the quantile mobility matrix is an identity matrix, and therefore mobility is zero.

In this example, the discrepancy arises for practical reasons as opposed to conceptual ones. If we had constructed an $N \times N$ transition matrix rather than a 10×10 or a 5×5 one, we would have seen positive mobility. It is because we do not do this in practice that no mobility is observed.

Example 4.   Proportionate Income Change

Consider two different situations. In situation one, everyone's income is unchanged, so $x \to x$. In situation two, everyone's income becomes the same non-zero multiple of base year income $\lambda, \lambda > 0$, which we write as $x \to \lambda x$. How do the mobilities in $x \to x$ and $x \to \lambda x$, $\lambda \neq 1$, compare with each other?

It turns out to make a stunning difference which approach is adopted. To wit:

• By the *time dependence approach*, $x \to x$ and $x \to \lambda x$ have the *same* mobility as each other—namely, none.

• By the *positional movement approach*, $x \rightarrow x$ and $x \rightarrow \lambda x$ have the *same* mobility as each other—namely, none.

• By the *share movement approach*, $x \rightarrow x$ and $x \rightarrow \lambda x$ have the *same* mobility as each other—namely, none.

• By the *symmetric income movement approach*, $x \rightarrow x$ and $x \rightarrow \lambda x$ have *different* mobility from each other. The first, $x \rightarrow x$, has *no mobility*. The second, $x \rightarrow \lambda x$, has *positive mobility*. Furthermore, the more different λ is from 1, the more mobility there is.

• By the *directional income movement approach*, $x \rightarrow x$ and $x \rightarrow \lambda x$ have *different* mobility from each other. The first, $x \rightarrow x$, has *no mobility*. The second, $x \rightarrow \lambda x$, has *nonzero mobility*. The mobility that there is is *positive* if $\lambda > 1$ and *negative* if $\lambda < 1$. Furthermore, the further λ is from 1, the more mobility there is.

These examples show clearly that the income movement approaches are fundamentally different from the others. This is because the income movement approaches say that income mobility takes place whenever someone's real income changes. Furthermore, the larger are these income changes in absolute value, the more income movement there has been. The other approaches characterize movement differently.

Example 5.   All Incomes Change by a Constant Dollar Amount

Suppose that everyone experiences an income change of $\$\alpha, \alpha \neq 0$, which is written as $x \rightarrow x + \alpha$. As was the case in example 4, the different mobility approaches give very different answers:

• By the *time dependence approach*, $x \rightarrow x + \alpha$ may or may not exhibit mobility—it depends on how time-dependence is measured.[19]

• Because no one's position in the income distribution changes, by the *positional movement approach*, $x \rightarrow x + \alpha$ has *no mobility*.

• Because the income shares of those below the mean rise and those above the mean fall, by the *share movement approach*, $x \rightarrow x + \alpha$ has *positive mobility*.

• All *income movement approaches* will say that $x \rightarrow x + \alpha$ exhibits *positive mobility*. Furthermore, the larger is α, the more mobility there is.

---

19. See section 6.3 of this chapter for a presentation of the different mobility measures.

We turn now to one final example.

Example 6.   Manna from Heaven

When manna drops from heaven[20] on some people's houses but not on others', those who get the manna enjoy a gain in income, a gain in income share, and possibly a gain in position. Those who do not get the manna have no change in income, a loss in income share, and possibly a loss in position. What do you want to say about the mobility experiences of *nonrecipients* in such a case? If your view is that the nonrecipients had downward mobility, you are a thoroughgoing relativist. At minimum you are a share movement adherent, and you may be a positional movement adherent as well. On the other hand, if, in your judgment, those who got no manna had no mobility, the share movement and positional movement approaches are not for you, and the income movement approach may be more suitable.

This section has shown that because the different approaches make fundamentally different judgments about certain key aspects of mobility, it makes a difference in theory which approach is used to gauge mobility. Thus, when you choose a mobility measure to take to data, you will want to be sure that it captures what for you is the right approach. The next section highlights the crucial distinctions among the measures.

6.3   Mobility Measures and Axioms

Some Mobility Measures

When we have data on a vector of base-year incomes $x = (x_1 x_2 \ldots x_n)$ and final-year incomes $y = (y_1 y_2 \ldots y_n)$, such that the ith income recipient occupies the same position in the two distributions, an income mobility measure may be defined as a function $m(x, y)$ defined on the

---

20. This is a culture-specific phrase. According to the biblical story, when the Israelites were starving in the desert, a food called manna dropped from the sky, enabling them to reinvigorate themselves. Those on whose houses manna dropped experienced a gain in economic well-being which came at no one's expense.

domain of vectors x and y.[21] There are a great many mobility measures. Among them are:

• The correlation coefficient between x and y

• The rank correlation coefficient, that is, the correlation between income recipients' ranks in distribution x and in distribution y

• The quantile immobility ratio, defined as the fraction of income recipients who remain in the same quintile, decile, or ventile of the income distribution (also called the "trace")

• Shorrocks's rigidity index, defined in the two period case as

$$R \equiv \frac{I(x+y)}{[\mu_x I(x) + \mu_y I(y)]/(\mu_x + \mu_y)},$$

where $I(.)$ is a particular scale-invariant inequality index.

• Fields and Ok's log-dollar per capita measure

$$m^{(2)}{}_n(x, y) = \frac{1}{n} \sum_{i=1}^{n} |\log x_i - \log y_i|. \tag{6.6}$$

• Fields and Ok's dollar per capita measure

$$m^{(1)}{}_n(x, y) = \frac{1}{n} \sum_{i=1}^{n} |x_i - y_i|. \tag{6.5.b}$$

Table 6.2 summarizes the performance of these six measures in the examples of subsection C.1. Some noteworthy differences appear. First, when a rank-preserving equalization of income takes place, the rank-correlation coefficient is unchanged. Thus, the rank-correlation is a measure of positional movement. Second, when people change ranks within given quantiles, the quantile immobility ratio is unchanged. This too is a measure of positional movement, but the positions here are broad groups rather than individual ranks. Third, when all incomes change proportionately, only the Fields-Ok measures declare that mobility has taken place. In this sense, the Fields-Ok indices measure income movement in ways that other indices do not. Fourth, when all incomes change by a constant dollar amount, the Fields-Ok indices capture that movement. Shorrocks's rigidity index changes too, because relative inequality is changed by a uni-

---

21. Different mobility measures can also be defined for the case when there are T years of data to be used.

Table 6.2
Mobility in some prototypic situations

	Is there mobility when					
	All incomes are unchanged?	A rank-preserving equalization takes place?	Some people change ranks within given quantiles?	All incomes change proportionately?	All incomes change by a constant dollar amount?	Some people gain income, others do not?
Correlation coefficient between income in year t and in year $t+1$	No	Yes	Yes	No	No	Yes
Rank correlation coefficient between income ranks in year t and in year $t+1$	No	No	Yes	No	No	Yes, if and only if someone changes rank
Quantile immobility ratio (quintile, decile, or ventile)	No	Yes, if and only if someone changes quantile	No	No	No	Yes, if and only if someone changes quantile
Shorrocks's rigidity index, two-period case	No	Yes	Yes	No	Yes	Yes
Fields and Ok's log-dollar measure	No	Yes	Yes	Yes	Yes	Yes
Fields and Ok's dollar measure	No	Yes	Yes	Yes	Yes	Yes

Note: All measures are defined in the text.

form increase or decrease in everybody's income. Finally, when manna drops from heaven, the various measures behave quite differently. Because incomes change, the two Fields-Ok measures indicate that there was mobility. The rank-correlation and quantile immobility ratio indicate mobility if and only if people change ranks or quantiles respectively. The correlation coefficient and Shorrocks's rigidity index will signal mobility because of the nonuniformity of the income changes.

These differences in behavior among the measures highlight their fundamental differences. The two Fields-Ok measures are income movement measures. The rank-correlation coefficient and quantile immobility ratio are measures of positional movement. Finally, the correlation coefficient and Shorrocks's R are measures of share movement. This distinction will be a useful one for you to keep in mind when you decide how best to measure mobility given your conception of what income mobility is.

Axiomatic Foundations

The axiomatic approach to mobility measurement was pioneered by Shorrocks (1978) and continued by King (1983), Cowell (1985), Chakravarty, Dutta, and Weymark (1985), Shorrocks (1993), and Fields and Ok (1996, 1999). The axiomatic foundations of the different measures may be compared and contrasted.

The earlier discussion exhibited one element of commonality: when everyone's income is unchanged, there is no mobility. Shorrocks (1993) suggested a normalization axiom whereby mobility is at a *minimum* when all incomes are unchanged, whereas Shorrocks (1978) suggested that a mobility measure should range from zero to one. Combined, these imply that when all incomes are unchanged, mobility is *zero*, which we write as:

NORMALIZATION AXIOM: $m(x, x) = 0$.

This axiom is hardly controversial: All of the mobility measures presented above satisfy it, as do all others that I know about

It is also essential to specify how mobility changes when people's incomes change. Four different concepts will be considered.

The first concept is *level-sensitivity*. In all conceptions of income mobility, when everyone's income remains the same, there is no mobility. Such a situation can be thought of as fulfilling two conditions: Income shares are maintained and the income level is maintained. Now keep just one of these: Keep everyone's income share the same but change the income level. In some mobility conceptions, there is no mobility in such a case. Such a notion can be defined formally as:

NORMALIZED LEVEL-INSENSITIVITY AXIOM: $m(x, \lambda x) = m(x, x) = 0$ for all $\lambda > 0$.

Note carefully what this implies: Not only is there no mobility in $(1, 2, 3) \rightarrow (1, 2, 3)$ but there is no mobility either in $(1, 2, 3) \rightarrow (2, 4, 6)$. Let us call the measures that fulfill this axiom the (normalized) *level-insensitive measures*.

A second concept is *relativity*. A mobility concept is defined to be relative if multiplying everyone's base-year and final-year income by the same positive scalar leaves mobility unchanged:

RELATIVITY AXIOM: $m(\lambda x, \lambda y) = m(x, y)$ for all $\lambda > 0$.

If you accept the relativity axiom, you are obligated to say that there is the same degree of mobility in the situation

$(1, 2, 3) \rightarrow (2, 4, 6)$

as there is in the situation

$(2, 4, 6) \rightarrow (4, 8, 12)$,

and likewise the situation

$(1, 2, 3) \rightarrow (6, 4, 2)$

has the same mobility as the situation

$(2, 4, 6) \rightarrow (12, 8, 4)$.

The third concept is what has been called *intertemporal scale invariance*, although I prefer to call it *strong relativity*. If you think of mobility as a function of income shares, you can convert the vectors x and y to their corresponding share equivalents by multiplying x by $1/\mu_x$ and y by $1/\mu_y$, obtaining $s_x = x/\mu_x$ and $s_y = y/\mu_y$. You can then define your mobility measure as a function of these shares: $m(s_x, s_y)$. Now, if two different x, y pairs x^1, y^1 and x^2, y^2 have the same s_x, s_y vectors, then $m(x^1, y^1) = m(x^2, y^2)$. More generally, if you choose *any* multiple $\gamma > 0$ of base year income and *any* other multiple $\lambda > 0$ of final year income and conclude that mobility is necessarily the same in going from γx to λy as in going from x to y, you have a strongly relative mobility notion, that is, $m(\gamma x, \lambda y) = m(x, y)$ for all $\gamma, \lambda > 0$. Combining strong relativity with the normalization axiom produces:

NORMALIZED STRONG RELATIVITY: $m(\gamma x, \lambda y) = m(x, y) = 0$ for all $\gamma, \lambda > 0$.

Measures possessing the normalized strong relativity property work in a particular way. To illustrate, take the following mobility situations:

$$(1, 2, 3) \rightarrow (2, 4, 6)$$

$$(1, 2, 3) \rightarrow (3, 6, 9)$$

Strongly relative measures would say that these have the same mobility as each other; normalized strongly relative measures would say that the common amount of mobility that they both have is zero.

The final concept is *translation invariance*. If a given amount α is added to or subtracted from everybody's base year and final year income, a translation-invariant mobility measure would declare the new situation to be as mobile as the original one:

TRANSLATION INVARIANCE AXIOM: $m(x + \alpha, y + \alpha) = m(x, y)$ for all $\alpha > 0$.

So for example, the situation $(1, 2, 3) \rightarrow (2, 4, 6)$ would have the same mobility as the situation $(2, 3, 4) \rightarrow (3, 5, 7)$, and so too would $(0, 1, 2) \rightarrow (1, 3, 5)$.

The preceding examples bear careful examination. They will help guide you in deciding whether you want to use a measure that is level-insensitive, relative, strongly relative, or translation-invariant. The choice depends, of course, on what you yourself understand the very concept of mobility to be.

Which Mobility Measures Satisfy Which Axioms?

Before choosing a mobility measure to take to data, you will want to know which measures satisfy which properties. Table 6.3 displays this. You see that you are free to choose measures satisfying all four of the preceding normalized axioms, just three, just two, or just one.

Table 6.3 also deals with a technical point. You can see that (normalized) level insensitivity ($m(x, \lambda x) = m(x, x) = 0$ for all $\lambda > 0$) is a special case of (normalized) strong relativity ($m(\gamma x, \lambda y) = m(x, y) = 0$

Table 6.3
Properties of some two-period mobility measures

	Normalization $m(x, x) = 0$	Level-Insensitivity $m(x, \lambda x) = m(x, x)$	Relativity $m(\lambda x, \lambda y) = m(x, y)$	Strong Relativity $m(\gamma x, \lambda y) = m(x, y)$	Translation Invariance $m(x + \alpha, y + \alpha) = m(x, y)$
Correlation coefficient between income in year t and in year $t+1$	Yes	Yes	Yes	Yes	Yes
Rank correlation coefficient between income ranks in year t and in year $t+1$	Yes	Yes	Yes	Yes	Yes
Quantile immobility ratio (quintile, decile, or ventile)	Yes	Yes	Yes	Yes	Yes
Shorrocks's rigidity index, two-period case	Yes	Yes	Yes	No	No
Fields and Ok's log-dollar measure	Yes	No	Yes	No	No
Fields and Ok's dollar measure	Yes	No	No	No	Yes

Note: All measures are defined in the text.

for all $\gamma, \lambda > 0$). For the latter axiom to be interesting, there must exist a reasonable mobility measure that *is* level-insensitive but *is not* strongly relative. As table 6.3 shows, Shorrocks's R is precisely such a measure. This means that you are free to make independent choices among these different concepts and measures.

Finally, one may note that several mobility measures are both relative (in the sense of both relativity and strong relativity) and absolute (in the sense of translation-invariance). This contrasts with the case of inequality measures, which may be relative or absolute but not both (Eichhorn and Gehrig 1982).

6.4 Conclusions

This chapter began by emphasizing that "income mobility" is a generic concept connoting a wide range of ideas. Five such notions were distinguished: time dependence, positional movement, share movement, nondirectional income movement, and directional income movement.

We then went on to consider what these different mobility concepts would say in certain stylized examples. Only when everyone's income stays the same do they all give the same answer. In other cases, they give different answers, because they are gauging fundamentally different concepts.

The next section compared measures and axioms. We saw that the correlation coefficient and Shorrocks's R are measures of share movement, the rank-correlation coefficient and quantile immobility ratio are measures of positional movement, and the Fields-Ok indices are measures of income movement. We also considered several possible axioms for income mobility, including axioms for normalization, level insensitivity, relativity, strong relativity, and translation invariance and showed that different mobility measures satisfy these different axioms.

The results of this chapter show that how mobility is measured makes an important difference *in theory*. Does it also make an important difference *in practice*? We turn now to empirical mobility studies for developing countries.

7

Growth and Income Mobility: Some Initial Evidence for the Developing World

Previous chapters looked at changes in inequality and poverty in the course of developing countries' economic growth. We are interested in this section in the parallel question for mobility: What is the relationship between income mobility and economic growth? Although mobility studies in developing countries are still in their infancy, owing in part to the very limited availability of panel data, there nonetheless are some interesting country studies, each of which illustrates in different ways the potential richness of economic mobility analysis.

7.1 Peru

The most comprehensive economic mobility study for a developing country is the one conducted by Herrera (1999) for Lima, Peru explicitly following the methods described in chapter 6. Using data from the Peruvian Living Standards Measurement Survey conducted by the Instituto Cuánto S.A., a panel of 421 households in Lima in 1990, 1994, and 1996 is matched with an earlier panel of 721 households in 1985/1986–1990. Economic status is measured by household expenditures, both total and per adult-equivalent.

The Peruvian economy went through three major phases during this period. First, 1985–1990 was characterized by the neopopulist government of Alan García, marked by two years of high growth followed by a dramatic recession and hyperinflation. Following this, 1990–1994 was a period of shock adjustment under the presidency of Alberto Fujimori. Third, 1994–1996 was marked by the resumption of economic growth and the abatement of inflation. In order to make mobility comparisons using periods as equal as possible in length,

Table 7.1
Lima, Peru: Quintile mobility matrix for households based on total expenditures per capita

A. Transition matrix between 1985–1986 and 1990

Quintile in 1985/86	Quintile in 1990				
	I	II	III	IV	V
I	48.3%	24.1%	16.6%	6.2%	4.8%
II	29.9%	23.6%	25.0%	11.8%	9.7%
III	11.8%	25.7%	29.2%	25.0%	8.3%
IV	7.6%	15.3%	17.4%	32.6%	27.1%
V	2.8%	11.1%	11.8%	24.3%	50.0%

B. Transition matrix between 1990 and 1996

Quintile in 1990	Quintile in 1996				
	I	II	III	IV	V
I	43.5%	30.6%	15.3%	8.2%	2.4%
II	22.6%	15.5%	29.8%	23.8%	8.3%
III	22.6%	25.0%	22.6%	19.1%	10.7%
IV	7.4%	23.8%	20.2%	25.0%	23.8%
V	4.8%	4.8%	11.9%	23.8%	54.8%

Source: Herrera 1999.

the presentation that follows uses the 1985–1990 and 1990–1996 results.

Herrera first analyzed positional movement using quintile transition matrices, reproduced here in table 7.1. Between 1985–1990 and 1990–1996 the immobility rate rose in the highest quintile (quintile V) and fell in the lowest quintile (quintile I). This means that positional movement did not unambiguously rise or fall. This ambiguity is borne out by the specific mobility figures in table 7.2. Positional movement increased by most of these measures but not all of them.

The study then turned to dominance analysis of mobility changes; see chapter 6 and Fields, Leary, and Ok 1998, 2000 for details of this method. Figure 7.1 plots symmetric expenditure movement for household expenditures per adult-equivalent (figure 7.1.a) and total (figure 7.1.b). Directional expenditure movement is plotted in figure 7.2, first for directional change in household expenditures per adult-equivalent (figure 7.2.a) and then total (figure 7.2.b). We see that symmetric expenditure movement *fell* from 1985–1990 to 1990–1996 but directional expenditure movement *rose* during the same period.

Table 7.2
Lima, Peru: Measures of positional movement

Index	1985–1990	1990–1996	Change in positional movement
Immobility ratio – diagonal	36.7%	32.3%	Mobility increased
Immobility ratio – diagonal + two adjacent cells	76.4%	71.3%	Mobility increased
Moved one quintile	39.7%	39.0%	Mobility decreased
Moved two or more quintiles	23.6%	28.7%	Mobility increased
Mean absolute jump (as a percentage of perfect mobility)	0.968 (60.5%)	1.052 (65.8%)	Mobility increased
One minus Spearman rank correlation coefficient	.511	.468	Mobility decreased

Source: Herrera 1999.

This highlights the importance of clarifying the mobility concept to measure.

Herrera's final step was to estimate microeconometric models of poverty persistence. One was a logistic regression model of chronic poverty, defined as being below the per adult-equivalent expenditure poverty line in 1990, 1994, and 1996. Another was an ordered logit model. The variables found to be significant determinants of chronic poverty were the household's demographic composition, the education of the head of the household, and initial wealth. Those that were insignificant were ethnic origin, sex of the head of the household, and place of residence.

One issue not addressed in Herrera's research is the relationship between growth and mobility. His work concentrates on comparing the mobility experiences under two different macroeconomic regimes: the neopopulist period between 1985 and 1990 and the orthodox adjustment period from 1990 to 1996. Since both periods include some years of growth and some years of stagnation, it is not possible to test for a link between growth and mobility.

Economic mobility in the earlier period of Peru's economic history (1985–1990) has been analyzed by Glewwe and Hall (1998). Between 1985 and 1990, real GNP per capita fell by 30 percent, while real wages declined by 50–70 percent. These authors used panel data from the World Bank's Living Standards Measurement Survey for Lima, Peru to study income mobility of urban households during this recessionary period.

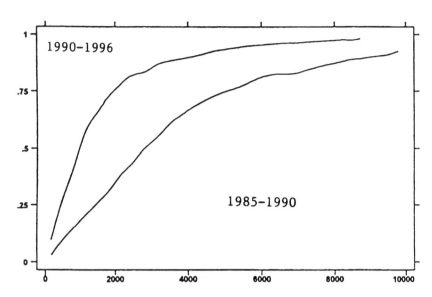

Figure 7.1.a
Lima, Peru: Nondirectional expenditure changes per adult-equivalent, 1985–1990 and
1990–1996

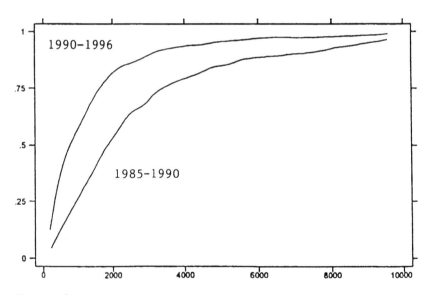

Figure 7.1.b
Lima, Peru: Nondirectional changes in total household expenditures, 1985–1990 and
1990–1996

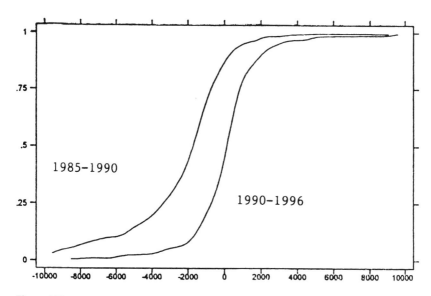

Figure 7.2.a
Lima, Peru: Directional expenditure changes per adult-equivalent, 1985–1990 and 1990–1996

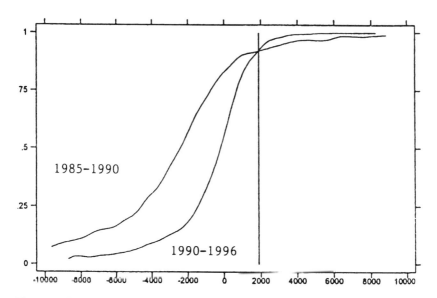

Figure 7.2.b
Lima, Peru: Directional changes in total household expenditures, 1985–1990 and 1990–1996

Table 7.3
Lima, Peru: Movement among quintiles of per capita consumption expenditure

		1990 Quintile				
		1	2	3	4	5
1985 Quintile	1	7.7%	4.4%	3.4%	2.6%	1.0%
	2	4.4%	5.2%	4.0%	2.9%	1.7%
	3	2.8%	4.3%	6.3%	4.7%	3.0%
	4	1.0%	2.8%	4.7%	5.9%	5.5%
	5	0.6%	1.8%	2.6%	5.9%	11.0%

Percentage on diagonal: 36.0%.
Percentage that moved by one quintile: 37.8%.
Percentage that moved by two or more quintiles: 26.2%.

They began by examining positional movement using a quintile mobility matrix, reproduced here in table 7.3. The household's economic well-being is measured using consumption expenditures per capita. Two-thirds of Peruvian households changed quintiles between 1985/1986 and 1990; and one-fourth moved two quintiles or more.

To see which households experienced how much change and why, the authors then performed two sets of statistical analyses of directional income movement. First, they regressed the percentage change in the household's per capita consumption on a number of correlates, taken one at a time. Those that exhibited statistically significant simple regression coefficients were the household head's years of education (positive), the proportion of household members who were elderly (positive), the proportion of household members who were children (negative), and the proportion of household members who were ill or invalids (negative).[1] The authors report these results but give them little weight, because they see them as mere description without explanatory content.

For their causal analysis of the determinants of vulnerability to macroeconomic shocks, they turned to multiple regression and estimated the determinants of the change in (the logarithm of) per capita household consumption. The more negative/less positive are these changes, the more "vulnerable" the household is said to be. Their main results are:

1. Here, "positive" means that a larger value of the variable is associated with a smaller income loss or a larger income gain, while "negative" means that a larger value of the variable is associated with a larger income loss or a smaller income gain.

• Households headed by relatively well-educated persons are less vulnerable.

• Female-headed households are less vulnerable.

• Households with more children are more vulnerable.

• Domestic transfer networks do not protect the poor.

• Peru's Social Security system is not targeted either to the vulnerable or to the poor.

These studies of Peru are more comprehensive than those conducted for any other country to date. We turn now to the case of Malaysia, where substantial work has been done, but not as much as in Peru.

7.2 Malaysia

The Malaysian Family Life Survey is a retrospective survey of approximately 1,000 households in Peninsular Malaysia, carried out in 1976. In a pair of papers, Randolph and Trzcinski (1989) and Trzcinski and Randolph (1991) studied the earnings mobility of prime-aged men (15–55 years of age) for the period 1967–1976. The Malaysian economy grew by 6 percent annually during the 1960s and by 8 percent annually during the first part of the 1970s.

Their first finding concerns positional movement. The decile mobility matrix for Malaysian males is reproduced here in table 7.4. (Deciles are numbered from 1 for poorest to 10 for richest.) We see that 50 percent of the males who began in the richest earnings decile remained there nine years later, and another 27 percent moved down just one decile. Likewise, 41 percent of those who began in the poorest decile were still there after nine years, and another 16 percent had moved up just one decile. Overall then, the majority of those who started in the poorest groups remained there, and likewise for the richest. On the other hand, fewer than 20 percent of Malaysian men who started in the four middle deciles remained in the same decile. These patterns typify what is found when decile mobility matrices have been calculated in other countries: Much higher rates of immobility are found in the highest and lowest income deciles than in the middle.

Other aspects of positional movement are elucidated with the aid of table 7.5. This table shows that Malaysian men moved an average

Table 7.4
Malaysia: Decile mobility matrix for Malaysian males, 1967–1976

Decile in 1967	1	2	3	4	5	6	7	8	9	10	Total
1	**40.9**	15.9	11.4	6.8	2.3	5.7	10.2	3.4	2.3	1.1	100.0
2	27.0	**24.7**	9.0	9.0	7.9	5.6	7.9	4.5	2.3	2.3	100.0
3	11.4	23.9	**26.1**	12.5	4.6	4.6	4.6	4.6	2.3	5.7	100.0
4	4.6	19.5	19.5	**11.5**	13.8	8.1	9.2	4.6	6.9	2.3	100.0
5	2.3	5.7	21.6	19.3	**18.2**	9.1	10.2	9.1	2.3	2.3	100.0
6	5.6	3.4	5.6	13.5	21.4	**14.6**	15.7	14.6	3.4	2.3	100.0
7	2.3	2.3	2.3	15.9	12.5	21.6	**19.3**	9.1	8.0	6.8	100.0
8	0.0	1.1	1.1	5.6	12.4	22.5	11.2	**21.4**	16.9	7.9	100.0
9	3.5	1.2	1.2	4.7	3.5	4.7	9.3	24.4	**29.1**	18.6	100.0
10	1.1	2.3	2.3	2.3	3.4	3.4	3.4	4.6	27.3	**50.0**	100.0
Total	100.0	100.0	100.0	100.0	100.0	100.0	100.0	100.0	100.0	100.0	

Table 7.5
Malaysia: Summary measures of mobility, 1967–1976

1967 Decile rank	Mean absolute change	Mean algebraic change
1	2.10	2.10
2	2.00	1.46
3	1.76	0.83
4	1.97	0.52
5	1.66	−0.11
6	1.71	−0.43
7	1.74	−0.83
8	1.61	−0.96
9	1.56	−1.19
10	1.35	−1.35
Overall mean	1.75	0.00

of 1.75 deciles, with the number of deciles moved being largest (in absolute value) for the poorest men and decreasing as relative earnings increase (column (a)). Men in the first decile necessary moved up if they changed category, while those in the tenth decile necessary moved down when they changed. This produces the +2.10 figure for mean decile change for the poorest decile and the −1.35 figure for the richest decile (column (b)). In between, as we move from poorer to richer deciles, the mean changes are monotonically decreasing—that is, those Malaysian men who began in the poorest four earnings

deciles on average improved their relative earnings position while those who began in the richer six earnings deciles on average dropped in the distribution. This kind of regression to the mean—those in relatively low positions moving up on average at the same time that those in relatively advantaged positions moved down relatively—is a common feature of income mobility data.

The third aspect of mobility studied for Malaysia was an analysis of determinants of directional positional change. Malaysian men who began in the middle eight deciles of the earnings distribution could theoretically have moved either up or down in relative position. Trzcinski and Randolph (1991) used a multinomial logit model to estimate whether a man moved up in decile terms, down in decile terms, or did not change decile. Ceteris paribus, a higher level of education made a man significantly more likely to start in one of the top earnings deciles and remain there over time, whereas a higher level of labor market experience (squared) made a man significantly less likely to start in one of the top earnings deciles and significantly more likely to move downward over time. Men who moved to a less urbanized area were more likely to experience downward relative earnings mobility, ceteris paribus, while those who changed jobs were less likely to move downwards. Finally, controlling for these and other variables, men who started in higher income deciles were less likely to move upward in relative terms, while those who started in lower income deciles were less likely to move downward. From this, the authors concluded: "Only one action enhanced an individual's prospect for relative mobility. By actively searching out new jobs in response to changing economic circumstances, an individual could increase the prospects for upward mobility."

The Malaysia studies provide an informative analysis of several aspects of income mobility during one particular time interval as well as an analysis of some of the individual factors associated with income change or lack thereof. Somewhat different aspects of income mobility have been examined for the case of Chile, to which we now turn.

7.3 Chile

In 1968, households in nine rural communities were interviewed and measures of their economic status were ascertained. In eight of these

Table 7.6
Chile: Movement among absolute income classes using per capita household income, 1968 and 1986

		Income class in 1986				
		1	2	3	4	5
Income class in 1968	1	0.08	0.32	0.20	0.28	0.12
	2	0.12	0.09	0.24	0.33	0.21
	3	0.11	0.25	0.11	0.21	0.32
	4	0.04	0.11	0.26	0.26	0.33
	5	0.03	0.03	0.12	0.24	0.58

Source: Scott and Litchfield 1994 (table 12).
Note: The income classes (measured according to per capita household income, y) are:
1: $y \leq 10,000$
2: $10,000 < y \leq 20,000$
3: $20,000 < y \leq 30,000$
4: $30,000 < y \leq 50,000$
5: $y > 50,000$
These income figures are in 1985 Chilean pesos.

communities, households were reinterviewed in 1986, producing a workable panel of 146 households. Scott and Litchfield (1994) analyzed income changes for these households. Between 1968 and 1986, household income per capita increased by 39 percent among this sample of households.

The first part of their mobility analysis was the calculation of various measures of movement among income classes. The households were divided into five absolute income classes according to their per capita incomes in 1968 and were then cross-classified into the same five absolute income classes in 1986. The transition matrix among these absolute income classes is shown in table 7.6. The diagonal entries increase sharply as we move from upper left to lower right. Thus, for example, only 8 percent of the households with per capita income below 10,000 pesos in 1968 remained in that income category in 1986. This is because of upward income movements: 32 percent of those in the lowest income category moved up to the next income category, 20 percent to the category above that, and so on. In growing economies, such "absolute income transition matrices" show sizable movements up and out of the low-income categories and low rates of continuance in the lowest categories—a feature not shared by quantile mobility matrices such as table 7.1.

The next part of their mobility analysis was to calculate both directional and nondirectional measures of movement among income classes. They found that actual mobility was about one-fourth of maximum possible mobility, that mobility was greater for poorer households, and that there was more upward than downward mobility. In their words, these data show that in the course of Chilean economic growth, "the absolute immiserisation hypothesis ... is refuted for this sample."

Their third contribution was to model the determinants of directional income movement. Two such models were formulated: (1) an ordered logit model in which the dependent variable was whether the household moved to a higher income class, moved to a lower income class, or stayed in the same income class;[2] and (2) a regression model in which the dependent variable was the change in the household's real per capita income. The variables found to be significant determinants of upward income movement were age of the head of the household, education of the household head (significant in the logit only), amount of land owned (significant in the logit only), and per capita household income in 1968 (the richer the household in 1968, the smaller the growth of income from 1968 to 1986). This result is, in the authors' words, "inconsistent with the polarisation thesis of cumulative advantage."

The Chile study shows that when economic growth took place, the specific households that were followed over time generally moved upward into higher income categories. In this sense, economic growth brought about upward income mobility for the great majority of those sampled, especially for those who started out at the bottom. Unfortunately, this was not the case in China, which we examine next.

7.4   China

China has undergone an enormous amount of economic and institutional change. At the same time, the economy has grown rapidly, especially in the coastal provinces. As a market society has emerged, income mobility has been taking place, and the mechanism of socioeconomic stratification has been changing.

---

2. Households in the highest or lowest income classes were excluded from this analysis, so that a movement up, a movement down, or nonmovement were all possibilities.

These processes have been analyzed in a series of papers by Nee (Nee 1994, 1996; Nee and Liedka 1997) based on a survey conducted by the Chinese Academy of Preventive Medicine (CAPM) covering 7,950 households living in 138 villages in 25 Chinese provinces in 1989. The respondents reported their income, total and from various sources, in 1989, 1983, and 1978. These income changes were in turn related to various characteristics of the respondents themselves and of the communities and provinces in which they lived.

Table 7.7 shows the quintile transition matrices for 1978–1983, 1983–1989, and 1978–1989 respectively. According to Nee (1994, pp. 23–24), these data show "considerable" income mobility in the early reform period, faster economic mobility when the pace of economic reform increased, and a "great transformation" in China's rural stratification. He sums up thus: "The transition to a mixed redistributive and market economy was accompanied by a quickening pace of change in relative economic standing among rural households. The findings (in table 7.7) are consistent with the view that institutional change resulted in a dramatic shake-up of the rural stratification order."

To probe into the institutional and economic factors in the movement of households through the income distribution, two statistical analyses were performed. Nee and Liedka (1997) estimated a cumulative logit model. In this model, the dependent variable was whether the household fell into the top income quintile versus the other four, the top two quintiles versus the other three, and so on, and a standard logistic model was then fit to each of these four alternative binarizations under the constraint that the effects of the covariates were identical across the four alternative ways of binarizing the response. The covariates included various measures of the institutional environment, the economic environment, individual-level covariates, and the household's base-year income quintile. They found that the variables that increase the probability that a household will fall into a higher income quintile are village economic growth, industrial per capita output, diffusion of private property forms and market institutions, human capital, and the presence of a communist party cadre in the household. Finally, other things equal, the higher the household's base-year (1978) income, the greater the likelihood of being in a high income quintile in 1989.

The other statistical analysis (Nee 1996) was an examination of changing household earnings (in yuan) in different groups of prov-

Table 7.7
China: Income mobility of rural households, 1978 to 1989

Panel A: 1978 to 1983

| | Income quintile in 1983 | | | | | |
	Top	2	3	4	Bottom	Total
Income quintile in 1978						
Top	61.3	29.8	7.3	1.0	0.6	100
2	20.9	38.8	30.3	8.6	1.4	100
3	10.6	18.1	33.1	32.6	5.7	100
4	5.7	9.4	19.2	34.8	30.9	100
Bottom	4.9	6.8	11.3	22.9	54.1	100

Panel B: 1983 to 1989

| | Income quintile in 1989 | | | | | |
	Top	2	3	4	Bottom	Total
Income quintile in 1983						
Top	48.5	25.2	12.7	6.6	7.1	100
2	23.1	28.9	23.4	13.9	10.8	100
3	16.5	20.1	23.2	24.2	16.0	100
4	9.8	15.7	24.0	28.6	21.9	100
Bottom	4.7	10.9	16.9	26.7	40.9	100

Panel C: 1978 to 1989

| | Income quintile in 1989 | | | | | |
	Top	2	3	4	Bottom	Total
Income quintile in 1978						
Top	40.3	24.4	16.2	10.4	8.7	100
2	23.6	26.3	21.0	16.7	12.4	100
3	19.6	21.8	21.0	20.8	16.8	100
4	12.7	17.2	21.5	26.2	22.4	100
Bottom	7.7	12.8	20.0	24.3	35.1	100

Source: Nee 1994 (table 3).

inces (inland, coastal redistributive, coastal corporatist, and laissez-faire) between 1983 and 1989. Variables that were found to be statistically significant ($p < .05$ or less) determinants of changing household earnings in at least one of the provincial groups were logged 1983 household income (positive effect), age and its square (inverted-U effect), participation in the labor market (positive effect), entrepreneurial activity (positive effect), being a political cadre (positive effect), and community income (positive effect). Nee concludes (1996, p. 942):

The analysis here confirms that the stratification order of rural China began a transformative change during the 1980s. Especially in the marketized coastal region, households moved up and down in relative economic standing, driven by new rules and mechanisms for getting ahead. The old rules of the game no longer worked as they did in the Maoist era, and households that followed those rules discovered that they fell in relative economic standing. However, households that were quick to adjust to an emergent market economy discovered new rules for getting ahead ... Even in the absence of regime change, a rapid shift to markets incrementally causes a relative decline in the significance of positional power based on redistribution and relative gain in the power of producers and entrepreneurs.

More generally, the results are seen as confirming the new institutional theory in sociology, which maintains that "institutions shape the structure of incentives and thereby establish the constraints within which rational actors identify and pursue their interests." (Nee 1996, p. 909).

The results amassed by Nee and associates offer a careful and thought-provoking examination of the factors underlying relative economic mobility in China. Yet, nothing presented thus far answers what is perhaps the most important mobility question of all: Were people in China getting richer or poorer absolutely? The evidence that can be assembled on this question is not encouraging.

The earnings of rural households are determined to a large degree by agricultural prices. In real terms, the price of grain sold to the state fell relative to the cost of production, lowering real agricultural incomes (Zhao 1993). Those rural households who were able to adjust by obtaining off-farm rural employment or by entering private entrepreneurship were able to get richer in the growing market economy (see the findings reported above), but those households that were not able to move into such activities were squeezed. Nee and Liedka (1997, p. 223) report that households in the bottom quintile suffered "a slight decline" in real income from 1978 to 1989, which they regard as a "special case of adverse price scissors affecting farmers still locked in the redistributive economics of grain production for the state." The stagnation of poverty in China in the latter 1980s is also documented by Ahuja et al. (1997, pp. 11–12), who find that deteriorating terms of trade for farmers was a major factor responsible for the lack of progress toward reducing poverty at this time.

This question of whether the rural poor in China did or did not achieve income gains as the rest of the economy grew has been analyzed by Chen and Ravallion (1996) and Jalan and Ravallion (1999). Their data come from a reprocessing of the Rural Household Surveys conducted by the State Statistical Bureau for the period 1985–1990. Incomes and expenditures are measured much more carefully in the SSB surveys than in the CAPM data used by Nee and associates.

Chen and Ravallion find for the four provinces for which they have data that, comparing 1985 with 1990, there was "little or no net gain to the poor." They then performed a statistical decomposition of the change in poverty. This showed that "in the two provinces where poverty fell over the period—namely Guangdong and Guizhou—this was mainly due to growth, while in the two provinces where poverty rose—Guangxi and Yunnan—the bulk of this was due to redistribution; a relative lack of growth in the latter two provinces was accompanied by poverty-increasing redistributions." Underlying these trends were "rising rural inequality and regional divergence with little gain to the poor in the lagging inland regions."

In follow-up work on the same data set, Jalan and Ravallion (1998, 1999) performed a microlevel analysis. The poverty line is defined on the basis of consumption per capita and the poverty measure is P_2. Poverty is decomposed into chronic poverty (viz., the poverty the household would have experienced if it received its mean income each year) and transient poverty (defined as the difference between the household's actual poverty and its chronic poverty). Transient poverty is found to be very important in rural China, much more so than in rural India. Comparing Chinese provinces, higher total poverty is found to be associated with higher chronic poverty. Examining households within provinces, chronic poverty is found to be a function of household structure, the age and education of the head, labor market participation variables, county-level variables (agriculture, wealth, and geography), and regional dummies, but few of these are found to be significant determinants of transient poverty. On this basis the authors conclude: "Our results suggest that different models are determining chronic versus transient poverty in this setting."[3] As for policy, they state: "There is a case for considering more finely targeting programs, although not as a means of fighting chronic poverty but rather as a way of stabilizing incomes by making assistance contingent on adverse events."

Overall, then, the mobility analysis for rural China has been complemented by analysis of cross-sectional data. Both show, unfortunately, a lack of progress for the rural poor in China in the latter 1980s.[4]

7.5   Côte d'Ivoire

Like many African economies, the economy of Côte d'Ivoire suffered a severe economic decline in the 1980s. In the second half of the decade, per capita GDP fell by 28 percent, and the incidence of poverty rose from 30 percent in 1985 to 46 percent in 1988.

The Côte d'Ivoire Living Standards Survey (CILSS) covered the 1985–1988 period. The CILSS had three one-year panels for the years 1985–1986, 1986–1987, and 1987–1988. Using these data, Grootaert and Kanbur (1996) calculated poverty in each year and over a two-year period (averaging incomes with the second year's income discounted at 10 percent). They found that because of economic mobility, two-period poverty is less severe than poverty in a single year.

To gauge mobility further, they divided each year's population into three groups ("extreme poor," "mid-poor," and "non-poor") and examined three-by-three transition matrices for each of the one-year panels. Overall, about 30 percent of households *increased* their economic position during this period of sharp economic decline. In the authors' words, "the general message is loud and clear; the lucky 'few' are not so few!" (Exclamation point in the original.)

---

3. For a review of the existing literature and issues surrounding poverty dynamics in developing countries, see Yaqub 1999.

4. The China story in the text stops with the 1980s. This is because mobility data do not exist for the 1990s. However, we do have poverty data from successive household surveys for the 1990s, which show a downward trend (World Bank, 1997a). Rising prices paid to farmers for agricultural products coupled with subsidized inputs are held to be responsible (Ahuja et al. 1997).

Finally, to determine who these lucky few were, those households who changed category were classified according to geographic region and occupation. The lucky few were found to be widely dispersed geographically and to come disproportionately from the poorer occupational groups.

In a subsequent study, Grootaert, Kanbur, and Oh (1997) used the same data to examine the determinants of change in economic status in Côte d'Ivoire. The dependent variable, termed "welfare," was change in per capita expenditure of the household. Explanatory variables included measures of base year condition, human capital, physical capital, region, socioeconomic status, segmentation variables, income composition, and change variables. For urban areas, human capital was the most important factor explaining welfare change, whereas in rural areas, physical capital mattered most. Household size and composition were also significant variables. Last, in both urban and rural areas, higher base-year economic status was related negatively to subsequent welfare change.

7.6   India

Finally, there have been two studies of income mobility in India. Coondoo and Dutta (1990) used panel data for more than 4,000 households from the National Council of Applied Economic Research for 1968/1969, 1969/1970, and 1970/1971 and reached the following principal conclusions. The first is that the three-year income distribution is distributed more equally than the single-year one, and thus income mobility in India acted to equalize the overall distribution of income. Second, poorer households' incomes increased at above-average rates, a finding also consistent with the equalizing role of income mobility. And third, using Shorrocks's index, they found that overall mobility was one-fourth of its maximum possible value.

A second India study was carried out by Drèze, Lanjouw, and Stern (1992) in the village of Palanpur. The advantages of such a village study are that income data were collected over a very long period of time (four times between 1957/1958 and 1983/1984), and the researchers could literally track every household by name and by personal acquaintance to assure that accurate matches over time were made. From quintile mobility matrices for 1957/1958–1962/1963, 1962/1963–1974/1975, and 1974/1975–1983/1984, the authors concluded that per capita incomes in different years are only "weakly correlated" with each other, because in an agricultural economy, current income in a particular year is a poor indicator of the household's "normal" earnings level.[5]

7.7 Conclusion

Economic mobility studies use panel data—that is, at least two observations on the same households or individuals over time. Various aspects of income mobility have been examined using panel data including: quintile and decile mobility matrices; comparisons of mobility rates across time periods, base income groups, and regions; mobility dominance comparisons; microeconometric models of change in economic well-being and persistence of poverty; and decomposition of poverty into chronic and transitory components. Among the findings are:

• In Peru positional movement fell over time but directional income movement increased at the same time.

• In Malaysia men with more education were more likely to start in a high earnings decile and remain there over time. Men who moved to a less urbanized area and those who did not change jobs were less likely to move downwards. Controlling for these and other variables, men who started in higher income deciles were less likely to move upward, while those in lower income deciles were less likely to move downward.

• In Chile there were sizable movements up and out of the low-income categories. Significant determinants of upward movement were age and education of the head of the household and base year household income.

• In China the transition to a mixed redistributive and market economy accelerated the rate of change of relative economic standing among rural households. Chronic poverty was found to be a function of household structure, the age and education of the household head, labor market participation variables, and county-level variables, but few of these were found to be significant determinants of transient poverty.

5. This study also examined occupational mobility and concluded that there was very little of it.

• In Côte d'Ivoire, during a period of sharp declines in per capita GDP and rising poverty, 30 percent of households increased their economic position.

• In the village of Palanpur, India a household's current economic status was found to be only weakly correlated with status in other years.

More economic mobility studies will be possible as new panel data sets become available for developing countries. The studies reviewed here give a flavor of the rich potential that this type of study has to offer.

8

The Meaning and Measurement of Economic Well-Being

In previous chapters, we examined ways of determining whether one income distribution is *more unequal* than another, whether one income distribution has *more poverty* than another, and whether a change from one income distribution to another has more *economic mobility* than another change. This chapter asks a different question: When is one income distribution *better* than another? Here, the "better" society is that into which you would choose to be born, or that which you would choose if you were a social planner.[1] It bears mention that the analytical methods introduced in this chapter apply not only to income distributions but to evaluations of economic states in general.

The chapter begins with an introduction to the types of approaches involved. We then turn our attention to social welfare functions defined first on vectors of utilities or of incomes and then to abbreviated social welfare functions. Some useful theorems on social welfare dominance are then presented. The chapter concludes by demonstrating how the various approaches can lead to different qualitative assessments.

8.1 Types of Approaches

In this book, we shall consider *outcome-based* evaluation criteria—that is, we will base our evaluations on measures calculated for the resultant income distributions, as economists nearly always do. But before proceeding to such measures, it is worth briefly discussing the alternative, which is to assign primacy to the *process* generating the

---

1. We are excluding purely self-interested choices of the type "I prefer A to B, because my income is higher in A than in B."

results. Here are some examples. Libertarians argue for a minimalist state, and therefore some would rank income distributions according to which has less government involvement of an undesirable type (Nozick 1974). Trade unionists and their supporters sometimes argue that a wage-employment package is good if and only if it is union-negotiated. And nearly all of us regard any economic state involving slavery as inferior to one without slavery. It lies outside the scope of this volume to debate such process-based criteria. They are brought up here so that they will not be overlooked.

Turning our attention to an evaluation of *outcomes* (or in Nozick's terminology, *end-states*), one might naturally seek guidance from the fundamental theorems of welfare economics. These may be stated as follows (Atkinson and Stiglitz 1980, p. 343):

FIRST WELFARE THEOREM: *If* (1) households and firms act perfectly competitively, taking prices as parametric, (2) there is a full set of markets, and (3) there is perfect information, *then* a competitive equilibrium, if it exists, is Pareto-efficient.

SECOND WELFARE THEOREM: *If* household indifference maps and firm production sets are convex, if there is a full set of markets, if there is perfect information, and if lump-sum transfers and taxes may be carried out costlessly, *then* any Pareto-efficient allocation can be achieved as a competitive equilibrium with appropriate lump-sum transfers and taxes.

The logical validity of these theorems is unquestioned. The issue is their usefulness.

Figure 8.1 depicts a simple two-person economy in which the participants (indexed by i) have utility levels U_1 and U_2 respectively. Three possible states are depicted: state A, which lies inside the utility possibility frontier, and states B and C which lie on it.[2] Our task is to choose the *best* of the three states.

We know from the first welfare theorem that under the stated conditions, the competitive equilibrium would not be a point like A (which is Pareto-inefficient). Rather, competition would lead to a point like B or C. One criterion for social welfare rankings is to judge

---

2. Points lying on the utility possibility frontier are said to be *Pareto-optimal* or *Pareto-efficient*. This means that one person cannot be made better off (in utility terms) without making another person worse off. A *Pareto-improvement* takes place when somebody is made better off and nobody else is made worse off. Moving from A to B in figure 8.1 would be a Pareto-improvement, as would a move from A to C.

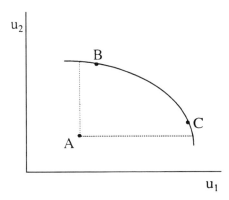

Figure 8.1

income distributions on the basis of *Pareto-improvements*. That is, social welfare is said to have increased if everybody's utility is at least as great and somebody's utility is strictly greater. By this criterion, either B or C is superior to A. But which is better, B or C? The second welfare theorem is of no help. It says that under the stated conditions, B can be achieved as a competitive equilibrium, and so too can C. Even if the "appropriate" lump-sum taxes and transfers could be made (which in the real world does not ever seem to be the case), the standard welfare theorems provide no basis for choosing among Pareto-optima.[3]

If we are going to make headway on this problem, we need a different way of thinking. In the next two sections, we consider two types of approaches based on social welfare functions.

8.2   Social Welfare Functions Based on Vectors of Utilities or Incomes

We begin with the class of *welfaristic social welfare functions*. By definition, a social welfare function is *welfaristic* if (i) its arguments are the utilities of the various individuals

$$W = f(U_1, \ldots, U_n) \tag{8.1}$$

---

3. There is, however, another criterion which *does* provide a ranking. This is the rule suggested by Buchanan and Tullock (1962) (see also Sen 1970), which states that if x is neither Pareto-superior nor Pareto-inferior to y, then x and y are socially *indifferent*. As a practical matter, Pareto-superiority is rarely attained, so by the Buchanan-Tullock criterion, nearly every social state would be ranked as indifferent to nearly every other.

and (ii) only the utilities of the various individuals enter the social welfare function.[4] Such a welfare function is also called individualistic and, in view of its origins in the work of Bergson (1938) and Samuelson (1947), a *Bergson-Samuelson social welfare function*. The indifference curves coming from this class of functions are called *Bergson-Samuelson community indifference curves*, about which more will be said later.

The class of Bergson-Samuelson social welfare functions is too general to be of use, so restrictions must be put on it. One is to limit oneself to *Paretian social welfare functions*. A social welfare function is Paretian if it approves of any Pareto-improvement:

$$W = f(U_1, \ldots, U_n), \, f(.) \text{ increasing in all } U_i. \tag{8.2}$$

One special type of Paretian social welfare function is the class of *utilitarian (or Benthamite) social welfare functions*, in which social welfare is taken to be the sum of the individual utilities

$$W = U_1 + U_2 + \cdots + U_n. \tag{8.3}$$

All Paretian social welfare functions regard any state which is Pareto-superior to another as being better in social welfare terms than the other. Notice, however, that the opposite is not true (i.e., if a state is better than another using the Benthamite social welfare function (8.3), this does *not* imply that it is also Pareto-superior). For instance, consider two ordered utility distributions such as $X = (1, 2, 3)$ and $Y = (1, 2, 4)$. Y is Pareto-superior to X: One individual is better off and nobody is worse off. Using a social welfare function like (8.3), social welfare in Y is also higher than in X. On the other hand, if we compare $X = (1, 2, 3)$ to $Z = (4, 2, 1)$ we find no Pareto-improvement, but social welfare function in Z is also higher than in X by (8.3). This is why Paretian social welfare functions provide a wider scope of comparison among states than the strict Pareto-improvement criterion.

Not all social welfare functions are Paretian. A social welfare function may be non-Paretian, because although it is welfaristic, that

---

4. The U_is in (8.1) are usually thought of as literal representations of the utility functions of the individuals themselves. However, U_i is also used to denote the individual component of social welfare that is associated with each individual, for example, the weight the evaluator assigns to the ith individual's income or consumption (Atkinson 1970; Sen 1973; Foster and Sen 1997, p. 116). Atkinson himself has expressed regret for not having used a letter other than U in this context (Atkinson 1983b, p. 5).

is, $W = f(U_1, \ldots, U_n)$, it is not increasing in all utilities. An example is the *egalitarian social welfare function* which, in a two-person economy, takes the form:

$$W = g(|U_1 - U_2|), \, g' < 0. \qquad (8.4)$$

This and other non-Paretian functions are sometimes called an *observer's social welfare function*, because the observer cares about something different from what the participants care about: In this case, the observer cares about $|U_1 - U_2|$ whereas the ith participant cares about U_i alone.

Another reason that a social welfare function may be non-Paretian is that it does not judge all Pareto-improvements to be strictly better. An example is the *Rawlsian social welfare function* in which social welfare depends only on the utility of the worst-off person (denoted by [1], the brackets indicating the individual's position in the utility distribution):

$$W = f(U_{[1]}), f(.) \text{ increasing.} \qquad (8.5)$$

This is not Paretian, because if a Pareto-improvement leaves the worst-off person's utility unchanged, the Rawlsian social welfare function says that welfare is unchanged.[5] What *is* Paretian, however, is the *lexicographic Rawlsian function*, defined as follows: If the poorest person's utility is unchanged, look at the next poorest person's utility, and so on until you find a change. Denote the poorest person whose utility has changed by [i]. Social welfare changes as $U_{[i]}$ changes:

$$W = f(U_{[i]}), f(.) \text{ increasing.} \qquad (8.6)$$

By this criterion, *any* Pareto-improvement would be judged as welfare-increasing.

Some social welfare functions not only are not Paretian but they are not even welfaristic. A social welfare function is *nonwelfaristic* if it is not a function of the utilities of the individuals involved, that is, it does not accept their preferences. Why might you not want to accept the utility functions of the participants? Suppose the participants exhibit malevolence (sometimes called "envy").[6] Let us represent

---

5. Recall the comment on Rawlsians' perceptions of poverty measures in chapter 2, note 15.
6. "Envy," though, has come to be used in economics in the specific sense that an individual prefers someone else's bundle of goods to his or her own. For a discussion of the concept of envy, see Hammond 1989.

these malevolent preferences in a two-person economy by the utility functions:

$$U_1 = h(Y_1, Y_2), \; h_1 > 0, \; h_2 < 0 \tag{8.7.a}$$

and

$$U_2 = i(Y_1, Y_2), \; i_2 > 0, \; i_1 < 0. \tag{8.7.b}$$

Malevolence enters in here by writing that the utility of one individual depends negatively on the income of the other. The observer may not want to accept this malevolence; such censoring has been suggested by Harsanyi (1955) and Goodin (1995), among others. An alternative is to use a social welfare function which is monotonic in each person's *income* (but not utility):

$$W = j(v(Y_1), v(Y_2), \ldots), \tag{8.8.a}$$

$$v(.) \text{ increasing in } Y_i \tag{8.8.b}$$

$$j(.) \text{ increasing in all } v(.). \tag{8.8.c}$$

This function is nonwelfaristic, because the *v*s are the weights used by the evaluator and not the individuals' own utility functions. Equations (8.8.a–c) also introduce a subtle but vitally important change: Social welfare is now expressed as a function of *incomes* (on which we have data) and not as a function of *utilities* (on which we do not).

To see how this makes a difference, suppose we have a *quasi-Pareto improvement*, defined to be a situation where somebody's income goes up and everybody else's income stays the same. (As always, incomes are assumed here to be expressed in real dollars.) When somebody's income has risen, holding others' incomes the same, (8.8) would say that social welfare has increased, and accordingly we may say that (8.8) is a quasi-Paretian social welfare function. However, the welfaristic social welfare function

$$W = f(U_1, \ldots, U_n) \tag{8.1}$$

coupled with malevolent utility functions

$$U_1 = h(Y_1, Y_2), \; h_1 > 0, \; h_2 < 0 \tag{8.7.a}$$

and

$$U_2 = i(Y_1, Y_2), \; i_2 > 0, \; i_1 < 0 \tag{8.7.b}$$

is incapable of rendering a social welfare judgment about an increase in one individual's income, holding constant the income of the other.[7]

Figure 8.2.a depicts a situation similar to that in figure 8.1 except that the comparison is now between different points on the space of *incomes* rather than on the space of *utilities*. Moving from A to B or from A to C constitutes a quasi-Pareto improvement, and as such raises welfare for the class of functions given by (8.8).

What about a comparison between B and C? At first, it might appear that a solution could be found by working with those community indifference curves derived from social welfare functions of type (8.1), but this is not so, because some members of this class of social welfare function rank B as better than C (figure 8.2.b) while others rank B as worse than C (figure 8.2.c). An answer needs to be sought elsewhere.

8.3   Abbreviated Social Welfare Functions

A different way of making welfare judgments—one that builds directly on the inequality and poverty analysis in chapters 2 through 5—is to use what are called *abbreviated social welfare functions* (Lambert 1993). A social welfare function is *abbreviated* if welfare is expressed as a function of statistics calculated from the income distribution vector, for example,

$$W = w(\text{GNP}, \text{INEQ}, \text{POV}), \tag{8.9.a}$$

where GNP is a measure of gross national product (in real dollars per capita), INEQ is a measure of inequality, and POV is a measure of poverty. When such functions are applied, it is usually with the stipulation (typically implicit) that social welfare increases if GNP rises, INEQ falls, or POV falls, and thus, assuming differentiability of the $w(.)$ function:

$$w_1 > 0, \ w_2 < 0, \text{ and } w_3 < 0.^8 \tag{8.9.b}$$

Empirically, GNP often increases while INEQ and POV decrease, permitting a welfare statement to be made using the class of functions (8.9). But about as often, a different pattern of changes is found— about half the time, INEQ increases in the course of GNP growth,

---

7. This is because although the recipient's utility has increased, the nonrecipient's utility has decreased, rendering the welfaristic social welfare function (8.8) ambiguous.
8. But for an alternative view on inequality, see Welch 1999.

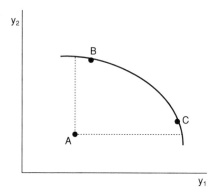

Figure 8.2.a

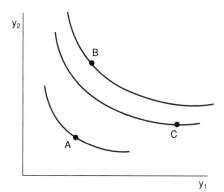

Figure 8.2.b

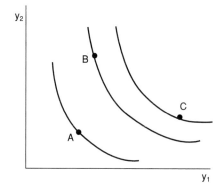

Figure 8.2.c

which means that the welfare judgment about the distributional effects of economic growth is ambiguous in such cases. The analyst can either accept the ambiguity rendered by (8.9) or seek another criterion for making comparisons of economic well-being. The next section presents the welfare dominance alternative.

8.4   Welfare Dominance Results

In certain situations, it may be possible to rank the welfare of one income distribution relative to another for a broad class of social welfare functions. Three theorems are particularly useful for this purpose.[9]

First, consider ranking two income distributions that have the same mean. The following theorem pertains to such situations:

THEOREM 8.1   WELFARE COMPARISONS WHEN MEANS ARE EQUAL (ATKINSON 1970; DASGUPTA, SEN, AND STARRETT 1973):   Let X and Y be two income distributions such that $\mu(X) = \mu(Y)$. Let $L_X(p) > L_Y(p)$ indicate that X Lorenz-dominates Y. Let W_E denote the class of anonymous, increasing, and S-concave social welfare functions. Then, $L(X) > L(Y)$ if and only if $w(X) > w(Y)$ for all $w \in W_E$.

Note carefully what this says: When the means are equal, an income distribution that Lorenz-dominates another is not only more equal but *better* in welfare terms—provided, that is, that we accept the properties of class W_E.[10]

What if the means are *not* equal? Two theorems apply in such cases.

THEOREM 8.2   FIRST-ORDER WELFARE DOMINANCE (SAPOSNIK 1981): Let X and Y be any two income distributions. Define $X(p) \equiv \inf\{x : F(x) \geq p\}$ (i.e., the smallest value of x such that $F(x) \geq p$) and define $Y(p)$ similarly. Let $X \succ_{FOD} Y$ indicate that X first-order

---

9. This discussion is based on work by Shorrocks (1983), Kakwani (1984), Pyatt (1989), Lambert ([1989] 1993), and Bishop and Formby (1994).

10. Taking the household as the unit of analysis, "anonymous" means that all households are treated identically regardless of which particular ones receive how much income. "Increasing" means that social welfare increases whenever one household's income increases, holding other households' incomes the same. "S-concave" means that the function registers higher economic well-being whenever a transfer of income is made from someone who is relatively high-income to someone who is relatively low-income.

dominates $\mathbf{Y}$, that is, $\mathbf{X}(p) \geq \mathbf{Y}(p)$ for all $p \in [0,1]$ with strict inequality for some p. Let $\mathbf{W}_P$ denote the class of anonymous, increasing social welfare functions. Then, $\mathbf{X} \succ_{\text{FOD}} \mathbf{Y}$ if and only if $w(\mathbf{X}) > w(\mathbf{Y})$ for all $w \in \mathbf{W}_P$.

First-order dominance is also called "rank dominance," because in the case of populations of equal size, the income of the person in each rank in $\mathbf{X}$ is at least as great as the income of the person with the corresponding rank in $\mathbf{Y}$ and strictly greater someplace. In other words, the person who ranks poorest in each distribution has a higher income in $\mathbf{X}$ than in $\mathbf{Y}$, and likewise for the second person, the third person, and so on. In the case of aggregate data divided, say, into centiles, for one income distribution to first-order dominate another, the income in the first centile of $\mathbf{X}$ must be higher than in $\mathbf{Y}$, the income in the second centile of $\mathbf{X}$ must be higher than in $\mathbf{Y}$, and so on up to the ninety-ninth centile. First-order dominance implies first-order poverty dominance (cf. chapter 6), that is, when one income distribution is better than another in the sense of theorem 8.2, the better one necessarily has less poverty than the other.

Note what makes first-order dominance different from Pareto dominance: In first-order dominance, we are comparing anonymous people in particular positions, whereas for Pareto dominance, we need to compare the before and after incomes for named persons.[11]

First-order dominance is an easy-to-use criterion in aggregate data. To implement it, check whether the real income is higher at the first quantile (decile or centile) in $\mathbf{X}$ than in $\mathbf{Y}$, likewise for the second quantile, the third quantile, and so on. Applications of this method appear in chapter 9.

It may turn out that the $\mathbf{X}(p)$ and $\mathbf{Y}(p)$ curves cross, as in figure 8.3. In this case, welfare rankings may still be possible, based on the following result:

THEOREM 8.3 SECOND-ORDER WELFARE DOMINANCE (SHORROCKS 1983, BASED ON KOLM 1976): Let $\mathbf{X}$ and $\mathbf{Y}$ be any two income distributions. Define the Generalized Lorenz curve $GL_x(p) \equiv \mu_x L_x(p)$, that is, the ordinary Lorenz curve multiplied by the mean, and define

---

11. The following example illustrates the difference. In distribution $\mathbf{X}$ let person α have \$100 and person β have \$200. In distribution $\mathbf{Y}$ let person β have \$150 and person α have \$300. Because both the poorest person and the second poorest person have higher incomes in $\mathbf{Y}$ than in $\mathbf{X}$, we may say that $\mathbf{Y}$ first-order dominates $\mathbf{X}$. But because person β is worse off in $\mathbf{Y}$ than in $\mathbf{X}$, $\mathbf{Y}$ does not Pareto-dominate $\mathbf{X}$.

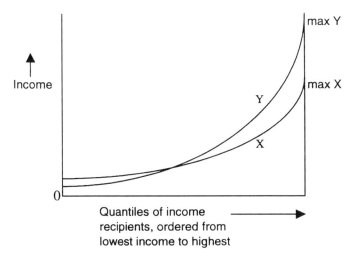

Figure 8.3
Crossing of quantile functions

$GL_y(p)$ similarly. One distribution **X** is said to second-order domi-
nate another **Y** (which we write as $\mathbf{X} \succ_{SOD} \mathbf{Y}$) if and only if $GL_x(p) \geq$
$GL_y(p)$ for all $p \in [0, 1]$ with strict inequality for some p. Then for the
class of anonymous, increasing, and S-concave social welfare func-
tions $\mathbf{W}_E$, $\mathbf{X} \succ_{SOD} \mathbf{Y}$ if and only if $w(\mathbf{X}) > w(\mathbf{Y})$ for all $w \in \mathbf{W}_E$.

Theorem 8.3 gives another easy-to-use criterion for making welfare
comparisons of two income distributions **X** and **Y**. Draw the two
generalized Lorenz curves, that is, the ordinary Lorenz curves multiplied by their respective means. One income distribution is judged
to be *better* than another (i.e., it gives higher welfare) if its generalized Lorenz curve lies somewhere above and nowhere below the
other's, and for this reason, second order welfare dominance is also
called "Generalized Lorenz curve dominance."[12] By the Shorrocks-
Kolm theorem, ranking by generalized Lorenz curves is equivalent to
using social welfare functions which:

1. are anonymous,
2. are increasing in all incomes,
3. are S-concave.

---

12. However, if generalized Lorenz curves cross, this criterion cannot be used to determine which income distribution is better. Thus, the SOD welfare ordering is partial in
the same way that inequality comparisons using ordinary Lorenz curves are partial.

This tells us what is required to justify welfare comparisons using generalized Lorenz curves. But before using this criterion, you will have to think whether *your* social welfare function satisfies these three properties.[13]

Before concluding this section, it is important to remark on the relationship between first- and second-order welfare dominance. Observe that the class of social welfare functions in theorem 8.3 is a subclass of the class in theorem 8.2. It follows that first-order welfare dominance implies second-order welfare dominance, or in different terminology, that rank dominance implies Generalized Lorenz dominance. It is an empirical question how often first order dominance fails but second order dominance holds. Empirical results on this issue are presented in chapter 9.

8.5   Similarities and Differences among the Various Approaches

Section 8.2 considered several types of social welfare functions defined on participants' utilities. The absence of utility information in data renders such functions unusable in practice.

The abbreviated social welfare function approach of section 8.3 and the welfare dominance approaches of section 8.4 both provide income-based criteria for helping determine if one income distribution is better or worse than another. (Again, please remember that "income" is being used in this book as shorthand for whichever indicator of economic well-being one chooses to use.)

The usefulness of the two approaches, as well as the differences between them, will be illustrated theoretically in this section and empirically in chapter 9. A useful heuristic device for doing this is to consider the three stylized economic growth types first introduced in Fields (1979a).[14]

Keeping within the dualistic development tradition of Lewis (1954), Fei and Ranis (1964), and Kuznets (1966), let us suppose that there are two economic sectors, which we shall call "modern" and "traditional." The workers in these sectors each earn incomes y_M and y_T respectively, $y_M > y_T$. The two sectors respectively comprise population shares f_M and $f_T = 1 - f_M$.

---

13. If you are not sure about the definitions, look again at footnote 10.
14. The welfare analysis that follows builds on that contained in Fields 1979a but moves beyond it to include certain additional features that didn't yet exist at that time.

Now let us define three stylized growth types. *Traditional sector enrichment* entails an increase in y_T, holding y_M and f_M constant. *Modern sector enrichment* involves an increase in y_M, holding y_T and f_M constant. Finally, *modern sector enlargement* occurs when f_M increases, holding y_M and y_T constant.

Traditional sector enrichment results in an increase in GNP, a reduction in inequality (by virtue of a Lorenz-improvement), and reduced poverty (for any of the poverty measures discussed in chapter 4, using any poverty line z, $y_T \leq z < y_M$). The class of abbreviated social welfare functions given by (8.9) deems such growth to be welfare-improving.

Modern sector enrichment produces an increase in GNP, an increase in inequality (by virtue of Lorenz-worsening), and no change in poverty (again, provided that the poverty line z falls in the range $y_T \leq z < y_M$). The class of social welfare functions given by (8.9) evaluates the increase in GNP positively and the increase in inequality negatively, and therefore cannot generate a verdict as to whether this type of growth is welfare-improving or not.

Modern sector enlargement also raises GNP. The Lorenz curves for the initial and final distributions can be shown to cross each other (Fields 1979a). When Lorenz curves cross, an inequality measure can always be found which registers an increase in inequality and another can be found which registers a decrease in inequality. Furthermore, as f_M varies from zero to one, a number of commonly used inequality measures first increase up to a critical value f_{M^*} and then decrease.[15] If you choose one of those measures, as f_M increases, you will then have an increase in GNP, a fall in poverty, and an increase in inequality for modern sector enlargement growth in the range $f_M < f_{M^*}$. Modern sector enlargement growth is therefore evaluated ambiguously in this range. It is only once $f_M > f_{M^*}$ that GNP grows, INEQ falls, and POV falls, so that this type of growth can be judged by the abbreviated social welfare function approach to be welfare-enhancing.

What if we instead use the welfare dominance approaches of section 8.4? Theorem 8.2 applies to each of the three stylized growth typologies, and in each, it registers an unambiguous verdict: *in traditional sector enrichment, in modern sector enrichment, and in modern*

---

15. This follows from a result contained in Anand and Kanbur 1993b, applied to the special case of zero within-sector inequality. See also Robinson 1976, Knight 1976, and Fields 1979a.

sector enlargement, economic growth is welfare-enhancing according to the welfare dominance approaches. This is because some real incomes have increased and none have decreased, producing first-order dominance.

The abbreviated social welfare function approach and the welfare dominance approaches diverge in the following way. The abbreviated social welfare function approach allows for the possibility that increased inequality might possibly overpower GNP growth, in the sense that an observer who is sufficiently inequality-averse might prefer a no-growth situation to an inequality-increasing pattern of growth. On the other hand, the welfare dominance approaches do not allow this—for those who adhere to such methods, any time some real incomes increase holding other real incomes the same, social welfare must be deemed to have increased, regardless of whether inequality has increased or not. It is this different treatment of inequality that is the critical factor distinguishing the abbreviated social welfare function approach from the first- and second-order welfare dominance methods.

8.6   Conclusions

This chapter has considered several methods for judging whether one income distribution is *better* than another—better in the sense that if you could choose, you would choose to belong to or bring about the first income distribution rather than the second. Your first decision is whether to choose which is preferred on the basis of the income distributions themselves or on the basis of the processes by which these distributions were generated. Assuming that your basis will be a comparison of the income distributions, your next decision is what kind of social evaluation function to use. Utility-based social welfare functions, while fine in theory, cannot be used empirically. You need to use something that can be calculated from available data on incomes or expenditures.

Two approaches for dealing with census or survey data were distinguished: abbreviated social welfare functions and welfare dominance methods. These were shown to make a difference in certain stylized growth types. The crucial distinguishing feature is the different ways in which these two approaches treat inequality.

Does the choice make a difference empirically? Chapter 9 shows that it does.

9   Empirical Comparisons of Economic Well-Being

Two empirically implementable ways of deciding whether one income distribution is better or worse than another were presented in chapter 8. The first used an abbreviated social welfare function in which economic well-being depends positively on gross national product (in real dollars per capita) and negatively on changes in inequality and poverty. The second approach involved dominance methods. This chapter applies these methods to a number of country cases from the developing world, comparing and contrasting the findings empirically.

9.1   Comparisons of Economic Well-Being: The Methods Reviewed

The "abbreviated social welfare functions" introduced in chapter 8 were of the form

$$W = w(\text{GNP}, \text{INEQ}, \text{POV}), \ w_1 > 0, \ w_2 < 0, \ \text{and} \ w_3 < 0, \tag{8.9}$$

such that social welfare is a positive function of GNP (in real dollars per capita) and a negative function of inequality and poverty in the country. We found empirically in chapter 3 that income inequality increases about half the time when economic growth takes place and decreases about half the time. It follows that for about half the growth experiences in the world, the class of social welfare functions given by (8.9) would record *ambiguous* changes in economic well-being as these countries grow.

The welfare dominance approach was reflected in theorems 8.1–8.3. Theorem 8.1 dealt with the case where mean income is unchanged. Since empirically, the mean nearly always changes, this theorem is of little practical interest.

Theorems 8.2 and 8.3 apply to cases where the mean changes. One distribution first-order dominates another if, for each population group, the per capita income in the first distribution is higher than in the second. For instance, if the population groups are deciles, first-order dominance holds if the per capita income is higher in one distribution than another for the first decile, for the second decile, and so on. Theorem 8.2 states that if one distribution first-order dominates another, the first distribution is *better* than the second for all social welfare functions which are anonymous and increasing in all incomes.

If neither distribution first-order dominates the other, we may still have second-order dominance. One distribution second-order dominates another if, for each population group, the *cumulative* per capita income is higher in the first distribution than in the second for each cumulative population group. Again, illustrating for the case of deciles, second-order dominance holds if one distribution has higher per capita income than another for the first decile, for the first two deciles taken together, and so on. Theorem 8.3 states that if one distribution second-order dominates another, the first distribution is *better* than the second for all social welfare functions which are anonymous, increasing in all incomes, and S-concave.

Comparisons of economic well-being using dominance methods have been carried out for five developing countries: Taiwan, Thailand, Indonesia, Brazil, and Chile. These results are presented below, where they are compared and contrasted with the results using abbreviated social welfare functions.

9.2   The Case of Taiwan

Taiwan's economy has had one of the world's highest economic growth rates since the 1960s. A welfare dominance analysis for the period 1980–1992 has been conducted by Chiou (1996).

Between 1980 and 1992, per capita income in Taiwan grew at a 6.1 percent annual rate. However, Taiwan's income distribution became more unequal (figures 9.1 and 9.2). Because GNP increased and inequality did also, the class of abbreviated social welfare functions of the form

$$W = w(\text{GNP}, \text{INEQ}, \text{POV}), \ w_1 > 0, \ w_2 < 0, \text{ and } w_3 < 0$$

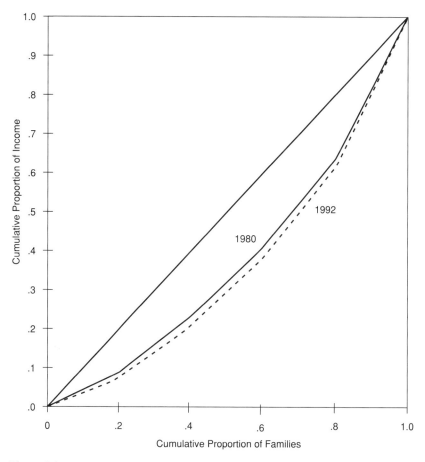

Figure 9.1
Taiwan: Lorenz curves of family income, 1980 and 1992
Source: Chiou 1996.

would be unable to say whether social welfare in Taiwan had improved or not.

First-order dominance testing gives an unambiguous answer. Table 9.1 and figure 9.3 show that the real incomes of each quintile of households in Taiwan were about double in 1992 what they had been in 1980. Thus, all evaluators who accept a social welfare function which is anonymous and increasing in all incomes would say that the 1992 income distribution in Taiwan was better (in a social welfare sense) than the 1980 distribution, notwithstanding the ambiguity recorded by the abbreviated social welfare function.

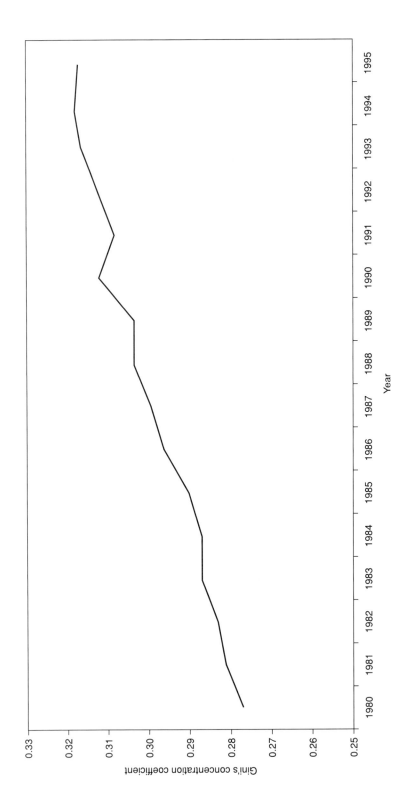

Figure 9.2
Taiwan: The rising Gini coefficient of household income
Source: Republic of China 1995 (table 4).

Table 9.1
Taiwan's mean income by quintile, 1980 and 1992 (mean family income per month in 1991 NT dollars)

	Quintile				
	1	2	3	4	5
1980	144,799	226,620	288,680	371,467	599,992
1992	225,600	405,159	536,331	710,493	1,183,164

Source: Chiou 1996.

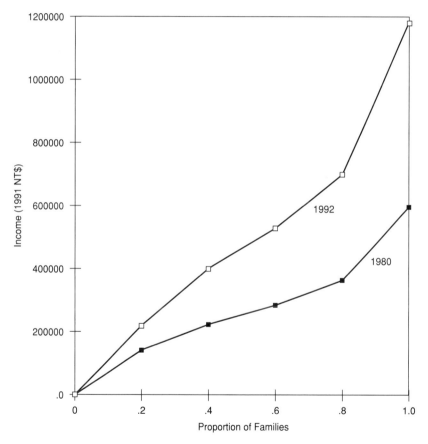

Figure 9.3
First-order dominance and Taiwan's income distribution, 1980 and 1992
Source: Chiou 1996.

Table 9.2
Thailand: Economic growth and changing inequality

	1975	1981	1986	1992
Mean expenditures	947.5	1250.0	1261.3	1911.4
	Economy grew		Economy grew	
Inequality measure				
Gini coefficient	35.74	39.71	42.62	45.39
	Inequality rose		Inequality rose	
Mean log deviation	0.209	0.259	0.301	0.342
	Inequality rose		Inequality rose	
Theil index	0.245	0.305	0.335	0.406
	Inequality rose		Inequality rose	
One-half of the square of the coefficient of variation	0.497	0.653	0.550	0.801
	Inequality rose		Inequality rose	

Source: Calculations by Ahuja et al. 1997 (table 4.2) based on Thai Socioeconomic Survey data.

9.3   The Case of Thailand

A welfare dominance analysis for Thailand has been presented in Ahuja et al. 1997 comparing four years: 1975, 1981, 1986, and 1992. GDP per capita in Thailand grew at an annual rate of 4.6 percent per capita between 1965 and 1980 and at 6.4 percent between 1980 and 1995; the corresponding per capita GDP growth rates in purchasing power parity (PPP) dollars were 4.4 percent for 1965–1980 and 5.5 percent for 1980–1995. However, this growth was quite uneven: Mean expenditure grew rapidly from 1975 to 1981, essentially stagnated from 1981 to 1986, and again grew rapidly between 1986 and 1992 (figure 9.4). Our question, therefore, is what distributional changes took place in Thailand during the 1975–1981 and 1986–1992 growth episodes?

Let us begin with the abbreviated social welfare approach. Inequality data appear in figure 9.5 and table 9.2. The Lorenz curves essentially coincide at the very lowest end of the expenditure distribution and then show Lorenz-worsenings during the 1975–1981 growth episode and again during the 1986–1992 growth episode. The increases in inequality during these growth episodes are confirmed by the four inequality measures presented in table 9.2, all of which increased when the economy grew from 1975 to 1981 and again when the economy grew from 1986 to 1992.

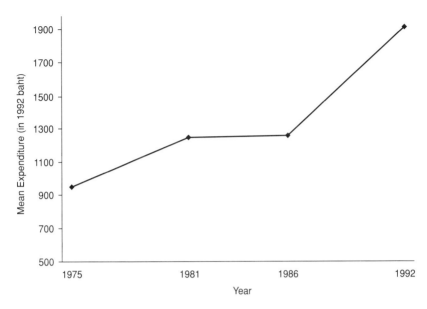

Figure 9.4
Thailand: Growth of mean expenditures, 1975–1992
Source: Calculations by Ahuja et al. (1997, table 4.2) based on Thai Socioeconomic Survey data.

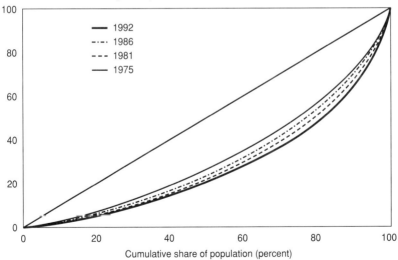

Figure 9.5
Thailand: Real expenditure Lorenz curves, 1975–1992
Source: Ahuja et al. (1997, figure 4.5) based on Thai Socioeconomic Survey data.

Table 9.3
Thailand: Economic growth and changing poverty

Poverty line/measure	1975	1981	1986	1992
Poverty line: $2 a day (1985 prices)				
P(0) Head-count	41.80	30.36	33.80	15.69
	Poverty fell		Poverty fell	
P(1) Poverty gap	12.09	7.87	10.05	3.45
	Poverty fell		Poverty fell	
P(2) Poverty severity	4.79	2.87	4.15	1.14
	Poverty fell		Poverty fell	
Poverty line: $1 a day (1985 prices)				
P(0) Head-count	5.92	2.84	5.49	0.97
	Poverty fell		Poverty fell	
P(1) Poverty gap	0.94	0.39	1.08	0.16
	Poverty fell		Poverty fell	
P(2) Poverty severity	0.25	0.09	0.34	0.04
	Poverty fell		Poverty fell	

Source: Calculations by Ahuja et al. 1997 (table 4.2) based on Thai Socioeconomic Survey data.

Poverty changes in a country reflect the combined effect of economic growth and inequality change; for a formal analysis of this, see section 5.2. Table 9.3 shows that despite the increase in inequality that took place in Thailand, economic growth nonetheless reduced poverty as measured by three different poverty indices for two alternative poverty lines. Figure 9.6 goes a step further: The graph shows that for all expenditure levels up to 360 baht per capita, the 1981 cumulative distribution function lies below the 1975 curve, and the 1992 curve lies below the 1986 one. Applying the poverty dominance methods presented in section 4.5, this means that poverty fell from 1975 to 1981 and again from 1986 to 1992 for *all* poverty measures in the class

$$P = \sum_{i=1}^{n} p(z, y_i)/n \text{ such that}$$

1. $p(z, y_i) = 0$ if $y_i \geq z$, and   (4.1)

2. $p(z, y_i) > 0$ if $y_i \leq z$

and for *all* poverty lines between 200 and 360 baht.

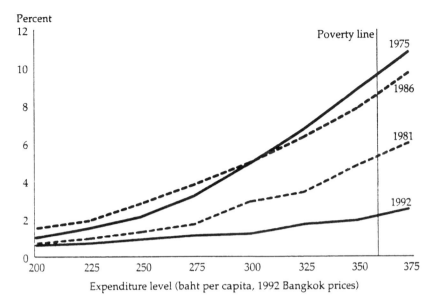

Figure 9.6
Thailand: Cumulative distribution functions, detail of low-income range, 1975–1992
Source: Ahuja et al. (1997, figure 4.7), based on Thai Socioeconomic Survey data.

Summing up what happened to the components of the abbreviated social welfare function approach, between 1975 and 1981 and again between 1986 and 1992, economic growth took place, inequality rose, and poverty fell. The abbreviated social welfare function

$$W = w(\text{GNP}, \text{INEQ}, \text{POV}), \ w_1 > 0, \ w_2 < 0, \text{ and } w_3 < 0, \qquad (8.9)$$

is therefore not able to say whether social welfare has improved or not.

Were we to instead use the welfare dominance method of theorem 8.2, we would get an unambiguous answer. As figure 9.7 shows, the 1981 curve dominates the 1975 curve and the 1992 curve dominates the 1986 one. Thus, by the first-order dominance criterion, the 1975–1981 economic growth led to a *better* distribution of economic well-being, as did economic growth during the 1986–1992 period.

9.4   The Case of Indonesia

Essentially the same result arises for Indonesia as arose for Thailand. Data from the Susenas surveys for Java have been analyzed by

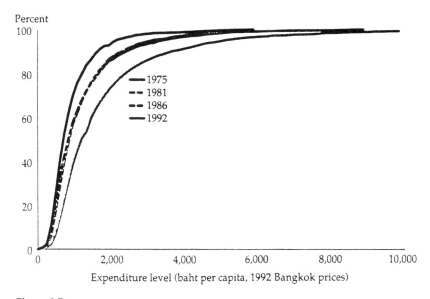

Figure 9.7
Thailand: Cumulative distribution functions, 1975–1992
Source: Ahuja et al. (1997, figure 4.6), based on Thai Socioeconomic Survey data.

Cameron (forthcoming) covering the years 1984 and 1990. Between 1984 and 1990, mean per capita income on Java grew by 23.5 percent. The three basic distributional facts she finds (figure 9.8) are:

1. The 1990 distribution first-order dominates the 1984 distribution.

2. The 1984 distribution Lorenz-dominates the 1990 distribution.

3. The 1990 distribution Generalized-Lorenz-dominates the 1984 distribution.

As we have learned, i implies iii. Thus, the dominance approach to economic well-being judges 1990 to be better than 1984. On the other hand, the abbreviated social welfare function approach records growth in mean income and rising inequality, and therefore evaluates the 1984–1990 experience ambiguously.

9.5   The Case of Brazil

Our next case is that of Brazil. Income inequality has been getting progressively more unequal, as gauged by successive Lorenz-worsenings from 1960 to 1970 to 1980 to 1990 (figure 9.9). Yet,

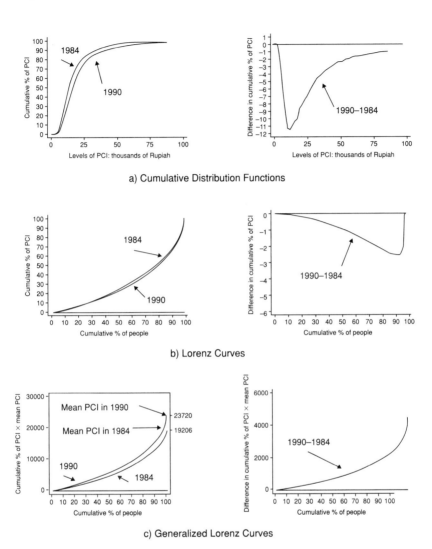

a) Cumulative Distribution Functions

b) Lorenz Curves

c) Generalized Lorenz Curves

Figure 9.8
Indonesia: Dominance comparisons, 1984 and 1990
Source: Cameron forthcoming.

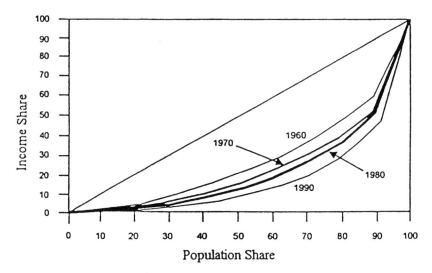

Figure 9.9
Brazil: Lorenz curves of income, 1960–1990
Source: Barros and Mendonça (1995, figure 7), based on Brazilian census data.

economic growth took place from 1960 to 1970 and again from 1970 to 1980 (figure 9.10). During these intervals, we see for Brazil, as we did for other countries, that the rising GNP and rising inequality are evaluated ambiguously by the abbreviated social welfare function

$$W = w(\text{GNP}, \text{INEQ}, \text{POV}), \ w_1 > 0, \ w_2 < 0, \text{ and } w_3 < 0.$$

Nonetheless, real incomes were higher in each decile of the Brazilian income distribution in 1980 than in 1960 (figure 9.11), so by the first-order dominance criterion, the 1980 distribution was better than the 1960 one.[1]

Let us now consider the 1980–1990 period in Brazil. In those years, GNP fell and inequality and poverty rose. The abbreviated social welfare function would therefore say that social welfare worsened in Brazil during this period of time. In addition, figure 9.11 shows that real incomes fell from 1980 to 1990 in every income decile, which means that by the first-order dominance criterion, the 1990 distribution of income was worse than the 1980 one. So in this case, the

---

1. For the price index used by Barros and Mendonça, growth was also positive between 1960 and 1970 for each decile except the seventh. For alternative price indices, income growth is recorded for that decile as well.

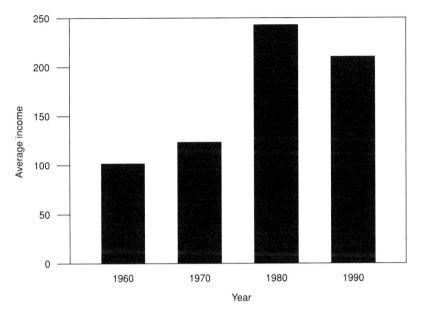

Figure 9.10
Brazil: Average income level of the economically active population (1960–1990)
Source: Barros and Mendonça (1995, figure 6), based on Brazilian census data.

abbreviated social welfare function approach and the first-order dominance approach are in agreement—unhappily, showing a *worsening* of economic well-being over the decade of the 1980s.

9.6   The Case of Chile

The final case to consider is Chile. Income distribution data at the national level are available for the period 1987–1994.[2]

Real per capita income grew at a 5.8 percent annual rate over these seven years. Between 1987 and 1994, the distributions of household income per capita and household income per adult-equivalent both showed Lorenz-improvements, and therefore falling inequality (table 9.4). Rapid economic growth accompanied by falling inequality would be expected to produce falling poverty. Table 9.5 shows that poverty did indeed fall for a variety of poverty lines and poverty

2. These are the CASEN (Caracterización Socioeconómica Nacional) data, covering all of Chile. (An earlier, 1985 survey is thought to be poorer in quality than and incomparable to the subsequent ones.) Earlier studies in Chile used data covering Greater Santiago only.

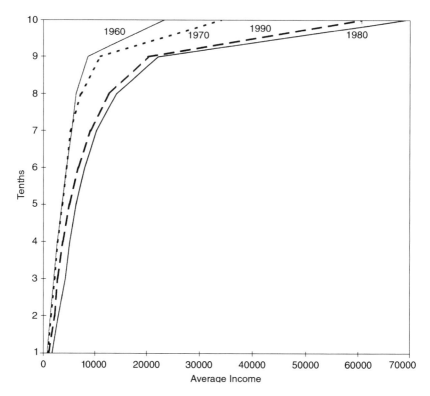

Figure 9.11
Brazil: Average income of each tenth of the distribution of economically active population with positive income
Source: Barros and Mendonça (1995, figure A.8.c), based on Brazilian census data.

measures. Because growth has taken place and inequality and poverty have fallen, all functions in the class of abbreviated social welfare functions

$$W = w(\text{GNP}, \text{INEQ}, \text{POV}), \quad w_1 > 0, \quad w_2 < 0, \quad \text{and } w_3 < 0$$

register improved economic well-being.

In view of these changes, it would not be surprising to find that the 1994 distribution dominates the 1987 distribution. Indeed, first-order dominance does arise (figure 9.12).

We may conclude that economic well-being in Chile improved by both the abbreviated social welfare function and the first-order-dominance criteria.

Table 9.4
Chile: Lorenz curves, 1987–1994

a) Decile income shares: Household incomes per capita

	1987		1994	
	Decile	Cumulative	Decile	Cumulative
Decile 1	1.21	1.21	1.28	1.28
Decile 2	2.19	3.40	2.33	3.61
Decile 3	2.95	6.35	3.11	6.72
Decile 4	3.77	10.12	3.96	10.68
Decile 5	4.72	14.84	4.96	15.64
Decile 6	5.94	20.78	6.22	21.86
Decile 7	7.66	28.44	7.91	29.77
Decile 8	10.37	38.81	10.60	40.37
Decile 9	15.89	54.70	15.95	56.32
Decile 10	45.30	100.00	43.66	99.98

b) Decile income shares: Household incomes per adult equivalent

	1987		1994	
	Decile	Cumulative	Decile	Cumulative
Decile 1	1.34	1.34	1.43	1.43
Decile 2	2.41	3.75	2.57	4.00
Decile 3	3.17	6.92	3.36	6.36
Decile 4	3.97	10.89	4.18	11.54
Decile 5	4.88	14.77	5.14	16.68
Decile 6	6.04	21.81	6.33	23.01
Decile 7	7.66	29.47	7.93	30.94
Decile 8	10.24	39.71	10.55	41.49
Decile 9	15.71	55.42	15.76	57.25
Decile 10	44.58	100.00	42.73	100.00

Source: World Bank 1997, pp. 11 and 13.

9.7   Conclusions

We found empirically in chapter 3 that income inequality increases about half the time when economic growth takes place and decreases about half the time. It follows that for about half the growth experiences in the world, the class of social welfare functions given by

$$W = w(\text{GNP}, \text{INEQ}, \text{POV}), \ w_1 > 0, \ w_2 < 0, \ \text{and} \ w_3 < 0 \qquad (8.9)$$

would report *ambiguous* changes in economic well-being in these countries' growth experiences.

Table 9.5
Poverty measures in Chile

a) Chile: Poverty measures: Household incomes per capita

	1987	1994
Indigence line P$15,050		
Headcount	0.2209	0.0996
Poverty deficit	0.0756	0.0336
FGT (2)	0.0382	0.0184
Poverty line L P$30,100		
Headcount	0.5137	0.3386
Poverty deficit	0.2274	0.1269
FGT (2)	0.1299	0.0663
Poverty line H P$34,164		
Headcount	0.5679	0.3940
Poverty deficit	0.2647	0.1554
FGT (2)	0.1560	0.0831

b) Chile: Poverty measures: Household incomes per adult equivalent

	1987	1994
Indigence line P$15,050		
Headcount	0.1268	0.0511
Poverty deficit	0.0412	0.0192
FGT (2)	0.0213	0.0118
Poverty line L P$30,100		
Headcount	0.4069	0.2308
Poverty deficit	0.1568	0.0762
FGT (2)	0.0822	0.0382
Poverty line H P$34,164		
Headcount	0.4726	0.2852
Poverty deficit	0.1905	0.0978
FGT (2)	0.1028	0.0492

Source: World Bank 1997, p. 18.

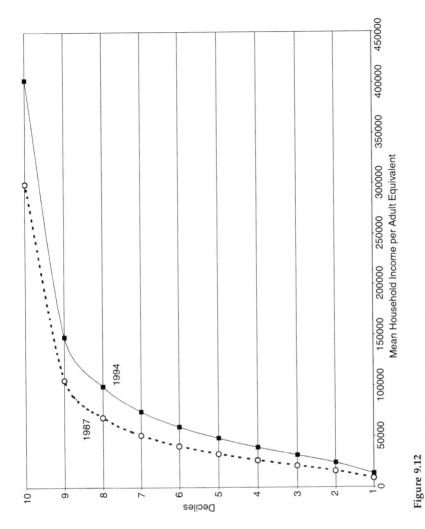

Figure 9.12
Chile: First-order dominance, 1987–1994
Source: World Bank 1997b (pp. 11–13).

What was not clear a priori is what dominance methods might reveal. What we have found is that dominance methods in fact give rankings for the five developing countries in which they have been applied, and what they show is that by the first-order dominance criterion, economic growth improved economic well-being in Taiwan from 1980 to 1992, in Thailand from 1975 to 1981 and again from 1986 to 1992, in Indonesia from 1984 to 1990, in Brazil from 1960 to 1980, and in Chile from 1987 to 1994.

It is sometimes thought that first-order dominance is such a stringent criterion that it is not likely to be fulfilled empirically very often. It may therefore come as a surprise to you, as indeed it did to me, that first-order dominance gives rankings in *all* of the cases we have reviewed.

The theoretical possibility that the abbreviated social welfare function method and dominance methods might disagree was noted in chapter 8. We now know that that in a number of cases—Taiwan, Thailand, Indonesia, and Brazil—the choice of method also makes an important *empirical* difference in evaluating the welfare effects of economic growth.

On the other hand, when it comes to evaluating the welfare effects of economic decline, the two methods may turn out to be in closer accord. We have looked at the case of Brazil for the 1980–1990 period. There, the two approaches were indeed in agreement: (1) All components of the abbreviated social welfare function changed in the direction of worsening welfare, so all functions of this class consequently show declines in economic well-being, and (2) The first-order dominance criterion produced falling real incomes for each decile of the population, which implies a decline in economic well-being for all social welfare functions which are anonymous and increasing in all incomes.

What distinguishes the conclusions reached by the two approaches is the way they treat inequality. In the abbreviated social welfare function approach, any increase in inequality will cause the welfare effects of economic growth to be evaluated ambiguously. By contrast, in the welfare dominance approach, as long as real incomes have increased for each quantile group, such as a decile or a quintile, it doesn't matter what has happened to their income shares. This is yet one more reason for you to consider carefully how important inequality is to you as compared with other aspects of income distribution.

10 Distribution and Development: Policies for Broad-Based Growth

10.1 Introduction

What policies and circumstances have helped countries achieve broad-based growth? This chapter addresses this question by inquiring into the sources of economic growth and policies to stimulate growth and by studying how policies affecting people in their roles as workers and as consumers have helped raise cash incomes and access to public services, especially among those at the bottom end of the income distribution. The chapter is accordingly divided into two major parts, the first examining policies for economic growth and the second policies affecting distribution. But because growth and distribution are affected by many of the same things and also affect one another, some overlap between the two parts is unavoidable.[1]

Four initial observations will be helpful in guiding our analysis. First, other things equal, a higher growth rate leads to more rapid improvements in economic well-being and faster reductions in absolute poverty. To achieve further such improvements, it is vital to seek out means for accelerating economic growth.

Second, other things equal, the more egalitarian the base, the greater the reduction in absolute poverty for growth of any given magnitude. But other things are not equal: According to the preponderance of the evidence presented below, the more equal the initial distribution of income, the faster is the subsequent rate of economic growth. It is then of great importance to establish mechanisms to assure that the economic growth that takes place is broadly based.

---

1. One study that has examined the determinants of economic growth and inequality together, using the same set of explanatory variables in the two regressions, is Lundberg and Squire 1999.

Third, some actions have proven to be helpful both for lowering poverty and inequality and for stimulating economic growth. For example, countries that paid early attention to education created the human capital infrastructure that contributed to more rapid economic growth and to a broader-based distribution of the benefits of growth. This illustrates a "virtuous circle," according to which actions favorable to distribution lead to higher growth, which leads in turn to continued distributional improvements.

Finally, if broad-based growth is to take place, the positive aspects of markets need to be harnessed. At the same time, nothing in economic theory enshrines the laissez-faire initial distribution of resources as being more ethically justifiable than some other starting point. What matters crucially is what private purchasing power people possess when they enter the market and what additional resources they receive from the state.

Let us now turn to studies of the sources of economic growth.

10.2   Stimulating Economic Growth

Growth Accounting

The standard starting point for understanding the sources of a country's economic growth is growth accounting. It is assumed that two inputs, capital and labor, are combined to produce output. Let K_t denote the amount of capital employed at time t and L_t the amount of labor. Both K_t and L_t are measured in efficiency units to standardize for quality improvements. The production function f_t links output Q_t to inputs:

$$Q_t = f_t(K_t, L_t).$$

Between time t and time $t+1$, the economy grows. Part of this growth comes from increased employment of capital and part from increased employment of labor. However, in general,

$$Q_{t+1} \neq f_t(K_{t+1}, L_{t+1}).$$

Rather, the left-hand side exceeds the right-hand side, because of technical change. That is, the production function $f_{t+1}(.)$ produces more output for given inputs than does the production function $f_t.(.)$.

To gauge the sources of economic growth, the following model has proven insightful (Griliches 1996). In the absence of technical progress,

$$Q_{t+1} - Q_t \approx \text{MPK}(K_{t+1} - K_t) + \text{MPL}(L_{t+1} - L_t),$$

where MPK and MPL are the marginal products of capital and labor respectively. If we assume that the economy operates under conditions of perfect competition and constant returns to scale, then both factors are paid their marginal products, and furthermore the shares of national income accruing to capital and labor are respectively $s_K \equiv (\text{MPK} \cdot K_t)/Q_t$ and $s_L \equiv (\text{MPL} \cdot L_t)/Q_t$. Under these assumptions, the total additional payments made to capital and labor would exactly exhaust the growth of available product:

$$\%\Delta Q_t = s_K \%\Delta K_t + s_L \%\Delta L_t, \tag{10.1}$$

the notation $\%\Delta$ signifying the percentage change in the variable in question.

If the left hand side of (10.1) is found empirically to exceed the right hand side, the residual may be attributed to technical change. The underlying production function may then be represented as

$$Q_t = f_t(K_t, L_t, \theta_t),$$

where θ_t indicates the "knowledge" or "technology level" in the economy at time t. Applying the preceding techniques to this new production function produces a decomposition of economic growth into three terms

$$\%\Delta Q_t = s_K \%\Delta K_t + s_L \%\Delta L_t + \text{TFPG}_t, \tag{10.2}$$

the last of which is called *total factor productivity growth*. It is a residual, bringing the left- and right-hand sides into equality.

Equation (10.2) provides a way of breaking down total output growth into components reflecting increased employment of capital, increased employment of labor, and total factor productivity growth. This permits an assessment of the role of increased availability and utilization of productive factors vis-à-vis technical change.

The sources of different developing countries' economic growth have been evaluated in this way. Particularly interesting analyses have been done for East Asia, where conflicting results have been found. On the one hand, the World Bank's *East Asian Miracle* study (1993) and Page (1994) estimated that two-thirds of the economic growth observed in Hong Kong, Korea, Singapore, and Taiwan was accounted for by increased utilization of labor and capital (including human capital) and one-third was due to TFP growth. However, even this one-third estimate is judged to be too high for these econ-

omies: Young (1995) adjusted the World Bank calculations by a) fac-
toring in the rising labor force participation rate in these economies,
b) adjusting for agriculture's falling share of employment, and
c) weighting the labor input by educational characteristics. Each
of these adjustments raises the contribution of measured inputs to
economic growth, thereby lowering the contribution of TFP growth.
The net effect is that while all of these East Asian economies grew
by more than 7 percent per year, Young estimates much smaller
economy-wide TFP growth: 2.3 percent per year in Hong Kong,
2.1 percent in Taiwan, 1.7 percent in Korea, and just 0.2 percent in
Singapore. Furthermore, in Singapore's manufacturing sector, the
estimated TFP growth was a *negative* 1.0 percent. Thus, according to
Young, there is nothing miraculous about East Asian growth; by his
reckoning, investment in physical and human capital and increased
labor force participation were overwhelmingly responsible for the
growth that took place.[2]

Similar growth accounting has been done for seven Latin American countries. In this study, Elias (1990) calculated annual TFP
growth rates ranging from 2.3 percent in Mexico and 1.9 percent in
Brazil down to 0.5 percent in Venezuela and 0.0 percent in Peru. In
Latin America too, TFP growth is a factor of some importance in accounting for economic growth, but these effects are swamped by the
contributions of capital and labor accumulation.

Growth accounting tells us the relative importance of growth of
capital, growth of labor, and growth of TFP, but it doesn't indicate
what factors may have caused these changes. Further insights can be
gained from growth regressions, to which we now turn.

Cross-Country Growth Regressions

Cross-country growth regressions have been used extensively in
recent years to study the sources of economic growth. Pioneering
papers include the works of Barro (1991), Levine and Renelt (1992),
and Mankiw, Romer, and Weil (1992). The by-now massive literature
in this area is surveyed by Barro and Sala-i-Martin (1995), Mankiw
(1995), Bénabou (1996), Perotti (1996), Benhabib and Spiegel (1997),
Barro (1997), and Temple (1999).

Most of the growth regression literature uses the Barro-Lee data
set or updates thereof (available online from the National Bureau of

2. See also Krugman 1994 and Kim and Lau 1994.

Economic Research at www.nber.org). The dependent variable in the growth regressions is some measure of aggregate economic growth between a base year and a final year, sometimes for a single growth period (e.g., 1965–1985) and sometimes for a number of growth periods (e.g., 1965–1975, 1975–1985, and 1985–1990). A wide range of explanatory variables appear on the right-hand side; these are discussed further below. Estimation methods that have been used in the growth regressions include ordinary least squares, extreme bounds tests, fixed effects estimation, seemingly unrelated regressions, instrumental variables, generalized method of moments, and three-stage least squares.

Barro (1997) has surveyed this literature and reached the following empirical conclusions about economic growth rates:

• The data strongly support conditional convergence. That is, the higher is the initial level of output relative to its "target level" (as determined by fundamentals), the lower is the growth rate.

• For a given starting level of real per capita GDP, a higher growth rate is accompanied by higher initial schooling and life expectancy, lower fertility, lower government consumption, better maintenance of the rule of law, and improvements in the terms of trade.

• When the extent of democracy is low, an increase in political rights increases growth.

• Higher inflation produces lower economic growth.

In an extensive empirical investigation, Sala-i-Martin (1997) explained countries' growth rates by region, political factors, religion, market distortions and market performance, types of investment, primary sector production, openness, type of economic organization, and an indicator variable for former Spanish colonies. Other variables that have been included in other studies are measures of financial market development, tariff rates, the quality of political institutions, military expenditures, scale effects, geographic variables, resource endowments, and an index of institutional quality. Most of these have been reported to be statistically significant determinants of economic growth.

In addition, there are other variables that are suspected to be important determinants of economic growth but which could not be included in cross-country regressions because of lack of data for a large number of countries. These include such public policies as tax distortions, public pension and other transfer programs, and government regulations and also such other economic circumstances as infrastructure investments, outlays on research and development, the quality of education, and the distribution of wealth.

Explaining Physical and Human Capital Accumulation

The total factor productivity calculations and the growth regressions presented above show us that accumulation of physical and human capital is vital to economic growth. What these techniques leave unanswered are the mechanisms by which countries accumulate inputs and improve total factor productivity. For this, we need to look into economic fundamentals—preferences, technology, public policies, and initial conditions—and their effects on factor accumulation.

In one such study, Benhabib and Spiegel (1997) examined the rates of investment in physical capital and human capital in a cross section of countries. They found that investment in physical capital is determined by GDP, political instability, and financial development. They also found that human capital investment is affected by financial development interacted with initial income levels and by the level of financial sector liquidity. Several other factors that might have played a role—income inequality, for example—proved to be statistically insignificant. The authors interpret these results as demonstrating the strong importance of financial sector variables and political stability as determinants of both total factor productivity growth and levels of investment.

Another study of the determinants of investment is by Barro and Sala-i-Martin (1995, chapter 12). They found that a higher investment ratio in a country is generated by more schooling, more health, higher life expectancy, and lower market distortions.

It is clear from studies such as these that economic growth can be accelerated by the choice of appropriate policies that encourage factor accumulation and TFP growth. We turn now to a brief look at these and other policies for economic growth.

Growth Policies

Some of the main ingredients of successful economic growth are now well-understood. Countries must adopt sound macroeconomic policies. They must produce goods and services that those who have the

purchasing power want to buy. They must save, invest, and accumulate capital. They must make full use of their labor forces. They
must invest in the human capital of their people. And they must
achieve technological change which raises productivity.

What policies help achieve these conditions? In answering this
question, I shall sample from the writings of the most important
writers in different branches of the field.

Let us begin with Anne Krueger's 1997 Presidential Address to
the American Economic Association. She observes that the favored
development policy in the 1950s and 1960s was one of import substitution, whereby countries aimed to produce domestically goods
that previously had been imported. They did this by instituting
tariffs, quotas, and other protectionist measures. Krueger shows us
how these policy prescriptions were based on a number of stylized
facts and premises which, though widely accepted at the time, were
later shown to be flawed. Research and theoretical modeling has now
produced an almost complete turnaround in thinking, so that "it is
now widely accepted that growth prospects for developing countries
are greatly enhanced through an outer-oriented trade regime and
fairly uniform incentives (primarily through the exchange rate) for
production across exporting and import-competing goods."[3] Her
paper offers an informative recounting of the contribution of research
in the last three decades to the formulation of improved policies.

Arnold Harberger, in his 1998 Presidential Address to the American Economic Association, draws the following policy prescriptions.
First, people must perceive real costs in order to reduce them. The
danger of inflation is that it blurs economic agents' perceptions of
relative prices. Second, price distortions drive a wedge between
social and private costs. Consequently, what may be a saving of private costs may not be a genuine saving from the point of view of the
economy as a whole. Third, ill-conceived regulations and bureau-
cratic hurdles can greatly slow an economy down. Fourth, international trade distortions impose burdens, whereas trade liberalization
opens up new paths of real cost reduction. Fifth, privatizations also
permit real cost reductions. Sixth, a sound legal and institutional
framework is needed to protect individuals against arbitrary incur-

---

3. This and other policy prescriptions have been dubbed the "Washington consensus"
by Williamson (1990). The main points of the Washington consensus are enumerated
by Harberger (1998a). For a challenge to this consensus view, see Stiglitz 1998a.

sions on their property and other economic rights. Finally, for economic policy to be effective and remain so, a political consensus on the broad outlines of economic policy is needed.

Gustav Ranis has done a lifetime of work analyzing the economic successes of Taiwan and other East Asian economies (e.g., Ranis 1974, 1978, 1995; Fei, Ranis, and Kuo 1979). In the case of Taiwan, the initial conditions were favorable and included well-developed rural infrastructure (roads, drainage, irrigation, and power), a sound institutional infrastructure (agricultural research, experiment stations, and farmers' associations), high literacy rates, extensive land reforms, and private ownership of major large-scale industries (mining, cement, pulp, and paper). The early phase of import substitution was unusually mild and contributed to strong linkages between agricultural and non-agricultural activities in a geographically decentralized fashion. Labor markets were flexible and relatively undistorted, enabling workers to be redeployed to those growing sectors that had the most pressing labor requirements. Once the Lewis-Fei-Ranis turning point was reached, the economy's comparative advantage shifted and increasingly well-educated labor was needed. In response, the period of compulsory schooling was lengthened in Taiwan and higher education was reoriented toward engineering and the natural sciences and away from traditional humanities and agricultural instruction. Finally, government policies facilitated entry into the technological era at the proper time. In Ranis's view, these public policies in Taiwan, and similar ones in other East Asian economies, succeeded in stimulating economic growth by accommodating the changing needs of the economy and not by specifically directing its path.

Amartya Sen has written extensively about policies for expanding people's capabilities and improving their functionings (e.g., Sen 1984, 1985, 1992, 1997, 1999). He and Jean Drèze have analyzed the policies leading to broad-based growth in China and contrasted these with the more limited successes in India (Drèze and Sen 1995). Market-oriented economic reforms, they note, came *after* China had already achieved land reform, near-universal literacy in the younger age groups, a radical reduction of endemic morbidity and undernutrition, the foundations of a social security system, a functioning system of local governance, and a major expansion on the basis of high participation of women in the labor force. By contrast, India has too much government interference in some fields (regulation, controls, stifling of competition) and too little government involvement in others (including basic education, health care, social security, land reform, and the promotion of social change). Without these foundations, Drèze and Sen argue, it will be more difficult for India to achieve economic development and improve social opportunity.

Finally, Joseph Stiglitz (1997, 1998a, 1998b) has offered a penetrating analysis of the role of government in the growth process. His main points are these. Markets work to organize the production and dissemination of goods and services, but sometimes they fail; government action is important in working with markets, complementing them, and even helping to create them. Government can take actions which promote both equity and growth in the context of individual responsibility and economic opportunity. Technological changes necessitate changes in the role of government. There is need to reexamine both what the government does and how it does it. Governments should focus on the fundamentals—economic policies, basic education, health, roads, law and order, environmental protection, as well as appropriate regulation, social protection, and welfare. The experiences of transition economies demonstrate that government is essential to establishing and maintaining the institutional infrastructure required for market economies to function effectively. Government itself can be reformed to improve its efficiency and efficacy. Finally, government has played a critical role in fostering economic development in a variety of countries and in a wide range of areas, including promoting education and technology, supporting the financial sector, investing in infrastructure, preventing environmental degradation, and creating and maintaining social safety nets. Summing up, what would accelerate economic growth? One way of putting it is that "market-friendly" policies are needed—ones that emphasize investing in people, improving the climate for enterprise, opening economies to international trade and investment, and getting macroeconomic policy right (World Bank 1991; Fischer 1998).

Turning the issue around, it is clear that many things can go wrong, any *one* of which can prevent economic growth from taking place.[4] Inappropriate macroeconomic policies have been studied at

---

4. Kremer (1993) has graphically labeled this the "o-ring theory of economic development," after the simple piece on the Challenger space shuttle that failed, causing the spacecraft to explode upon liftoff.

great length; see, for instance, Fischer 1993. Economic growth in the world's two most populous countries, India and China, was retarded by policies that stifled private sector initiative, but following large-scale policy reforms, both countries have achieved unprecedented rates of economic growth and expanded social opportunities (e.g., Drèze and Sen 1995; United Nations 1997). Prematurely high prices of labor and unstable industrial relations can lead multinational enterprises elsewhere and impede development (World Bank 1995; Pencavel 1996; Kuruvilla 1996). Kleptocracies and bad governance can bring an economy to a standstill (Klitgaard 1990; Mauro 1995; Kaufmann 1997; Bardhan 1997; Tanzi 1998; Rose-Ackerman 1999). Populism can lead to great excesses (Sachs 1990; Dornbusch and Edwards 1990; Iglesias 1998; Harberger 1998a). Finally, the sad fact is that some countries just start with so little that very little can be done to help them; in these cases, bad policies make a bad situation even worse (Sachs and Warner 1997; Krugman 1998; Collier and Gunning 1999; Freeman and Lindauer 1999).

Finally, I should say that I do not want to give the impression that our discipline has reached agreement on all aspects of growth policy. Several controversies remain, especially about the growth successes in East Asia (Amsden 1989; Wade 1990; World Bank 1993; Bradford 1994; Fishlow et al. 1994; Page 1994; Rodrik 1995b; Stiglitz 1996; Stiglitz and Uy 1996; Bhagwati 1996; Leipziger 1997; Stallings, Bird-sall, and Clugage 1998). Did the East Asian economies grow because they got the prices right or because governments intervened so as to govern the market and get the prices wrong? How important was the strategy of "picking winners," and to the extent that it was important, did it aid or hinder development? Exporting is clearly of importance to growth; is protection of domestic industries important to exporting? Was growth export-led or investment-led? I just want to mention these issues and leave it to others to try to resolve them.

From Income Distribution to Economic Growth

There is now a substantial literature on how income inequality and poverty affect economic growth. Early growth models posed the possibility—indeed, likelihood—that beyond some point, growth and equality are conflicting objectives. The basic mechanism, articulated in a series of papers by Kaldor (1956, 1957, 1958), focused on the process of capital accumulation. In his class-based model, capitalists have a higher marginal propensity to save than workers do. Thus, the larger is capital's share of national income, the higher will be the economy's savings rate. These higher savings, in turn, translate into greater investment, increased capital formation, and faster economic growth. In this way, a higher income share of capital may be presumed to lead to higher subsequent growth. And by a similar argument, if the marginal propensity to save rises with income, greater inequality in the size distribution of income will *raise* the economy's subsequent growth rate.

Other authors have proposed many channels through which inequality might be *harmful* for growth:

• High inequality increases the ability of high-income people to use their wealth to secure political outcomes favorable to themselves. Such actions include political contributions, lobbying, cronyism, bribery, and other forms of "rent-seeking." To the extent that resources are allocated to these activities, less is available for productive investment, which lowers growth.

• High inequality strengthens the economic and political bargaining power of the rich, both directly and through the implied threat of capital flight.

• High inequality contributes to political and macroeconomic instability.

• High inequality stifles agricultural output. This is because land productivity tends to be higher on smaller farms than on large ones.

• High inequality increases the demand for luxury goods relative to basic goods. If luxury goods are produced with more capital-intensive technologies than basic goods are, then the demand for factors of production is skewed in favor of capital and against labor, perpetuating the initial inequality.

• High inequality causes the median voter to favor populist social programs. To help finance such redistributive programs, taxes on capital may be raised, which acts as a disincentive to investment.

• High inequality gives the poor the ability to limit, via the political system, the private appropriability of investments in skills or technology.

• High inequality may lead the poor to engage in rent-seeking or predatory behavior at the expense of the middle and upper classes.

• High inequality leads to investments in higher education and advanced health care for the few rather than primary and secondary education and primary health services for the many. The resultant low levels of basic human capital retard economic growth.

• High inequality of income or of collaterable assets such as land limits the ability of the poor to acquire the resources they need (land, draft animals, machinery, equipment, and fertilizer) in order to operate small farms efficiently. In this way, high inequality worsens the growth-impeding effects of capital market imperfections.

Besides these mechanisms which lead from high inequality to low growth, there also are mechanisms leading from poverty to low economic growth (Bliss and Stern 1978; Behrman and Deolalikar 1988; Drèze and Sen 1990, 1995; Dasgupta 1993; Ray 1993; Basu 1997). In a country with a high level of poverty to start with:

• The poor may be so badly nourished that they are too weak to perform up to their full physical potential. Low nutrition thus engenders low productivity and continued low incomes.

• The poor may be unable to undertake economically worthwhile investments, owing to the underdevelopment of capital markets.

• The poor may be unable to afford to forego the labor of their children, so they do not send them to school, passing on the heritage of low human capital to the next generation.

• If the poor constitute a majority of a country's people, the country may be too poor to afford to build sufficient schools, health clinics, and physical infrastructure.

Through such mechanisms, poverty begets low growth which begets continued poverty. We have, in short, a "poverty trap."[5]

Much empirical research has now been done on the effect of income distribution on economic growth. Inequality and poverty are taken up in turn.

A negative empirical relationship between initial income inequality and subsequent growth was first noted by Fields (1989), but this was statistically insignificant owing to a very small sample size.

---

5. The idea of a poverty trap dates back to Myrdal (1944), Nurkse (1953), Nelson (1956), and Leibenstein (1957). These authors used such terms as "cumulative causation," "circular constellation of forces," and "low-level equilibrium trap." Theoretical models of such traps are reviewed in Banerjee and Newman 1994.

Working with larger samples in a multiple regression framework, Persson and Tabellini (1992, 1994), Alesina and Rodrik (1992, 1994), and Perotti (1992) all found a statistically significant relationship whereby high income inequality *reduces* economic growth. This result has been reaffirmed in many studies including Benhabib and Spiegel (1994), Bourguignon (1994), Perotti (1994, 1996), Clarke (1995), Keefer and Knack (1995), Birdsall, Ross, and Sabot (1995a, 1995b), Bénabou (1996), and Deininger and Squire (1998). Additionally, in the specification preferred by Barro (1999), the effect of inequality on growth is negative up to per capita GDP of $2,070 in 1985 U.S. dollars—the income level of Portugal, Malaysia, or South Africa—and positive thereafter. But very recently, several studies have appeared in which inequality is found to be *positively* related to economic growth; see Brandolini and Rossi (1998) for a sample of developed countries and Li and Zou (1998) and Forbes (1999) for a subsample of the Deininger-Squire data. It thus remains an open question which way this effect actually runs.

Besides income inequality, asset inequality has also been shown to be a determinant of growth. Alesina and Rodrik (1994) and Deininger and Squire (1998) found that higher inequality of land slows subsequent growth. This finding was reaffirmed by Birdsall and Londoño (1997), who reached two additional conclusions: Higher educational inequality also slows subsequent growth, and inequality of assets causes the inequality of income to become statistically insignificant.

Finally, the effect of poverty on economic growth has been examined, with a conclusively inconclusive result. The hypothesis of "unconditional convergence"—namely, that poorer countries tend to catch up with richer ones—has been tested and rejected (Barro 1991; Ray 1998; Durlauf and Quah, forthcoming). But the evidence does not support the contrary hypothesis either. As we see in figure 10.1, the data reveal *no pattern in the averages*: countries that were richer in the beginning grew at the same average rate as initially poorer countries. But we see also that the initially poorer countries had a much *more dispersed* growth pattern than the initially richer countries did.

Why some countries grow at faster rates than others is a crucial question in macroeconomics. The evidence presented here shows that inequality and poverty have no systematic effect. An understanding of why these effects go one way in some countries and the other way in others lies at the research frontier of our profession.

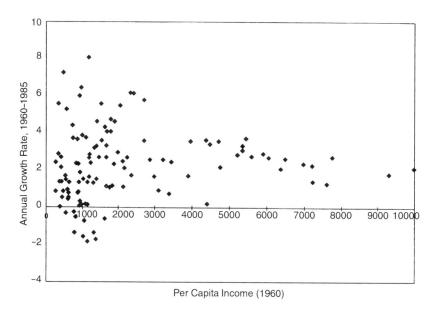

Figure 10.1
Growth rate of countries versus initial income
Source: Ray 1998 (figure 3.10).

10.3 Distributional Policies

Increasing Earnings in the Labor Market

The poor in developing countries derive the overwhelming share of their incomes from the work they do. There are four main ways in which economic growth can raise the returns from their labor. One is that economic growth may stimulate the growth of employment in the relatively high-paying sectors of the economy. Second, labor demand may tighten to the point that employers compete vigorously against one another to retain existing workers and attract new ones, creating generalized wage increases throughout the economy. Third, for those (in most developing countries, a substantial majority) who remain engaged in self-employment activities, their incomes will be enhanced if they have more complementary resources with which to work on their family farms and in their family businesses. Finally, all of these mechanisms are enhanced if workers come to possess more human capital.

Trade and the Demand for Wage Labor

Manufacturing is a vital sector in developing country labor markets. Rates of employment and wage growth in manufacturing are very different in different parts of the developing world. In those economies that have grown the fastest, manufacturing employment and real earnings per worker have increased the most.

All of the high-growth, low-inequality countries in the world are in East Asia (Page 1994). For decades now, the East Asian economies have maintained higher economic growth rates than any other economies in the world. Exports have been an important part of their success because of their strategies of export-push. More open economies have achieved higher rates of economic growth. They have also achieved higher productivity growth. For details on these points, see Sachs and Warner 1995, Frankel, Romer, and Cyrus 1997, Pack 1997, Krueger 1997, Edwards 1998, and McNab and Moore 1998; but for more skeptical views, see Harrison and Revenga 1995 and Bruton 1998.

One aspect of the East Asian experience has been misperceived, with potentially damaging policy inferences sometimes being drawn. It is sometimes said that workers have not participated in the economic growth of East Asia. It is also said that even if workers could participate in economic growth in the past, given the high level of competition in today's world economy, they cannot continue to do so. Finally, it is argued that as a matter of public policy, wages must be kept down, lest competitive advantage be lost.

What I would like to suggest is that these claims about the labor market are fundamentally wrong. In past research (Fields 1984, 1994), I presented data showing that in Hong Kong, Singapore, Korea, and Taiwan, labor market conditions *improved rapidly*. This came about both through a process of enlargement of production in the modern sector and consequent intersectoral shifts of labor (Kuznets 1955, 1966; Lewis 1954, 1984) and through a process of generalized wage increases in integrated labor markets. Early on in these economies, when labor was still abundant relative to the needs of these economies' leading sectors (primarily manufacturing), economic growth led to fuller employment at essentially constant wages. But then, once the Lewis-Fei-Ranis turning point was reached and the "labor surplus" phase came to an end, the labor market tightened, but in a different way. Full employment was maintained, with unemployment rates hovering between one and four percent for decades. The types of jobs in which people were employed improved: Agriculture (a low wage sector) fell as a share of total employment; the labor force became better-educated; the better occupations expanded to employ a larger fraction of the labor force; a smaller percentage of workers were engaged in self-employment or in unpaid family work. And perhaps, most important, real earnings rose sharply, so that workers' real earnings doubled approximately every ten years.

A not-very-well-known fact is that in Hong Kong, Korea, Singapore, and Taiwan, real earnings grew in line with real per capita GDP. Workers in these economies benefited and benefited handsomely from the economic growth that took place. As a result, living conditions in East Asia are very much better now than they were a generation ago.[6] At the same time that real manufacturing wages in a group of export-oriented East Asian economies were rising by 170 percent in real terms, real wages of agricultural laborers in India grew by 70 percent, wages of industrial workers in Latin America grew by just 12 percent, and modern sector wages fell in many sub-Saharan African countries (World Bank 1995).

Unfortunately, the Asian crisis that began in 1997 has reversed some of the earlier progress. Unemployment rose sharply and real wages fell in such countries as Indonesia, Thailand, Korea, and the Philippines (Asian Development Bank 1999). Only time will tell how quickly the crisis will be reversed.

Recent difficulties notwithstanding, countries *can* succeed and the people in them *can* enjoy substantially higher standards of living if their economies are able to expand into profitable new markets. Even the United Nations Development Program, long a holdout in this regard, has accepted this message: "Indeed, poor countries can leapfrog several decades of development if they combine their low wages with basic education, technical skills and export-led growth, taking advantage of the rapidly opening global markets. This is the policy message of the East Asian tigers" (United Nations 1997, p. 10).

We turn now to education and other forms of human capital.

---

6. Nonetheless, Korean workers remain discontented, because of suppression of the labor movement. See, for instance, Lindauer et al. 1997, Lee 1998, and Park 1999.

Human Capital

The term "human capital" refers to the education, health, and other productive capacities embodied in human beings. The importance of human capital has come up many times already in this chapter.

The positive effects of increased human capital have been documented throughout the world. Everywhere, people with more education earn more in wage employment than people with less education (Schultz 1988; Psacharopoulos 1994). Education has also been shown to have an important role in augmenting the productive abilities of the self-employed: The higher the education of the farmer or the business proprietor, the higher his or her self-employment income tends to be (Lockheed, Jamison, and Lau 1980; Behrman 1990a). In addition, more education, especially of females, improves the ability of households to manage their health and nutrition needs and control their fertility (Dasgupta 1993; Strauss and Thomas 1995, 1998).

The East Asian countries paid early attention to primary and then secondary education (e.g., Behrman and Schneider 1994). In fact, the East Asian countries had higher levels of literacy in 1960 than India does now (Drèze and Sen 1995).[7] Investments in human capital affect income distribution primarily through the labor market. Greater human capital facilitates the adoption of technology from abroad. An export-oriented trade and industrialization strategy is more likely to work precisely because a country's workers are well endowed with human capital. Employment and wages are likely to be higher as a result.

High human capital investment has often been held up as an important cause of the East Asian development success (e.g., Krause 1988; Turnham 1993; World Bank 1993; Ranis 1995). The reasons for this "virtuous circle" include the direct productivity-augmenting effects of education, the ability of a well-educated labor force to produce world class products for export, the reduction of scarcity rents to education, consequent low income inequality, and resultant beneficial effects of low inequality on economic growth and public spending. By contrast, the Latin American countries were caught in a "vicious circle" of low education (in terms of both quantity and quality), slow economic growth, high inequality, and continued slow

7. On the other hand, on a per capita basis, India has six times as many students in universities and other institutions of higher education as China does.

growth. For more on such circles, see Bourguignon 1994, Birdsall, Ross, and Sabot 1995a, 1995b), and United Nations 1996.

These and other considerations have led analysts to conduct studies of "social rates of return" to education. These studies, which have now been done for a great many countries and are summarized in Psacharopoulos 1994, have found three main patterns. First, the social rates of return to education exceed the opportunity uses of funds. Second, the social rates of return are higher in the developing countries than in the developed ones. And third, the social rates of return are highest for primary education, intermediate for secondary education, and lowest for higher education. Policy conclusions have been drawn from these findings: More resources should be devoted to education in the world; more resources should be focused on improving educational attainments in the developing nations as opposed to the developed ones; and more of the developing countries' resources should be devoted to primary education and less to higher education. But because of questions concerning the extent to which these estimates are associative as opposed to causal, these conclusions are not universally accepted (e.g., Behrman 1990a, 1990b, 1993).

We shall return to public spending patterns later in this chapter.

Land and the Agricultural Sector

Agriculture accounts for 61 percent of employment in the developing countries as a whole; in the least developed countries, the percentage is 74 percent (*Human Development Report 1997*, table 16). For this reason, among the most important determinants of economic well-being in developing economies are the volume of and returns to agricultural employment and the distribution of land and other productive assets for the self-employed.

Both Korea and Taiwan began their modern development epochs with relatively equal distributions of land. Figure 10.2 demonstrates that in an international comparison circa 1960, Korea and Taiwan were the two economies with the most equal distributions of land ownership and with two of the most equal distributions of income.

As has often been noted, in both of these cases (as well as in Japan and China), equal land ownership was brought about by thoroughgoing land reforms. On the other hand, owing to lack of land reform, landlessness and near-landlessness are pervasive throughout

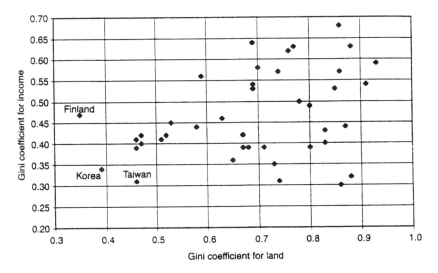

Figure 10.2
Measures of income and land inequality around 1960
Source: Rodrik 1995a (figure 13).

the developing world, and especially so in South Asia and in Latin America (Griffin 1981; Khan and Lee 1983; Sheahan 1987; IFAD 1992; Quibria and Srinivasan 1994). Landholdings are distributed much more unequally in Latin America than in other developing regions (Otsuka, Chuma, and Hayami 1992).

A more equal distribution of landholdings produces a more equal distribution of income through two channels: the direct effect of a more equal distribution of acreage, and the indirect effect of higher productivity per acre on small holdings. As was first suggested by John Stuart Mill, in country after country, land productivity has been found to be higher on small farms than on large ones, often considerably so (Yotopoulos and Nugent 1976; Lipton 1977, 1993; Berry and Cline 1979; Squire 1981; Binswanger, Deininger, and Feder 1995). Furthermore, around the world, family farms using family labor have been found to be more efficient than large scale agriculture, in part because of reduced transactions costs in search, screening, and supervision in labor markets (Sen 1966; Putterman 1989; Lipton 1993; van Zyl et al. 1996). Thus, a more equal distribution of land would be expected to lead not only to greater income equality but also to a higher level of agricultural output and lower poverty, which has been confirmed empirically (Lundberg and Squire 1999).

In view of these economic benefits, why then does land continue to be distributed so unequally and inefficiently? The answer is a mix of historical circumstance and political power. Taking the case of Latin America as an example, the unequal pattern of landownership, as represented by the *latifundia* system, dates back to the time of the Spanish and Portuguese *conquistadores*. Other large landholdings are of more recent vintage; for example, in the case of Brazil, land could be titled only in minimum lots of 988 acres (Binswanger and Elgin 1989). Once these large landholdings were amassed, a powerful oligarchy was established, which used its wealth and power to keep a hold on their land and to acquire additional lands through private purchases and with the acquiescence, or even the encouragement, of the state (de Janvry 1981).

While some land reforms have been successful, many have not, for reasons both of power and of design (Powelson and Stock 1987; de Janvry and Sadoulet 1990; Lal and Myint 1996; Binswanger and Deininger 1997). In many countries, the landed aristocracy has been able to resist land reform entirely. In many others, they have subverted it—for example, when it appeared that workers would be guaranteed certain rights, landlords preempted this process by evicting tenant farmers and hired laborers from the land. When land actually was distributed, often it was the political cronies who were given land, while others not so well-connected got nothing. Finally, some land reforms proved to be ineffective, because even though the poor did receive allotments of land, more was needed; complementary policies in such areas as marketing, credit, and inputs to small farmers were also required.

In those circumstances where land reform is simply not possible, other policies are needed to raise the productivity and incomes of the rural poor. Gardner (1997) reviews agricultural reforms in seven countries (Chile, Ghana, Hungary, Indonesia, Madagascar, Mexico, and New Zealand). He concludes that: Sustained reforms in agriculture are rare and typically not market-oriented; agricultural price policy reforms can be stymied by appreciation of the real exchange rate; reforms that are appropriately supported through macroeconomic policy will lead to improved agricultural performance; and failed or incomplete reform efforts outnumber successes. As an illustration of the mechanisms at work, Heath and Binswanger (1996) draw an interesting contrast between Kenya and Ethiopia. Kenyan farmers were granted secure land rights, access to infrastructure and markets, reasonable terms of trade, and cash income from sales of crops or labor. Agricultural output grew faster than population growth—this, in a country with one of the highest population growth rates in the world. On the other hand, in Ethiopia, the absence of such institutions discouraged investments by farmers, and the agricultural sector consequently stagnated.

National policies often work against the development of the agricultural sector (e.g., Thorbecke and Morrisson 1989; Krueger, Schiff, and Valdés 1991; Johnson 1991; Binswanger and Deininger 1997). Comparative studies have been carried out for a wide range of countries including Indonesia, Malaysia, Thailand, Taiwan, Korea, China, Argentina, Ghana, Nigeria, Tanzania, Uganda, Zambia, India, Kenya, Mexico, Brazil, Colombia, Guatemala, South Africa, Mali, Burkina Faso, Nepal, and Sri Lanka. These studies show that countries' agricultural sectors are stifled and earning opportunities for the poor reduced by a variety of mechanisms:

• The agricultural sector often faces high direct taxation via land taxes and export taxes.

• The agricultural sector is often subject to high indirect taxation via overvalued exchange rates and import duties.

• Comparative advantage is jeopardized, as internationally competitive products such as coffee and tea are taxed, while uncompetitive products such as food crops are protected.

• The resources devoted to the agricultural sector are often directed to providing property rights, public investment, services, credit, and subsidies to large modern enterprises and not to small farmers.

• Inadequate resources have been made available for irrigation, inputs, research, and credit.

Much can be done to overcome these barriers and improve the performance of developing countries' agricultural sectors. What is lacking is not knowledge, but rather resources and political will.

Credit and Financial Markets

What the poor own is their labor. What they lack is capital. The poor's lack of capital is sometimes taken as a sign that the capital goods market has failed, and that what is needed are greater investments in plant and equipment, increased raw materials and inventories for businesses, and additional farm equipment and fertilizer for farms. The latter part of this statement is true: Capital goods such as these are in fact needed. However, it is not because the capital goods market has failed; in the great majority of cases, these goods are available for sale or rent in virtually unlimited quantity to anyone prepared to pay the going market price. The problem arises, rather, because the poor lack the means to buy or rent these capital goods, even for manifestly worthwhile activities.

Failures in credit and financial markets are endemic and militate against the availability of credit for the poor, with consequent slower overall economic growth (Bencivenga and Smith 1991; Levine and Zervos 1993; Hoff and Stiglitz 1993; Besley 1995; Ray 1998). Lack of information is pervasive, so that lenders find it very difficult to identify which potential borrowers are more credit-worthy and which less so. The transactions costs of lending are only somewhat higher for a large loan than for a small one; this causes lenders to prefer making fewer large loans rather than many small ones. The lack of specific collateral that the poor have to offer makes it much riskier to make a loan of any given amount to a poor person than to a richer one. There is also the fact that borrowers face limited liability rules, which make them propose risky projects since they (the borrowers) enjoy all of the upside gains but face only limited downside losses. Then too, a kind of moral hazard problem arises: so-called "strategic" or "opportunistic" defaults, as borrowers choose to default when it is in their economic interest even in cases where they could repay. In addition, borrowers may find only a very limited number of lenders—sometimes, none at all—so they are unable to shop for the best lending terms. Also, credit for the poor is typically rationed: Even those who are able to obtain loans are unable to get as much credit as they ask for at the going rate. Finally, loans, when available, may be interlinked with transactions in product markets, input markets, and labor markets.

These limitations in the credit market make things very difficult for the poor. When the poor are able to borrow, it is often at very high rates of interest: 12 percent is a low annual rate of interest in the developing world; 200 percent is not unheard of. Often, though, credit is not available at all. The results can be devastating. Take the case of poor farmers, who may wish to borrow for seeds, fertilizer, farm equipment or draft animals; for the hiring of labor in planting and harvesting season; and for the payment of school fees for their children. If the harvest turns out to be good, the loan has to be repaid, with interest. But if the harvest turns out to be bad, the farmer and his family may become trapped in perpetual indebtedness (which they may not escape even in death, because in many societies, the debts are passed on to one's descendants).

The alternative to being able to borrow only at high interest rates is not to borrow at all. The poor resort to coping strategies which may themselves be harmful. They may, in bad years, sell their assets (land, farm buildings, draft animals, claims on the harvest) at distress prices (Cain 1981; Rosenzweig and Wolpin 1993). They may withdraw their children from school to provide essential unpaid labor, but at the cost of reducing the children's future earning opportunities (Basu forthcoming). They may be so poor, and therefore so weak, that they are unable to produce up to their full physical potentials (Behrman and Deolalikar 1988).

In these ways, underdeveloped credit markets contribute to continued poverty, higher income inequality, and slower economic growth. It would therefore be expected that much would be gained by developing these markets. Experience has shown that rural credit needs cannot be fulfilled by relying on commercial banks and other large lending institutions (Besley 1995; Ray 1998). Furthermore, interlinkage of rural credit with other markets, though understandable, is also problematical (Bhaduri 1977; Bardhan and Rudra 1978; Braverman and Srinivasan 1981; Bardhan 1984; Bell 1987; Floro and Yotopoulos 1991; Sadoulet 1992). Rather more promising are microfinance schemes. One of the earliest and best-known of these, from which many others are now being modeled, is the Grameen Bank in Bangladesh.[8]

The Grameen Bank aims to target very small loans ($100 or so) at reasonable rates of interest (12–17 percent per annum) to the poor (operationalized as a household owning less than half an acre of land). Ninety-four percent of borrowers are women. A number of the problems plaguing developing country credit markets are overcome because loans are made to a self-formed groups of borrowers. Because the individuals who form these groups know much better than the Bank does who is likely to repay the loans and who is not, those members of the community who are poor credit risks will be excluded from these groups. Some of the informational problems that normally arise in developing country credit markets are thus

---

8. For a comprehensive description, see Khandker 1996.

overcome. Furthermore, the bank makes loans to group members in sequence, only making a loan to a second person in a group after the first person's loan has been repaid. Group members therefore have a strong incentive to prevent their peers from borrowing for excessively risky projects or defaulting opportunistically. Consequently, loan recovery rates exceed 90 percent.

Evaluation studies have shown that the Grameen Bank has been a successful means of channeling credit to the poor at reasonable cost (Osmani 1991; Pitt and Khandker 1995; Khandker 1996, 1998; Morduch 1998). Lipton (1998) has drawn thirteen rules for successful pro-poor credit from the Grameen bank and other similar programs: Respect fungibility of credit; seek a poverty focus, but by means other than direct targeting; avoid antipoor rules and actions; find alternatives to physical collateral; cut poor borrowers' transactions costs; reduce the covariance of repayment; avoid lending monopolies; ensure that extra credit can be productive before raising its supply; subsidize transactions costs and administration, not interest; avoid politicizing or softening repayment but anticipate emergencies; complement credit with infrastructure and education; impose savings requirements to improve borrowers' performance; and create incentives to lenders and borrowers for repayment.

These experiences show that it is possible to reach the poor through well-designed credit programs. The Grameen Bank is being studied and copied, with modification, around the world—even in the United States!

Reaching the Poor and the Vulnerable Through Public Spending

It is frequently said that development efforts should be targeted on the poor and the vulnerable. This phrase, "the poor and the vulnerable," is used so often that it is easy to forget that the two groups are not the same. On the one hand, many of "the poor" have an *assured* low income—for example, those with steady, low-paying jobs. On the other hand, some of those with the greatest vulnerability to income shocks face fluctuations around a quite *high mean*—international traders, for example.

The distinction between "the poor" and "the vulnerable" becomes particularly important when officials need to decide to whom to devote scarce resources. Take the case of displaced civil servants, who are often aided through structural adjustment programs and sector adjustment loans. These people have often been among the highest earners in the economy, and many have skills and connections that enable them to find new jobs or self-employment opportunities on their own. So although they suffer undeniable losses when their government jobs come to an end, the case can nonetheless be made that they are *not* the most deserving of scarce development funds. These funds, rather, might be channeled towards the poor.

There are three major ways of doing this: targeted government spending and user charges, self-targeting, and well-designed economic security programs.

Targeted Government Spending and User Charges

The principles of targeting have been developed and exposited by Besley and Kanbur (1993), van de Walle and Nead (1995), Lipton and Ravallion (1995), Besley (1996), and van de Walle (1997). This work starts with the fact that the needs of developing countries are much greater than the resources available with which to meet them. If a country is unable to meet all of its needs, where should it put its money?

First, a guiding principle is needed. One such principle is to use resources on the margin to help the poor. "A World Free of Poverty" is an excellent guiding slogan for such efforts. Another principle is to assure that different groups benefit from government spending in proportion to their numbers (Harberger 1998a). The world would look very different if the poorest 20 percent of the people got 20 percent of the benefits of government programs.

Once such a principle is selected, certain conclusions immediately follow. A presumption is created in favor of certain patterns of spending and charges. By following what is sometimes called "broad targeting," key sectors are selected. Then, within those sectors, emphasis is given to those activities that are likely to benefit the poor the most.

This approach may be illustrated by considering the education sector. The studies of social rates of return to education cited above aim to measure the efficiency aspects of investments in different levels of education. When distributional aspects are introduced, they reinforce the presumption in favor of primary education. Unit costs of higher education are many, many times greater than those of primary education; a given amount of spending therefore produces

benefits spread over many more people if it used for primary education than for higher education. In addition, taking account of who
is now being included in school systems and who is excluded, it is no
surprise to find that the sons and daughters of the poor are the ones
left out. Expenditures on higher education benefit the children of the
well-to-do disproportionately, whereas expanded primary or secondary education would have a much greater effect on the children of
the poor.

A very simple rule of thumb can be used to indicate which level of
education is likely to produce the largest social benefits per dollar
spent. First, find the unit cost of each level of education. Then spec-
ulate on the benefits. In Brazil, for example, the per student cost of
university education is thirty-five times the per student cost of secondary education (IPEA, cited in Birdsall and James 1993). If higher
education costs thirty-five times as much per student as secondary
education does, then for higher education to be the better use of
scarce public funds, the social benefits of having more trained engi-
neers, economists, and humanists must be thirty-five times as large
as the benefits of having more clerks, small businesspeople, and farm
operators with secondary level skills. How likely is this?

These considerations lead to the presumption that additional investments in primary education (or secondary education if a country's primary education needs have already been fulfilled) would
have a greater effect on development than does the same amount
invested in higher education. In the same way, broad targeting
would lead to an emphasis on primary health care, not hospital
facilities, and on feeder roads, not airline terminals. These pre-
sumptions may be overturned in certain instances—for instance, if
the country's poor are very well-suited to growing flowers or man-
gos for export to developed country markets, but the country lacks a
runway for jumbo cargo jets—but then the case has been made that
the poor benefit *more* from such types of public spending in ways
that are not at first immediately obvious.

Yet, many countries' patterns of spending and charges are demonstrably *not* pro-poor. Continuing with the case of the education sector, many countries have incomplete primary education
systems, for which fees are charged, while university education is
entirely subsidized. Contrast Korea, which spent 10 percent of its
public educational budget on higher education, with Venezuela,
which spent 43 percent (Birdsall, Ross, and Sabot 1995a). Tan and

Mingat (1992) found that in eleven Asian countries, the 10 percent best-educated received 36.3 percent of public educational spending. Schultz (1988), Behrman and Schneider (1994, 1996), and van de Walle and Nead (1995) demonstrate that many countries favor higher education, which benefits the well-to-do, rather than primary education, which would help the poor.

Jimenez (1995) reviews spending patterns and charges, and concludes that while many public expenditures contribute to a more equal distribution of income, many others do not. Lipton (1993) offers evidence that government investment favors the urban upper and middle classes and the rural elite rather than the small family operator. Birdsall and James (1993) provide numerous examples of governments which choose to provide universities and hospitals rather than primary schools and health clinics, because they believe that the latter are of lower quality and because they are unable to withstand the pressure imposed upon them by powerful elites. Ferroni and Kanbur (1990) find that "the poverty focus and the poverty reduction impact of public spending in Africa is very low." Demery and Squire (1996) report that public social expenditures are much less targeted in Côte d'Ivoire and Ghana than in Colombia and Malaysia.

Van de Walle (1995, pp. 615–616) sums up thus: "Spending on *basic* services—notably primary and secondary education and basic health care—is found to reach the poor almost universally ... However, many programs whose stated rationale is to reduce poverty have instead been dismal and expensive failures." (Emphasis in the original.)

What can be done about this? Jimenez (1995) recommends five policies:

• Across sectors, prioritize those used primarily by the poor.

• Within sectors, do likewise.

• Mobilize more resources in nondistortionary ways.

• Improve program management and internal efficiency.

• Improve targeting to the poor.

Based on cross-country regression analysis, Devarajan, Swaroop, and Zou (1996) conclude that capital expenditures have been excessive and that the mix should be shifted somewhat in favor of efficient current expenditures.

One difficult issue is the pricing of social services. On the one hand, offering social services for free can be very costly. On the other hand, even modest user charges can seriously reduce usage by the poor (Gertler and van der Gaag 1990; Stewart 1995). Before leaving the topic of targeted government spending, two final points should be made. One is that we should consider the *costs* of targeting as well as the benefits. Targeting entails administrative cost associated with means-testing, such as gathering the financial information needed to decide whom to include in the program and whom to exclude. There also are political costs: Those excluded from the program may fail to support it or may even turn against it. For example, free public universities may engender support for the entire education system, even if certain groups have very low probabilities of actually sending their children to such universities. For these reasons, in certain instances, the poor may be helped more by an untargeted program which enjoys broad popular support and hence greater funding than by a targeted program which ends up being funded at a much lower level.

Second, mention should be made of *indicator targeting*. Indicator targeting offers benefits to all who possess certain easily observable characteristics. Examples are residence in a poor geographic area, belonging to a disadvantaged racial or ethnic group, or owning less than a certain amount of land. Indicator targeting comes out ahead of finer targeting in terms of lower administrative costs, but this comes at the expense of reduced target efficiency.

Indicator targeting is most efficient in reducing poverty when most of those with particular characteristics are poor and most of the poor have that particular characteristic. This is sometimes the case, but rarely. Take the issue of race. In South Africa, 33–40 percent of the variance in income is between races and the rest is within races (Leibbrandt, Bhorat, and Woolard 1998). Race-based targeting will be much more effective there than in Malaysia, where only 10 percent of the variance is between races and 90 percent is within races (Anand 1977).

Self-Targeting

The basic principle of self-targeting is that people are offered a program in which they may *choose* to participate. If the aim is to create opportunities for the poor, incentives can be constructed so that the poor, and only the poor, elect to enroll in such programs.

One self-targeted scheme is the Employment Guarantee Scheme (EGS) which has operated since 1973 in the Indian state of Maharashtra, which includes Mumbai (formerly Bombay). Public works jobs are offered to all who want them, but the wage is sufficiently low that only those with very poor outside opportunities will find the EGS jobs attractive. Participants are put to work on such projects as road-building, irrigation, soil conservation, and forestation programs.

Evaluation studies show that the EGS has produced important benefits (World Bank 1990; Osmani 1991; Ravallion and Datt 1995; Drèze and Sen 1995). The effectiveness of the self-targeting feature is shown by the fact that more than 90 percent of the participants in the Maharashtra program came from households with incomes below the poverty line. An important benefit for these workers is that employment is available particularly when it is most needed—in slack seasons and when other opportunities are most limited. As a result, income variations for the poor are reduced. And because the EGS guarantees a job to all who want one, there are minimal opportunities for corrupt program administrators to achieve personal gain through favoritism, patronage, or bribes.

After a thorough review of public works programs to create employment for the poor in Maharashtra and elsewhere,[9] Lipton (1998) recommends the following design features: Design employment for low opportunity cost individuals; seek alternatives to direct targeting; use scheme rules and conditions to discriminate for the poor; allow for poor workers' frequent physical difficulties; minimize poor participants' transactions costs; reduce covariate stresses on public works resources; use retailer, employer, and public works competition "for the poor"; before starting, check that low demand for labor causes poverty; subsidize coverage, sustainability, and graduation; encourage grassroots pressure groups to improve the scheme; seek complementarities among employment schemes; build up capacity of schemes and workers before works begin; and use performance incentives for officials and participants.

It has not yet been established whether public works employment programs are *more* effective than other programs for the poor. Public works programs have costs, both direct administrative costs and the foregone earnings of participants. Simple income transfers to every-

9. Other large public works employment programs include those in Bangladesh, Bolivia, Chile, Honduras, Cape Verde, and Botswana.

one residing in overwhelmingly poor rural areas would economize on these costs. In the case of the Maharashtra program, Ravallion and Datt (1995) estimate that the net benefits of an untargeted, uniform transfer to households would be about as great as the benefits under the EGS.

In sum, targeted and self-targeted programs have advantages and disadvantages vis-à-vis poverty reduction. Whether to go for such programs or for unconditional ones depends upon the net impact of a particular program on poverty, which is not always easy to gauge. In the words of van de Walle (1995, p. 616): "Other things being equal, the more ways one discriminates between beneficiaries, the greater the impact of targeting on poverty. However, other things are not equal. Fine targeting sometimes comes at a cost to the poor. Administrative costs may escalate, political support may vanish, and behavioral responses may create extra costs to targeted interventions. There is no simple answer to how much targeting is desirable."

Economic Security Programs and Citizenship Benefits
Individuals face many sources of economic insecurity. These include: individual inability to command resources (e.g., unemployment, low and unreliable pay, infirmity); family transitions (e.g., divorce or death of a spouse, arrival of children); industrial shocks (e.g., decline in prices of traded goods, loss of former markets, downsizing); and regional and national conditions (e.g., being a citizen of a poor country with no opportunity to emigrate, inflation, banking crises, natural disasters, political turmoil). Economic security programs are intended to protect against some of these risks.[10]

The two basic kinds of economic security programs are social insurance and social assistance. *Social insurance programs* aim to insure people against losses in material standards of living caused by such circumstances as unemployment, disability, and old age. *Social assistance programs* (also called "social safety nets") aim to assure a basic standard of living for everyone. Social insurance programs typically aim to replace a certain fraction of lost income, whereas social assistance programs seek to provide a floor of protection.[11]

---

10. In British English, these are called "social security programs." In American English, "Social Security" has a more limited meaning, designating the government's old-age pension program.
11. This is the distinction between the Bismarckian and Beveridgean approaches (Pestieau 1994).

In some developing countries, social insurance and social assistance programs offer a broad base of coverage for workers. For example, the Republic of Korea has established a wide range of programs including minimum wages, occupational safety and health, and employment insurance in the labor market. Of course, it is the country's very success with economic growth that has enabled such programs to be introduced and enlarged.[12]

Then there are those who are unable to work. One way of reaching them is through categorical benefits: benefits to the old, the blind, the disabled, and so on. But such categorization has costs. Another possibility is to provide the types of goods that the poor consume in the places where the poor are located—in effect, what might be called "citizenship benefits."

Although such economic security programs and citizenship benefits are possible in principle, they are sadly lacking in practice. Burgess and Stern (1991, pp. 41–42) have summed up the situation in developing countries thus:

Unemployment insurance and State pensions rarely cover more than a minority, generally a small minority ... Health care, whilst often subsidized, may be thinly and haphazardly spread, State support for the infirm and disabled is generally negligible, and education seldom extends beyond primary school ... These differences in the level, coverage, and effectiveness of State provision of social security partly reflect acute resource constraints in developing countries ... The supply of social security is also restricted by the low level of institutional development of a kind which may help to facilitate effective provision of resources to the poor and vulnerable.

Taking worker benefits as a case in point, when only formal sector workers are covered, a great many people are left out. In Korea, as in most other Asian countries, these are workers in smaller firms (which, in the Korean context, are those with fewer than ten employees). In most of Latin America, the vaunted social security programs cover only a small minority of labor force—the so-called "labor aristocracy"—and the most needy are left uncovered in the great majority of countries (Mesa-Lago 1991).[13] In much of sub-Saharan Africa, social insurance and social assistance programs for

---

12. The Korean programs are detailed in Korea International Labour Foundation 1998 and the Editing Committee of White Paper on Welfare Reform (1998). For reviews of safety net programs in general, see Ahmad 1993 and World Bank 1997.

13. Chile is an exception, however, in that reforms were undertaken so that social programs for the poor could be maintained while budgetary cuts were made elsewhere (Castañeda 1992; Marcel and Solimano 1994).

wage employees simply do not exist. It therefore falls on families and communities to provide a social safety net, which they do throughout the developing world with only partial success.

Sri Lanka and the Indian state of Kerala are exceptional in that they do provide ample citizenship benefits.[14] For decades, Sri Lanka has provided its citizens with basic education, health services, and free food (first as a generalized rice ration, later as means-tested food stamps). As a result, Sri Lanka has achieved an impressive record of high life expectancy, low morbidity, and widespread literacy. In Kerala (a state of 29 million people, which is larger than most developing countries, including Sri Lanka), public support for the citizenry includes public health services, food distribution programs, and the achievement of high literacy. The results are impressive: 89 percent of two-year-olds have received vaccinations, 97 percent of births are preceded by a prenatal checkup, 92 percent of births take place in medical institutions, 96 percent of villages have medical facilities, 99 percent of rural children have attended school, and 87 percent of the population receives subsidized cereals from the public distribution system. Yet, both Sri Lanka and Kerala have achieved only sluggish economic growth.

In cross-country analysis, Anand and Ravallion (1993) related life expectancy to countries' levels of public health spending per capita. The relationship between these two variables is significantly positive; however, this relationship fades to insignificance when GNP per capita is included as an additional explanatory factor. Thus, economic growth enables public health spending to be increased, which raises life expectancy.

What services governments provide, and for whom they provide them, reflect not only national income but also fundamental political choices. Human development can be much enhanced if economic growth takes place and if the political will is present to assure that the additional resources are used in a broad-based way.

10.4 Conclusions

This chapter has drawn on country experiences to show that a wide range of policy options are available to accelerate economic growth

---

14. This paragraph is based on Drèze and Sen 1989, 1995, Anand and Kanbur 1990, and Ramachandran (1997).

and to assure a broad-based distribution of the available resources. To briefly recapitulate the main conclusions that have been reached:

First, economic growth is essential to improving the economic well-being of a nation's people. Countries must be able to: produce goods and services that their citizens and others' will want to buy; save, invest, and accumulate capital; reach full employment; build up the human capital of their people; and achieve technical change. All of this requires that a policy environment be created within which growth policies can flourish.

Policies to achieve economic growth are many. Sound macroeconomic policies include tight monetary policy, small fiscal deficits, and stable prices. Countries should avoid distorting prices, regulations, and the trade environment in ways that impede growth. An outward-oriented trade regime is desirable, because it gives countries access to world markets and to technological advances and facilitates learning. Governments can work with markets, complement existing ones, help create new ones, and work to overcome the deficiencies of certain market outcomes. Appropriate investments in human capital infrastructure need to be undertaken as a precondition to growth. Finally, low inequality has been shown to be good for growth.

At the same time, many things can go wrong. Among them: hostility toward private enterprise; stifling of private sector initiative; prematurely expensive labor; unstable industrial relations; bad governance; runaway populism; and an insurmountable poverty of resources.

Some actions to achieve broad-based growth work through the labor market by increasing employment opportunities and earnings. The demand for wage labor can be increased by choosing appropriate trade and other policies. Labor productivity can be enhanced by investing in the education, training, and health of the population, thereby increasing their human capital. The returns to self-employment can be raised by equalizing the distribution of land and other productive assets and by improving credit and financial markets.

Finally, governments can reach the disadvantaged as consumers and as citizens. Public spending can be targeted and user charges designed so that the poor benefit more, especially by giving priority to basic education, health care, nutrition, housing, potable water, sewerage, and public health measures. Programs can be set up to be self-targeted, so that the poor and only the poor will choose to participate. Economic insecurity can be lessened through well-designed social insurance and social assistance programs.

There are thus many development policy actions from which to choose. Countries must prioritize among these various options, and these priorities will differ across countries. Sadly, the poorer the country, the greater are its development requirements and the fewer the resources with which to satisfy them. This chapter has indicated where the policy priorities for broad-based growth are likely to be found. The economic well-being of several billion people lies in the balance.

References

Adams, Richard H., Jr., and Harold Alderman. 1992. "Sources of Income Inequality in Rural Pakistan: A Decomposition Analysis." *Oxford Bulletin of Economics and Statistics* 54(4) (November): 591–608.

Adelman, Irma, and Cynthia Taft Morris. 1973. *Economic Growth and Social Equity in Developing Countries*. Stanford: Stanford University Press.

Adelman, Irma, and Sherman Robinson. 1989. "Income Distribution and Development." In Hollis B. Chenery and T. N. Srinivasan, eds., *Handbook of Development Economics*, Vol. 2, Amsterdam: Elsevier Science Publishers B.V.

Aghion, Philippe, Eve Caroli, and Cecilia García-Peñalosa. 1999. "Inequality and Economic Growth: The Perspective of the New Growth Theories." *Journal of Economic Literature* 37(4): 1615–1660.

Ahluwalia, Montek S. 1974. "Income Inequality: Some Dimensions of the Problem." In Hollis B. Chenery et al., eds., *Redistribution with Growth*. Oxford: Oxford University Press.

Ahluwalia, Montek S. 1976a. "Income Distribution and Development: Some Stylized Facts." *American Economic Review* 66(2) (May): 128–135.

Ahluwalia, Montek S. 1976b. "Inequality, Poverty and Development." *Journal of Development Economics* 3: 307–342.

Ahluwalia, Montek S., Nicholas G. Carter, and Hollis Chenery. 1979. "Growth and Poverty in Developing Countries." In Hollis Chenery, *Structural Change and Development Policy*. New York: Oxford University Press.

Ahmad, Ehtisham. 1993. "Protecting the Vulnerable: Social Security and Public Policy." In Michael Lipton and Jacques van der Gaag, eds., *Including the Poor*. Washington, DC: World Bank.

Ahuja, Vinod, Benu Bidani, Francisco Ferreira, and Michael Walton. 1997. *Everyone's Miracle? Revisiting Poverty and Inequality in East Asia*. Washington, DC: World Bank.

Alesina, Alberto, and Dani Rodrik. 1992. "Distribution, Political Conflict, and Economic Growth: A Simple Theory and Some Empirical Evidence." In Alex Cukierman, Zvi Hercowitz, and Leonardo Leiderman, eds., *Political Economy, Growth, and Business Cycles*. Cambridge and London: MIT Press.

Alesina, Alberto, and Dani Rodrik. 1994. "Distributive Politics and Economic Growth." *Quarterly Journal of Economics*: 465–490.

Ali, Ali Abdel Gadir. 1997. "Dealing with Poverty and Income Distribution Issues in Developing Countres: Cross Regional Experiences." Paper presented at the African Economic Research Consortium Bi-Annual Research Workshop, Nairobi (December 1996; revised January 1997).

Ali, Ali Abdel Gadir, and Erik Thorbecke. 1998. "The State and Path of Poverty in Sub-Saharan Africa: Some Preliminary Results." Paper presented at the African Economic Research Consortium Bi-Annual Research Workshop, Nairobi (May).

Allison, Paul D. 1978. "Measures of Inequality." *American Sociological Review* 43 (December): 865–880.

Amiel, Yoram, and Frank Cowell. 1994. "Inequality Changes and Income Growth." In Wolfgang Eichhorn, ed., *Models and Measurement of Welfare and Inequality*. Berlin: Springer-Verlag.

Amsden, Alice. 1989. *Asia's Next Giant: South Korea and Late Industrialization*. New York: Oxford University Press.

Anand, Sudhir. 1977. "Aspects of Poverty in Malaysia." *Review of Income and Wealth* (March): 1–16.

Anand, Sudhir, and S. M. R. Kanbur. 1984. "Inequality and Development: A Reconsideration." In H. P. Nissen, ed., *Towards Income Distribution Policies: From Income Distribution Research to Income Distribution Policy in LDCs*. Padenburg: EADI.

Anand, Sudhir, and S. M. R. Kanbur. 1990. "Public Policy and Basic Needs Provision: Intervention and Achievement in Sri Lanka." In Jean Drèze, Amartya Sen, and Athar Hussain, eds., *The Political Economy of Hunger*. Oxford: Oxford University Press.

Anand, Sudhir, and S. M. R. Kanbur. 1993a. "Inequality and Development: A Critique." *Journal of Development Economics* 41(1): 19–43.

Anand, Sudhir, and S. M. R. Kanbur. 1993b. "The Kuznets Process and the Inequality-Development Relationship." *Journal of Development Economics* 40(1): 25–52.

Anand, Sudhir, and Martin Ravallion. 1993. "Human Development in Poor Countries: On the Role of Private Incomes and Public Services." *Journal of Economic Perspectives* (Winter).

Anand, Sudhir, and Amartya K. Sen. 1997. "Concepts of Human Development and Poverty: A Multidimendional Perspective." *Background Papers for Human Development Report 1997*. New York: United Nations.

Asian Development Bank. 1999. *Asian Development Outlook 1999*.

Atkinson, Anthony B. 1970. "On the Measurement of Inequality." *Journal of Economic Theory*.

Atkinson, Anthony B. 1983a. *The Economics of Inequality*, 2d ed. Oxford: Clarendon.

Atkinson, Anthony B. 1983b. *Social Justice and Public Policy*. Cambridge: MIT Press.

Atkinson, Anthony B. 1987. "On the Measurement of Poverty." *Econometrica* 55(4) (July): 749–764.

Atkinson, Anthony B. 1997. "Bringing Income Distribution in From the Cold." *The Economic Journal* (March).

Atkinson, Anthony B. 1998. *Poverty in Europe*. Oxford: Blackwell.

Atkinson, Anthony B., and François Bourguignon. 1999. "Poverty and Inclusion from a World Perspective." Paper presented at the Annual Bank Conference on Development Economics, Paris (June).

Atkinson, Anthony B., and Christian Morrisson. 1992. *Empirical Studies of Earnings Mobility*. Chur, Switzerland: Harwood.

Atkinson, Anthony B., Lee Rainwater, and Timothy B. Smeeding. 1995. *Income Distribution in OECD Countries: Evidence from the Luxembourg Income Study*. Paris: OECD.

Atkinson, Anthony B., and Joseph E. Stiglitz. 1980. *Lectures on Public Economics*. New York: McGraw-Hill.

Ayub, Mahmood. 1977. *Income Inequality in a Growth-Theoretic Context: The Case of Pakistan*. Unpublished doctoral dissertation, Yale University.

Banerjee, Abhijit, and Andrew Newman. 1991. "Risk Bearing and the Theory of Income Distribution." *Review of Economic Studies*: 211–265.

Banerjee, Abhijit, and Andrew Newman. 1993. "Occupational Choice and the Process of Development." *Journal of Political Economy*: 274–298.

Banerjee, Abhijit, and Andrew Newman. 1994. "Poverty, Incentives, and Development." *American Economic Association Papers and Proceedings* 84(2) (May): 211–215.

Bardhan, P. K. 1984. *Land, Labor and Rural Poverty*. New York: Columbia University Press.

Bardhan, P. K. 1997. "Corruption and Development: A Review of Issues." *Journal of Economic Literature* 35(3) (September): 1320–1346.

Bardhan, P. K., and A. Rudra. 1978. "Interlinkage of Land, Labour and Credit Relations: An Analysis of Village Survey Data in East India." *Economic and Political Weekly* 13 (February).

Barro, Robert J. 1991. "Economic Growth in a Cross-Section of Countries." *Quarterly Journal of Economics* (May): 407–443.

Barro, Robert J. 1997. *Determinants of Economic Growth: A Cross-Country Empirical Study*. Cambridge and London: MIT Press.

Barro, Robert J. 1999. "Inequality, Growth, and Investment." NBER Working Paper No. 7038 (April).

Barro, Robert J., and Xavier Sala-I-Martin. 1995. *Economic Growth*. New York: McGraw Hill.

Barros, Ricardo Paes de, and Rosane Silva Pinto de Mendonça. 1995. "The Evolution of Welfare, Poverty and Inequality in Brazil Over the Last Three Decades: 1960–1990." IPEA (March).

Bartholomew, D. J. 1982. *Stochastic Models for Social Processes*. New York: Wiley.

Basu, Kaushik. 1997. *Analytical Development Economics*. Cambridge: MIT Press.

Basu, Kaushik. 1999. "Child Labor." *Journal of Economic Literature* 37(3): 1083–1119.

Basu, Kaushik, and Phan Hoang Van. 1998. "The Economics of Child Labor." *American Economic Review* 88(3): 412–427.

Behrman, Jere. 1990a. *The Action of Human Resources and Poverty on One Another: What We Have Yet to Learn.* Washington: Population and Human Resources Department, World Bank.

Behrman, Jere. 1990b. *Human Resource Led Development?: Review of Issues and Evidence.* Delhi: ILO-ARTEP.

Behrman, Jere. 1993. *The Contribution of Human Capital to Economic Development: Some Selected Issues.* Geneva: International Labour Office (November).

Behrman, Jere, and Anil Deolalikar. 1988. "Health and Nutrition." In Hollis Chenery and T. N. Srinivasan, eds., *Handbook of Development Economics, Volume I.* Amsterdam: Elsevier.

Behrman, Jere, and Ryan Schneider. 1994. "An International Perspective on Schooling Investments in the Last Quarter Century in Some Fast-Growing East and Southeast Asian Countries." *Asian Development Review.*

Behrman, Jere R., and Ryan Schneider. 1996. "Where Does Brazil Fit?" In Nancy Birdsall and Richard H. Sabot, eds., *Opportunity Foregone: Education in Brazil.* Washington, DC: Inter-American Development Bank.

Bell, Clive. 1987. "Credit Markets and Interlinked Transactions." In Hollis Chenery and T. N. Srinivasan, eds., *Handbook of Development Economics, Volume 1.* Amsterdam: North-Holland.

Bénabou, Roland. 1991. "Equity and Efficiency in Human Capital Investment: The Local Connection." *Review of Economic Studies*: 237–264.

Bénabou, Roland. 1996. "Inequality and Growth." *NBER Macroeconomics Annual* 11: 11–74.

Bencivenga, Valerie R., and Bruce D. Smith. 1991. "Financial Intermediation and Endogenous Growth." *Review of Economic Studies* 58(2) (April): 195–209.

Benhabib, Jess, and Mark M. Spiegel. 1994. "The Role of Human Capital in Economic Development: Evidence from Aggregate Cross-Country Data." *Journal of Monetary Economics*: 143–173.

Benhabib, Jess, and Mark M. Spiegel. 1997. "Growth and Investment Across Countries: Are Primitives All That Matter?" Federal Reserve Bank of San Francisco, Working Paper 97-03 (July).

Bergson, Abram. 1938. "A Reformulation of Certain Aspects of Welfare Economics." *Quarterly Journal of Economics.*

Berry, R. Albert, and William R. Cline. 1979. *Agrarian Structure and Productivity in Developing Countries.* Geneva: International Labour Organisation.

Besley, Tim J. 1995. "Savings, Credit and Insurance." In Jere Behrman and T. N. Srinivasan, eds., *Handbook of Development Economics, Volume III (A).* Amsterdam: Elsevier Science.

Besley, Tim J. 1996. "Political Economy of Alleviating Poverty: Theory and Institutions." *Annual World Bank Conference on Development Economics 1996*: 117–144.

Besley, Tim J., and Ravi Kanbur. 1993. "The Principles of Targeting." In Michael Lipton and Jacques van der Gaag, eds., *Including the Poor*. Washington: World Bank.

Bhaduri, A. 1977. "On the Formation of Usurious Interest Rates in Backward Agriculture." *Cambridge Journal of Economics* 1: 341–352.

Bhagwati, Jagdish N. 1991. *The World Trading System at Risk*. Princeton: Princeton University Press.

Bhagwati, Jagdish N. 1996. "The 'Miracle' That Did Happen: Understanding East Asia in Comparative Perspective." Keynote speech, Cornell University Conference on East Asian Growth (May).

Bhagwati, Jagdish N., and T. N. Srinivasan. 1983. *Lectures on International Trade*. Cambridge: MIT Press.

Bhorat, Haroon, Murray Leibbrandt, and Ingrid Woolard. 1995. "Towards an Understanding of South Africa's Inequality." Paper prepared for presentation at the African Economic Research Consortium workshop, Johannesburg, South Africa (November and December).

Bigsten, Arne. 1984. *Income Distribution and Development*. London: Heinemann.

Bigsten, Arne. 1987. "Poverty, Inequality and Development." In Norman Gemmell, ed., *Surveys in Development Economics*. Oxford: Basil Blackwell.

Binswanger, Hans P., and Klaus Deininger. 1997. "Explaining Agricultural and Agrarian Policies in Developing Countries." *Journal of Economic Literature* 35 (December): 1958–2005.

Binswanger, Hans P., Klaus Deininger, and Gershon Feder. 1995. "Power, Distortions, Revolt and Reform in Agricultural Land Relations." In Jere Behrman and T. N. Srinivasan, eds., *Handbook of Development Economics*. Amsterdam: Elsevier.

Binswanger, Hans P., and Miranda Elgin. 1989. "What Are the Prospects for Land Reform?" In Allen Maunder and Alberto Valdés, eds., *Agriculture and Governments in an Interdependent World: Proceedings of the Twentieth International Conference of Agricultural Economists*: 739–754. Aldershot, UK: Dartmouth.

Birdsall, Nancy, and Estelle James. 1993. "Efficiency and Equity in Social Spending: How and Why Governments Misbehave." In Michael Lipton and Jacques van der Gaag, eds., *Including the Poor*. Washington, DC: World Bank.

Birdsall, Nancy, and Juan Luis Londoño. 1997. "Asset Inequality Matters: An Assessment of the World Bank's Approach to Poverty Reduction." *American Economic Association Papers and Proceedings* 87(2): 32–37.

Birdsall, Nancy, David Ross, and Richard Sabot. 1995a. "Inequality and Growth Reconsidered: Lessons from East Asia." *World Bank Economic Review* (September): 477–508.

Birdsall, Nancy, David Ross, and Richard Sabot. 1995b. "Inequality as a Constraint on Growth in Latin America." In David Turnham, Colm Foy, and Guillermo Larraín, eds.,

Social Tensions, Job Creation and Economic Policy in Latin America. Paris: Organisation for Economic Cooperation and Development.

Bishop, John A., and John P. Formby. 1994. "A Dominance Evaluation of Distributions of Income and the Benefits of Economic Growth." In J. H. Bergstrand et al., eds., *The Changing Distribution of Income in an Open U.S. Economy*. Amsterdam: Elsevier.

Blackburn, McKinley L. 1994. "International Comparisons of Poverty." *American Economic Association Papers and Proceedings* 84(2) (May): 371–374.

Bliss, Christopher J., and Nicholas H. Stern. 1978. "Productivity, Wages, and Nutrition: 1. The Theory; 2. Some Observations." *Journal of Development Economics* 5: 363–398.

Bourguignon, François. 1979. "Decomposable Income Inequality Measures." *Econometrica* 47(4) (July): 901–920.

Bourguignon, François. 1990. "Income Distribution, Development and Foreign Trade: A Cross-Sectional Analysis." *European Economic Review*.

Bourguignon, François. 1994. "Growth, Distribution, and Human Resources." In Gustav Ranis, ed., *En Route to Modern Growth*. Baltimore: Johns Hopkins University Press.

Bourguignon, François, and Christian Morrisson. 1989. *External Trade and Income Distribution*. Paris: Organisation for Economic Cooperation and Development.

Bourguignon, François, and Christian Morrisson. 1998. "Income Distribution, Development and Foreign Trade: A Cross-Sectional Analysis." *European Economic Review* 34: 1113–1132.

Bourguignon, François, and Christian Morrisson. 1998. "Inequality and Development: the Role of Dualism." *Journal of Development Economics* 57: 233–257.

Bradford, Colin I. Jr. 1994. "The East Asian Development Experience." In Enzo Grilli and Dominick Salvatore, eds., *Economic Development: Handbook of Comparative Economic Policies, Vol. 4*, 339–419. Westport, CT, and London: Greenwood Press.

Brandolini, Andrea, and Nicola Rossi. 1998. "Income Distribution and Growth in Industrial Countries." In Vito Tanzi and Ke-Young Chu, eds., *Income Distribution and High-Quality Growth*. Cambridge and London: MIT Press.

Braverman, Avishay, and T. N. Srinivasan. 1981. "Credit and Sharecropping in Agrarian Societies." *Journal of Development Economics* 9: 289–312.

Bruno, Michael, Martin Ravallion, and Lyn Squire. 1998. "Equity and Growth in Developing Countries: Old and New Perspectives on the Policy Issues." In Vito Tanzi and Ke-Young Chu, eds., *Income Distribution and High-Quality Growth*. Cambridge and London: MIT Press.

Bruton, Henry J. 1998. "A Reconsideration of Import Substitution." *Journal of Economic Literature* 36(2) (June): 903–936.

Buchanan, James, and Gordon Tullock. 1962. *The Calculus of Consent*. Ann Arbor: University of Michigan Press.

Burgess, Robin, and Nicholas Stern. 1991. "Social Security in Developing Countries: What, Why, Who, and How?" In Ehtisham Ahmad, Jean Drèze, John Hills, and Amartya Sen, eds., *Social Security in Developing Countries*. Oxford: Clarendon Press.

Burkhauser, Richard V., Douglas Holtz-Eakin, and Stephen E. Rhody. 1997. "Labor Earnings Mobility and Inequality in the United States and Germany During the Growth Years of the 1980s." *International Economic Review* 38: 75–94.

Burkhauser, Richard V., Douglas Holtz-Eakin, and Stephen E. Rhody. 1998. "Mobility and Inequality in the 1980s: A Cross-National Comparison of the U.S. and Germany." In Stephen Jenkins, Arie Kapteyn, and Bernard Van Praag, eds., *The Distribution of Welfare and Household Production: International Perspectives*. Cambridge: Cambridge University Press.

Burniaux, Jean-Marc, Thai-Thanh Dang, Douglas Fore, Michael Förster, Marco Mira d'Ercole, and Howard Oxley. 1998. *Main Trends in Income Distribution and Poverty: Evidence from Recent Studies*. Paris: OECD.

Cain, Mead. 1981. "Risk and Insurance: Perspectives on Fertility and Agrarian Change in India and Bangladesh." *Population and Development Review* 7: 435–474.

Cameron, Lisa. (n.d.). "Poverty and Inequality in Java: Examining the Impact of the Changing Age, Educational, and Industrial Structure." *Journal of Development Economics* (forthcoming).

Campano, Fred, and Dominick Salvatore. 1988. "Economic Development, Income Inequality and Kuznets' U-Shaped Hypothesis." *Journal of Policy Modeling* 10(2) (Summer): 265–288.

Capa, Cornell, and J. Mayone Stycos. 1974. *Margin of Life*. New York: Grossman.

Castañeda, Tarsicio. 1992. *Combating Poverty*. San Francisco: ICS Press.

Chakravarty, S. J., B. Dutta, and J. A. Weymark. 1985. "Ethical Indices of Income Mobility." *Social Choice and Welfare* 2: 1–21.

Champernowne, D. G. 1974. "A Comparison of Measures of Inequality of Income Distribution." *The Economic Journal* (December): 787–816.

Chen, Shaohua, Gaurav Datt, and Martin Ravallion. 1993. "Is Poverty Increasing in the Developing World?" World Bank Working Paper. (Abridged version published in *Review of Income and Wealth*. December 1994.)

Chen, Shaohua, and Martin Ravallion. 1996. "Data in Transition: Assessing Rural Living Standards in Southern China." *China Economic Review* 7(1): 23–56.

Chenery, Hollis, Montek S. Ahluwalia, C. L. G. Bell, John H. Duloy, and Richard Jolly. 1973. *Redistribution with Growth*. New York: Oxford University Press.

Chenery, Hollis, and Moises Syrquin. 1975. *Patterns of Development, 1950–1970*. New York: Oxford University Press.

Chiou, Jong-Rong. 1996. "A Dominance Evaluation of Taiwan's Official Income Distribution Statistics, 1976–1992." *China Economic Review*.

Chiswick, Barry. 1971. "Earnings Inequality and Economic Development." *Quarterly Journal of Economics* (February): 21–39.

Citro, Constance F., and Robert T. Michael. 1995. *Measuring Poverty: A New Approach*. Washington, DC: National Academy Press.

Clark, S., R. Hemming, and D. Ulph. 1981. "On Indices for the Measurement of Poverty." *Economic Journal* 91.

Clarke, George R. C. 1995. "More Evidence on Income Distribution and Growth." *Journal of Development Economics*: 403–428.

Cline, William. 1975. "Distribution and Development: A Survey of the Literature." *Journal of Development Economics* 1: 359–400.

Collier, Paul, and Jan Willem Gunning. 1999. "Explaining African Economic Performance." *Journal of Economic Literature* 37 (March): 64–111.

Coondoo, Dipankar, and Bhaskar Dutta. 1990. "Measurement of Income Mobility: An Application to India." In Bhaskar Dutta et al., eds., *Economic Theory and Policy: Essays in Honor of Dipak Banerji*. Bombay and New York: Oxford University Press.

Council of Economic Advisers. 1964. *Economic Report of the President*. Washington, DC: U.S. Government Printing Office.

Cowell, Frank A. 1985. "Measures of Distributional Change: An Axiomatic Approach." *Review of Economic Studies* 52: 135–151.

Cowell, Frank A. 1995. *Measuring Inequality*. London: Prentice Hall/Harvester Wheatsheaf.

Cowell, Frank A. 1999. "Measurement of Inequality." In Anthony B. Atkinson and François Bourguignon, eds., *Handbook of Income Distribution*. Amsterdam: Elsevier Science.

Dalton, H. 1920. "The Measurement of the Inequality of Incomes." *Economic Journal* 30: 348–361.

Dandekar, V. M., and N. Rath. 1971. *Poverty in India*. Pune: Indian School of Political Economy.

Danziger, Sheldon, and Peter Gottschalk. 1995. *America Unequal*. New York: Russell Sage Foundation.

Dasgupta, Partha. 1993. *An Inquiry Into Well-Being and Destitution*. Oxford: Oxford University Press.

Dasgupta, Partha, Amartya K. Sen, and David Starrett. 1973. "Notes on the Measurement of Inequality." *Journal of Economic Theory*.

Datt, Gaurav, and Martin Ravallion. 1992. "Growth and Redistribution Components of Changes in Poverty Measures: A Decomposition with Applications to Brazil and India in the 1980s." *Journal of Development Economics* 38(2): 275–295.

de Janvry, Alain. 1981. *The Agrarian Question and Reformism in Latin America*. Baltimore: Johns Hopkins University Press.

de Janvry, Alain, and Elisabeth Sadoulet. 1990. "Efficiency, Welfare Effects, and Political Feasibility of Alternative Antipoverty and Adjustment Programs." Development Centre Technical Papers No. 6. Paris: Organisation for Economic Cooperation and Development.

Deaton, Angus. 1997. *The Analysis of Household Surveys. A Microeconometric Approach to Development Policy*. Washington, DC: World Bank.

Deininger, Klaus, and Lyn Squire. 1996. "A New Data Set Measuring Income Inequality." *The World Bank Economic Review* 10: 3.

Deininger, Klaus, and Lyn Squire. 1997. "Economic Growth and Income Inequality: Reexamining the Links." *Finance and Development* (March): 38–41.

Deininger, Klaus, and Lyn Squire. 1998. "New Ways of Looking at Old Issues: Inequality and Growth." *Journal of Development Economics* 57(2) (December): 259–287.

Demery, Lionel, and Lyn Squire. 1996. "Macroeconomic Adjustment and Poverty in Africa: An Emerging Picture." *The World Bank Research Observer* 11(1): 39–59.

Demery, Lionel, Binayak Sen, and Tara Vishwanath. 1995. "Poverty, Inequality and Growth." ESP Discussion Paper Series 70 (June). World Bank.

Deutsch, Joseph, and Jacques Silber. 1999. "The Kuznets Curve and the Impact of Various Income Sources on the Link Between Inequalilty and Development." Bar-Ilan University, Ramat-Gan, Israel.

Devarajan, Shantayanan, Vinaya Swaroop, and Heng-fu Zou. 1996. "The Composition of Public Expenditures and Economic Growth." *Journal of Monetary Economics* 37: 313–344.

Dornbusch, Rudiger, and Sebastian Edwards. 1990. "Macroeconomic Populism." *Journal of Development Economics* 32(2).

Drèze, Jean, Peter Lanjouw, and Nicholas Stern. 1992. "Economic Mobility and Agricultural Labour in Rural India: A Case Study." *Indian Economic Review* (Special Number): 25–54.

Drèze, Jean, and Amartya K. Sen. 1989. *Hunger and Public Action*. Oxford: The Clarendon Press.

Drèze, Jean, and Amartya K. Sen. 1990. *The Political Economy of Hunger*. Oxford: Oxford University Press.

Drèze, Jean, and Amartya K. Sen. 1995. *India: Economic Development and Social Opportunity*. Oxford: The Clarendon Press.

Dumke, Rolf. 1991. "Income Inequality and Industrialization in Germany, 1850–1913: the Kuznets Hypothesis Re-Examined." In Y. S. Brenner, Harmut Kaelble, and Mark Thomas, *Income Distribution in Historical Perspective*. Cambridge: Cambridge University Press.

Durlauf, Steven N., and Danny T. Quah. n.d. "The New Empirics of Economic Growth." In John Taylor and Michael Woodford, eds., *Handbook of Macroeconomics*. Amsterdam: North-Holland.

Editing Committee. 1998. *Welfare Reform in Korea: Toward the 21st Century*. White paper on welfare reform (February) Seoul.

Edwards, Sebastian. 1998. "Openness, Productivity and Growth: What Do We Really Know?" *Economic Journal* 108(447) (March): 383–398.

Eichhorn, W., and W. Gehrig. 1982. "Measurement of Inequality in Economics." In Bernhard H. Korte, ed., *Modern Applied Mathematics: Optimization and Operations Research*. North-Holland.

Elias, Victor J. 1990. *Sources of Growth: A Study of Seven Latin American Economies*. San Francisco: ICS Press.

Eusufzai, Zaki. 1997. "The Kuznets Hypothesis: An Indirect Test." *Economics Letters* 54(1): 81–85.

Fei, John C. H., and Gustav Ranis. 1964. *Development of the Labor Surplus Economy*. Homewood, IL: Irwin.

Fei, John C. H., Gustav Ranis, and Shirley Kuo. 1978. "Growth and the Family Distribution of Income by Factor Components." *Quarterly Journal of Economics* (February): 17–53.

Fei, John C. H., Gustav Ranis, and Shirley W. Y. Kuo. 1979. *Growth with Equity: the Taiwan Case*. Oxford: Oxford University Press.

Feinstein, Charles. 1988. "The Rise and Fall of the Williamson Curve." *Journal of Economic History* 48: 699–729.

Ferroni, Marco, and Ravi Kanbur. 1990. "Poverty-Conscious Restructuring of Public Expenditure." World Bank.

Fields, Gary S. 1979a. "A Welfare Economic Approach to Growth and Distribution in the Dual Economy." *Quarterly Journal of Economics* (August).

Fields, Gary S. 1979b. "Income Inequality in Urban Colombia: A Decomposition Analysis." *Review of Income and Wealth*: 327–341.

Fields, Gary S. 1980. *Poverty, Inequality, and Development*. Cambridge: Cambridge University Press.

Fields, Gary S. 1984. "Employment, Income Distribution and Economic Growth in Seven Small Open Economies." *The Economic Journal* 94: 74–83.

Fields, Gary S. 1989. "A Compendium of Data on Inequality and Poverty for the Developing World." Cornell University.

Fields, Gary S. 1991. "Growth and Income Distribution." In George Psacharopoulos, ed., *Essays on Poverty, Equity, and Growth*. Oxford and New York: Pergamon.

Fields, Gary S. 1993. "Inequality in Dual Economy Models." *Economic Journal* 103: 420, 1228–1235.

Fields, Gary S. 1994. "Poverty Changes in Developing Countries." In Rolph van der Hoeven and Richard Anker, eds., *Poverty Monitoring: An International Concern*. New York: St. Martin's Press.

Fields, Gary S., and George H. Jakubson. 1994. "New Evidence on the Kuznets Curve." Cornell University.

Fields, Gary S., and Amanda Newton Kraus. 1996. "Changing Labor Market Conditions and Income Distribution in Brazil, Costa Rica, and Venezuela." Cornell University.

Fields, Gary S., and Jesse B. Leary. 1999. "Economic and Demographic Aspects of Taiwan's Rising Family Income Inequality." In Gustav Ranis, Sheng-Cheng Hu, and Yun-Peng Chu, eds., *The Economics and Political Economy of Development in Taiwan into the 21st Century*. Edward Elgar.

Fields, Gary S., and Jennifer O'Hara Mitchell. 1999. "Changing Income Inequality in Taiwan: A Decomposition Analysis." In T. N. Srinivasan and Gary Saxonhouse, eds., *Development, Duality, and the International Regime: Essays in Honor of Gustav Ranis*. Ann Arbor: University of Michigan Press.

Fields, Gary S., Jesse B. Leary, and Efe A. Ok. 1998. "Income Movement in the United States in the Seventies and Eighties." Working Paper, Cornell University and New York University.

Fields, Gary S., Jesse B. Leary, and Efe A. Ok. 1999. "Dollars and Deciles: Changing Earnings Mobility in the United States, 1970–1995." Cornell University.

Fields, Gary S., and Efe A. Ok. 1996. "The Meaning and Measurement of Income Mobility." *Journal of Economic Theory* 71: 349–377.

Fields, Gary S., and Efe A. Ok. 1999. "Measuring Movement of Incomes." *Economica* 66(264): 455–472.

Fields, Gary S., and Efe A. Ok. 1999. "The Measurement of Income Mobility: An Introduction to the Literature." In Jacques Silber, ed., *Handbook of Income Inequality Measurement*. Kluwer Academic Publishing.

Fischer, Stanley. 1993. "The Role of Macroeconomic Factors in Economic Growth." *Journal of Monetary Economics* 32(3) (December): 485–512.

Fischer, Stanley. 1998. "ABCDE: Tenth Conference Address." *Annual Bank Conference on Development Economics*. (April) World Bank.

Fishlow, Albert. 1972. "Brazilian Size Distribution of Income." *American Economic Review* (May).

Fishlow, Albert. 1995. "Inequality, Poverty and Growth: Where Do We Stand?" Paper presented at the Annual Bank Conference on Development Economics (May). World Bank.

Fishlow, Albert, 1996. "Inequality, Poverty and Growth: Where Do We Stand?" *Annual Bank Conference on Development Economics*.

Fishlow, Albert, Catherine Gwin, Stephan Haggard, Dani Rodrik, and Robert Wade. 1994. *Miracle or Design?: Lessons from the East Asian Experience*. Washington, DC: Overseas Development Council.

Flemming, John, and John Micklewright. 1999. "Income Distribution, Economic Systems and Transition." In Anthony B. Atkinson and François Bourguignon, eds., *Handbook of Income Distribution*.

Floro, M. S., and P. Yotopoulos. 1991. *Informal Credit Markets and the New Institutional Economics: The Case of Philippine Agriculture*. Boulder, CO: Westview.

Forbes, Kristin. 1999. "A Reassessment of the Relationship between Inequality and Growth," MIT.

Foster, James E. 1984. "On Economic Poverty: A Survey of Aggregate Measures." In R. Basmann and G. Rhodes, eds., *Advances in Econometrics*. Greenwich, CT: JAI Press.

Foster, James E. 1985. "Inequality Measurement." In H. Peyton Young, ed., *Fair Allocation*: 31–68. American Mathematical Society.

Foster, James E. 1998. "Absolute versus Relative Poverty." *American Economic Association Papers and Proceedings* 88(2) (May): 335–341.

Foster, James E., Joel Greer, and Erik Thorbecke. 1984. "A Class of Decomposable Poverty Measures." *Econometrica* 52: 761–766.

Foster, James E., and Efe A. Ok. 1999. "Lorenz Dominance and the Variance of Logarithms." *Econometrica* 67(4): 901–907.

Foster, James E., and Amartya Sen. 1997. "*On Economic Inequality* After a Quarter Century." In Amartya Sen, ed., *On Economic Inequality*, 2d ed. Oxford: Clarendon Paperbacks.

Foster, James E., and Anthony F. Shorrocks. 1988. "Poverty Orderings." *Econometrica* 56.

Frankel, Jeffrey, David Romer, and Teresa Cyrus. 1997. "Trade and Growth in East Asian Countries: Cause and Effect." NBER Working Paper 5732 (February).

Freeman, Richard, and David Lindauer. 1999. "Why Not Africa?" National Bureau of Economic Research Working Paper 6942 (February).

Friedman, Milton, and Simon Kuznets. 1954. *Income from Independent Professional Practice.* New York: National Bureau of Economic Research.

Fuchs, Victor. 1967. "Redefining Poverty and Redistributing Income." *The Public Interest.*

Fuchs, Victor. 1969. "Comment on Measuring the Size of the Low-Income Population." In Lee Soltow, ed., *Six Papers on the Size Distribution of Wealth and Income*: 198–202. New York: National Bureau of Economic Research.

Galenson, Walter. 1997. "Economic Growth, Income, and Employment." Cornell University.

Galor, Oded, and Joseph Zeira. 1993. "Income Distribution and Macroeconomics." *Review of Economic Studies*: 35–52.

Ganuza, Enrique, Samuel Morley, and Lance Taylor. 1998. *Politicas Macroeconomicas en América Latina y el Caribe, 1980–1996.* Mexico, D.F.: Fondo de Cultura Económica.

Gardner, Bruce L. 1997. "Policy Reform in Agriculture: An Assessment of the Results in Seven Countries." University of Maryland Working Paper (September).

Gertler, Paul, and Jacques van der Gaag. 1990. *The Willingness to Pay for Medical Care: Evidence from Two Developing Countries.* Baltimore, MD: Johns Hopkins University Press.

Gittleman, Maury, Michael Horrigan, and Mary Joyce. 1997. "Have Family Income Mobility Patterns Changed?" Paper presented at the Annual Meeting of the American Economic Association, New Orleans, LA (January).

Glewwe, Paul, and Gillette Hall. 1998. "Are Some Groups More Vulnerable to Macroeconomic Shocks than Others? Hypothesis Tests Based on Panel Data from Peru." *Journal of Development Economics* 56(1) (August): 181–206.

Glomm, Gerhard. 1997. "Whatever Happened to the Kuznets Curve? Is It Really Upside Down?" *Journal of Income Distribution* 7(1): 63–87.

Glomm, Gerhard, and B. Ravikumar. 1994. "Equilibrium Theories of the Kuznets Curve." Paper prepared for the Conference on Income Distribution and Economic Development, Madrid, Spain (December 15–18).

Glomm, Gerhard, and B. Ravikumar. 1995. "Teorías de Equilibrio de la Curva de Kuznets: Una Revisión." *Cuadernos Económicos* 61: 79–94.

Goodin, Robert. 1986. "Laundering Preferences." In Jon Elster and Aanund Hylland, eds., *Foundations of Social Choice Theory*: 75–101. Cambridge, New York, and Sydney: Cambridge Univesity Press. Paris: Maison des Sciences de l'Homme.

Goodin, Robert E. 1995. *Utilitarianism as a Public Philosophy*. New York: Cambridge University Press.

Gottschalk, Peter, and Robert Moffitt. 1994. "The Growth of Earnings Instability in the U.S. Labor Market." *Brookings Papers on Economic Activity* 2: 217–272.

Gottschalk, Peter, and Timothy M. Smeeding. 1997. "Cross-National Comparisons of Earnings and Income Inequality." *Journal of Economic Literature* 35: 632–687.

Gradstein, Mark, and Moshe Justman. 1993. "On the Political Economy of the Kuznets Curve." Ben Gurion University Working Paper (November).

Griffin, Keith. 1981. *Land Concentration and Rural Poverty*. London: Macmillan.

Griffin, Keith, and A. R. Khan. 1978. "Poverty in the Third World: Ugly Facts and Fancy Models." *World Development*.

Griliches, Zvi. 1996. "The Discovery of the Residual: A Historical Note." *Journal of Economic Literature* 34 (September): 1324–1330.

Grootaert, Christiaan, and Ravi Kanbur. 1996. "The Lucky Few Amidst Economic Decline: Distributional Change as Seen Through Panel Data." In Christiaan Grootaert, *Analyzing Poverty and Policy Reform: The Experience of Côte d'Ivoire*. Aldershot, UK: Avebury.

Grootaert, Christiaan, Ravi Kanbur, and Gi-Taik Oh. 1997. "The Dynamics of Welfare Gains and Losses: An African Case Study." *Journal of Development Studies* 33(5) (June): 635–657.

Hadar, J., and W. Russell. 1969. "Rules for Ordering Uncertain Prospects." *American Economic Review* 59.

Hammond, Peter. 1989. "Envy." In John Eatwell, Murray Milgate, and Peter Newman, *The New Palgrave: Social Economics*. New York: Norton.

Harberger, Arnold C. 1984. "Economic Policy and Economic Growth." In Arnold C. Harberger, ed., *World Economic Growth*: 427–466. San Francisco: ICS Press.

Harberger, Arnold C. 1998a. "Monetary and Fiscal Policy for Equitable Economic Growth." In Vito Tanzi and Ke-Young Chu, eds., *Income Distribution and High-Quality Growth*. Cambridge and London. MIT Press.

Harberger, Arnold C. 1998b. "A Vision of the Growth Process." *American Economic Review* 88(1) (March): 1–32.

Harrison, Ann, and Ana Revenga. 1995. "The Effects of Trade Policy Reform: What Do We Really Know?" National Bureau of Economic Research Working Paper Number 5225.

Harsanyi, John C. 1955. "Cardinal Welfare, Individualistic Ethics and Interpersonal Comparisons of Utility." *Journal of Political Economy.*

Heath, John, and Hans Binswanger. 1996. "Natural Resource Degradation Effects of Poverty and Population Growth are Largely Policy-Induced: The Case of Colombia." *Environment and Development Economics* 1 (February): 65–84.

Herrera, Javier. 1999. "Ajuste Económico, Desigualdad, y Movilidad." DIAL (July).

Hoff, Karla, and Joseph E. Stiglitz. 1993. "Imperfect Information in Rural Credit Markets: Puzzles and Policy Perspectives." *World Bank Economic Review* 4: 235–250.

Hungerford, Thomas L. 1993. "U.S. Income Mobility in the Seventies and Eighties." *Review of Income and Wealth* 39: 403–417.

IFAD (International Fund for Agricultural Development). 1992. *The State of World Rural Poverty.* New York: New York University Press.

Iglesias, Enrique. 1998. "Income Distribution and Sustainable Growth: A Latin American Perspective." In Vito Tanzi and Ke-Young Chu, eds., *Income Distribution and High-Quality Growth.* Cambridge and London: MIT Press.

Inter-American Development Bank. n.d. *Economic and Social Progress in Latin America.* (various years).

ILO. International Labour Office. 1976. *Meeting Basic Needs.* Geneva: ILO.

ILO. International Labour Office. 1987. *World Labour Report* 1-2. Geneva: ILO.

ILO. International Labour Office. 1998a. *The Social Impact of the Asian Financial Crisis.* (April) Bangkok: ILO Regional Office for Asia and the Pacific.

ILO. International Labour Office. 1998b. *The Future of Urban Employment.* Geneva: ILO.

Jalan, Jyotsna, and Martin Ravallion. 1998. "Transient Poverty in Postreform Rural China." *Journal of Comparative Economics* 26: 338–357.

Jalan, Jyotsna, and Martin Ravallion. 1999. "Do Transient and Chronic Poverty in Rural China Share Common Causes?" World Bank (February).

Jarvis, Sarah, and Stephen P. Jenkins. 1998. "How Much Income Mobility Is There in Britain?" *The Economic Journal* 108 (March): 1–16.

Jenkins, Stephen P. 1991. "The Measurement of Income Inequality." In Lars Osberg, ed., *Economic Inequality and Poverty.* Armonk, NY: Sharpe.

Jenkins, Stephen P., Arie Kapteyn, and Bernard M. S. van Praag, eds. 1998. *The Distribution of Welfare and Household Production: International Perspectives.* Cambridge: Cambridge University Press.

Jenkins, Stephen P., and Peter J. Lambert. 1997. "Three 'I's of Poverty Curves, with an Analysis of UK Poverty Trends." *Oxford Economic Papers* 49(3) (July): 317–327.

Jenkins, Stephen P., and Peter J. Lambert. 1998. " 'Three I's of Poverty' Curves and Poverty Dominance: Tips for Poverty Analysis." *Research on Economic Inequality* 8: 39–56.

Jha, Sailesh K. 1996. "The Kuznets Curve: A Reassessment." *World Development* 24(4): 773–780.

Jimenez, Emmanuel. 1995. "Human and Physical Infrastructure: Public Investment and Pricing Policies in Developing Countries." Chapter 43 in Jere Behrman and T. N. Srinivasan, eds., *Handbook of Development Economics, Volume III.* Amsterdam: Elsevier Science.

Johnson, D. Gale. 1991. *World Agriculture in Disarray.* New York: St. Martin's Press.

Kaelble, Hartmut, and Mark Thomas. 1991. "Introduction." In Y. S. Brenner, Hartmut Kaelble, and Mark Thomas, *Income Distribution in Historical Perspective.* Cambridge: Cambridge University Press.

Kakwani, Nanak. 1980. *Income Inequality and Poverty.* New York: Oxford University Press for the World Bank.

Kakwani, Nanak. 1984. "Welfare Rankings of Income Distributions." In R. Basmann and G. Rhodes, *Advances in Econometrics.* Greenwich, CT: JAI Press.

Kakwani, Nanak. 1993. "Poverty and Economic Growth with Application to Côte d'Ivoire." *Review of Income and Wealth* 39: 121–139.

Kaldor, Nicholas. 1956. "Alternative Theories of Distribution." *Review of Economic Studies* 23: 83–100.

Kaldor, Nicholas. 1957. "A Model of Economic Growth." *The Economic Journal* 67(268) (December): 591–624.

Kaldor, Nicholas. 1958. "Capital Accumulation and Economic Growth." Paper prepared for the Corfu meeting of the International Economic Association (August). (Reprinted in Kaldor 1978: 1–53).

Kaldor, Nicholas ed. 1978. *Further Essays on Economic Theory.* New York: Holmes and Meier Publishers.

Kanbur, Ravi. 1999. "Income Distribution and Development." In Anthony B. Atkinson and François Bourguignon, *Handbook of Income Distribution.* Amsterdam: Elsevier Science.

Kanbur, Ravi, and Nora Lustig. 1999. "Why Is Inequality Back on the Agenda?" Paper presented at the Annual Bank Conference on Development Economics, World Bank, Washington, DC (April).

Kaufmann, Daniel. 1997. "Corruption: The Facts." *Foreign Policy* (Summer): 114–131.

Keefer, Philip, and Stephen Knack. 1995. "Polarization, Property Rights and the Links Between Inequality and Growth." World Bank.

Khan, Azizur Rahman, and Eddy Lee. 1983. *Poverty in Rural Asia.* Bangkok: International Labour Organisation Asian Employment Programme.

Khandker, Shahidur. 1996. "Grameen Bank: Impact, Costs, and Program Sustainability." *Asian Development Review* 14(1): 97–130.

Khandker, Shahidur. 1998. *Fighting Poverty with Microcredit.* New York: Oxford University Press.

Kim, J. I., and L.J. Lau. 1994. "The Sources of Economic Growth of East-Asian Newly Industrialized Countries." *Journal of the Japanese and International Economies* 8: 235–271.

King, Mervyn A. 1983. "An Index of Inequality: with Applications to Horizontal Equity and Social Mobility." *Econometrica* 51: 99–115.

Klitgaard, Robert. 1990. *Tropical Gangsters*. New York: Basic Books.

Knight, John B. 1976. "Explaining Income Distribution in Less Developed Countries: A Framework and an Agenda." *Bulletin of the Oxford Institute of Economics and Statistics* (August).

Kolm, S. C. 1976. "Unequal Inequalities I and II." *Journal of Economic Theory*.

Korea International Labour Foundation. 1998. *Labor Reform in Korea: Toward the 21st Century*. (February) Seoul.

Krause, Lawrence B. 1988. "Hong Kong and Singapore: Twins or Kissing Cousins?" *Economic Development and Cultural Change* 36(3) (suppl.): S45–S66.

Kravis, Irving. 1960. "International Differences in the Distribution of Income." *Review of Economics and Statistics* (November): 408–416.

Kremer, Michael. 1993. "The O-Ring Theory of Economic Development." *Quarterly Journal of Economics*: 551–575.

Krueger, Anne O. 1997. "Trade Policy and Economic Development: How We Learn." *American Economic Review* 87(1) (March): 1–22.

Krueger, Anne O., Maurice Schiff, and Alberto Valdés, eds. 1991. *Political Economy of Agricultural Pricing Policy*. Baltimore: Johns Hopkins University Press.

Krugman, Paul. 1994. "The Myth of Asia's Miracle." *Foreign Affairs* 73(6): 62–78.

Krugman, Paul. 1998. "The Role of Geography in Development." Paper presented at the Annual Bank Conference on Development Economics, World Bank (April).

Kuruvilla, Sarosh. 1996. "Linkages Between Industrialization Strategies and Industrial Relations/Human Resource Policies: Singapore, Malaysia, the Philippines, and India." *Industrial and Labor Relations Review* 49(4) (July): 635–657.

Kuznets, Simon. 1955. "Economic Growth and Income Inequality." *American Economic Review* (March): 1–28.

Kuznets, Simon. 1963. "Quantitative Aspects of the Economic Growth of Nations: VIII, Distribution of Income By Size." *Economic Development and Cultural Change* (Part 2) (January): 1–80.

Kuznets, Simon. 1966. *Modern Economic Growth*. New Haven: Yale University Press.

Lal, Deepak, and Hla Myint. 1996. *The Political Economy of Poverty, Equity, and Growth: A Comparative Study*. Oxford: The Clarendon Press.

Lambert, Peter J. 1989. *The Distribution and Redistribution of Income: A Mathematical Analysis*. Oxford: Blackwell. Second edition published by University of Manchester Press, 1993.

Lecaillon, Jacques, et al. 1984. *Income Distribution of Economic Development: An Analytical Survey*. Geneva: International Labour Office.

Lee, Won-Duck. 1998. "Industrial Relations: Retrospect on the Past Decade and Policy Directions for the 21st Century." In Lee, Won Duck and Choi, Kang-Shik, eds., *Labor Market and Industrial Relations in Korea*. Seoul: Korea Labor Institute.

Leibbrandt, Murray, Haroon Bhorat, and Ingrid Woolard. 1998. "Understanding Contemporary Household Inequality in South Africa." University of Cape Town.

Leibenstein, Harvey. 1957. *Economic Backwardness and Economic Growth*. New York: Wiley.

Leipziger, Danny M., ed. 1997. *Lessons from East Asia*. Ann Arbor: University of Michigan Press.

Levine, Ross, and David Renelt. 1992. "A Sensitivity Analysis of Cross-Country Growth Regressions." *American Economic Review* (September): 942–963.

Levine, Ross, and Sara J. Zervos. 1993. "What Have We Learned About Policy and Growth from Cross-Country Regressions?" *American Economic Review* 83(2): 426–430.

Lewis, W. Arthur. 1954. "Economic Development with Unlimited Supplies of Labor." *The Manchester School*.

Lewis, W. Arthur. 1983. "Development and Distribution." In Mark Gersovitz, ed., *Selected Economic Writings of W. Arthur Lewis*. New York: New York University Press.

Lewis, W. Arthur. 1984. "The State of Development Theory." *American Economic Review* 74(1) (March): 1–10.

Li, Hongyi, and Heng-fu Zou. 1998. "Income Inequality is not Harmful for Growth: Theory and Evidence." Review of Development Economics 2(3) (October): 318–334.

Li, Hongyi, Lyn Squire, and Heng-fu Zou. 1998. "Income Inequality is Not Getting Worse After All: Evidence From Around the World." *The Economic Journal* 108 (January): 1–18.

Lindauer, David L., et al. 1997. *The Strains of Economic Growth: Labor Unrest and Social Dissatisfaction in Korea*. Cambridge: Harvard University Press.

Lindert, Peter H., and Jeffrey G. Williamson. 1985. "Essays in Exploration: Growth, Equality, and History." *Explorations in Economic History* 22: 341–377.

Lipton, Michael. 1977. *Why Poor People Stay Poor: Urban Bias in World Development*. London: Temple Smith.

Lipton, Michael. 1993. "Land Reform as Commenced Business: The Evidence Against Stopping." *World Development* 21(4) (April): 641–657.

Lipton, Michael. 1998. *Successes in Anti-Poverty*. Geneva: International Labour Office.

Lipton, Michael, and Martin Ravallion. 1995. "Poverty and Policy." In Jere Behrman and T. N. Srinivasan, eds., *Handbook of Development Economics, Volume III*. Amsterdam: Elsevier Science.

Lipton, Michael, and Jacques van der Gaag, eds. 1993. *Including the Poor*. Washington: The World Bank.

List, John A. and Craig Gallet. 1999. "The Kuznets Curve: What Happens After the Inverted-U?" *Review of Development Economics* 3(2): 200–206.

Lockheed, Maureen E., Dean T. Jamison, and Lawrence J. Lau. 1980. "Farmer Education and Farm Efficiency: A Survey." *Economic Development and Cultural Change* 29: 37–76.

Londoño, Juan Luís. 1990. *Human Capital and Long Run Swings of Income Distribution: Colombia 1938–1988* (August) mimeo.

Londoño, Juan Luís, and Miguel Székely. 1997. "Distributional Surprises After a Decade of Reforms: Latin America in the Nineties." Inter-American Development Bank.

Londoño, Juan Luís, and Miguel Székely. 1998. "Sorpresas Distributivas después de una década de reformas: América Latina en los noventa." *Revista de Economía Política* (Special Issue): 195–242. Pensamiento Iberoamericano.

Lorenz, M. C. 1905. "Methods of Measuring the Concentration of Wealth," *Publications of the American Statistical Association* (9): 209–219.

Lundberg, Mattias, and Lyn Squire. 1999. "Growth and Inequality: Extracting the Lessons for Policymakers." (June) World Bank.

Lydall, Harold. 1977. *Income Distribution During the Process of Development*. Geneva: International Labour Office.

Mankiw, N. Gregory. 1995. "The Growth of Nations." *Brookings Papers on Economic Activity* 1: 275–326.

Mankiw, N. Gregory, David Romer, and David N. Weil. 1992. "A Contribution to the Empirics of Economic Growth." *Quarterly Journal of Economics* (May): 407–437.

Manuelyan-Atinc, Tamar, and Michael Walton. 1998. "From Economic Crisis to Social Crisis," in World Bank, *East Asia: The Road to Recovery*.

Marcel, Mario, and Andrés Solimano. 1994. "The Distribution of Income and Economic Adjustment." In Barry P. Bosworth, Rudiger Dornbusch, and Raúl Labán, eds., *The Chilean Economy*. Washington: Brookings Institution.

Markandya, A. 1984. "The Welfare Measurement of Changes in Economic Mobility." *Economica* 51: 457–471.

Mauro, Paulo. 1995. "Corruption and Growth." *Quarterly Journal of Economics* 110(3) (August).

McMurrer, Daniel P., and Isabel V. Sawhill. 1998. *Getting Ahead: Economic and Social Mobility in America*. Washington, DC: The Urban Institute Press.

McNab, Robert M., and Robert E. Moore. 1998. "Trade Policy, Export Expansion, Human Capital and Growth." *Journal of International Trade and Economic Development* 7(2) (June): 237–256.

Mesa-Lago, Carmelo. 1991. "Social Security in Latin America and the Caribbean: A Comparative Assessment." In Ehtisham Ahmad, Jean Drèze, John Hills, and Amartya Sen, eds., *Social Security in Developing Countries*. Oxford: Clarendon Press.

Milanovic, Branko. 1994. "Determinants of Cross-Country Income Inequality: An 'Augmented' Kuznets Hypothesis," World Bank, Policy Research Working Paper 1246 (January).

Milanovic, Branko. 1999. "Explaining the Increase in Inequality During the Transition." *Economics of Transition* (May).

Mincer, Jacob. 1974. *Schooling, Experience, and Earnings*. New York: Columbia University Press for the NBER.

Minhas, B. S., L. R. Jain, S. M. Kansal, and M. R. Saluja. 1987. "On the Choice of Appropriate Consumer Price Indices and Data Sets for Estimating the Incidence of Poverty in India." *The Indian Economic Review* (January–June).

Morawetz, David. 1977. *Twenty-five Years of Economic Development, 1950 to 1975*. Baltimore: Johns Hopkins University Press for the World Bank.

Morduch, Jonathan. 1998. "The Grameen Bank: A Financial Reckoning." (August) Hoover Institution.

Morgan, James N. 1975. *Five Thousand American Families*. Ann Arbor, MI: Institute for Social Research, University of Michigan.

Myrdal, Gunnar. 1944. *An American Dilemma*. New York: Harper and Brothers.

Nee, Victor. 1994. "The Emergence of a Market Society: Changing Mechanisms of Stratification in China." *Working Papers on Transitions from State Socialism* 94.1 (April) Cornell University.

Nee, Victor. 1996. "The Emergence of a Market Society: Changing Mechanisms of Stratification in China." *American Journal of Sociology* (January).

Nee, Victor, and Raymond V. Liedka. 1995. "Institutions, Income Mobility and the Production of Inequality in Reforming State Socialism." Working Paper (September) Cornell University.

Nee, Victor, and Raymond V. Liedka. 1997. "Markets and Inequality in the Transition from State Socialism." In Manus I. Midlarsky, ed., *Inequality, Democracy, and Economic Development*. New York: Cambridge University Press.

Nelson, Richard R. 1956. "A Theory of the Low-Level Equilibrium Trap in Underdeveloped Economies." *American Economic Review* 46: 894–908.

Nielsen, François. 1994. "Income Inequality and Industrial Development: Dualism Revisited." *American Sociological Review* (October).

Nielsen, François, and Arthur S. Alderson. 1995. "Income Inequality, Development, and Dualism: results from an Unbalanced Cross-National Panel." *American Sociological Review* (October).

Nozick, Robert. 1974. *Anarchy, State, and Utopia*. Oxford: Basil Blackwell.

Nurkse, Ragnar. 1953. *Problems of Capital Formation in Underdeveloped Countries*. New York: Oxford University Press.

O'Higgins, Michael, and Stephen Jenkins. 1990. "Poverty in the EC: Estimates for 1975, 1980, and 1985." In Rudolph Teekens and Bernard M. S. van Praag, eds., *Analysing Poverty in the European Community: Policy Issues, Research Options, and Data Sources*.

OECD. Organization for Economic Cooperation and Development. 1993. "Earnings Inequality: Changes in the 1980s." *Employment Outlook* (July).

OECD. Organization for Economic Cooperation and Development. 1996. "Earnings Inequality, Low-Paid Employment and Earnings Mobility." *Employment Outlook* (July): 59–108.

OECD. Organization for Economic Cooperation and Development. 1997. "Earnings Mobility: Taking a Longer Run View." *Employment Outlook* (July).

Orshansky, Mollie. 1965. "Counting the Poor: Another Look at the Poverty Profile." *Social Security Bulletin* (January).

Oshima, Harry T. 1991. "Kuznets' Curve and Asian Income Distribution." In Toshiyuki Mizoguchi et al., eds., *Making Economies More Efficient and More Equitable: Factors Determining Income Distribution*. New York: Oxford University Press.

Oshima, Harry T. 1994. "The Impact of Technological Transformation on Historical Trends in Income Distribution of Asia and the West." *The Developing Economies* 22(3) (September): 237–255.

Osmani, S. R. 1991. "Social Security in South Asia." In Ehtisham Ahmad, Jean Drèze, John Hills, and Amartya Sen, eds., *Social Security in Developing Countries*. Oxford: Clarendon Press.

Otsuka, Keijiro, Hiroyuki Chuma, and Yujiro Hayami. 1992. "Land and Labor Contracts in Agrarian Economies: Theories and Facts." *Journal of Economic Literature* (December): 1965–2018.

Pack, Howard. 1997. "The Role of Exports in Asian Development." In Nancy Birdsall and Frederick Jaspersen, eds., *Pathways to Growth: Comparing East Asia and Latin America*. Washington: Inter-American Development Bank.

Page, John. 1994. "The East Asian Miracle: Four Lessons for Development Policy." In Stanley Fischer and Julio J. Rotemberg, eds., *NBER Macroeconomics Annual*: 219–269. Cambridge and London: MIT Press.

Papanek, Gustav F., and Oldrich Kyn. 1986. "The Effect on Income Distribution of Development, the Growth Rate, and Economic Strategy." *Journal of Development Economics* (September): 23, 55–65.

Parikh, Kirit, and T. N. Srinivasan. 1993. "Poverty Alleviation Policies in India." In Michael Lipton and Jacques van der Gaag, eds., *Including the Poor*. Washington: World Bank.

Park, Se-Il. 1999. "Labor Market Reform and the Social Safety Net in Korea." *Joint U.S.-Korea Academic Studies* 9.

Paukert, Felix. 1973. "Income Distribution at Different Levels of Development: A Survey of the Evidence." *International Labour Review* (August–September): 97–125.

Pencavel, John. 1996. "The Legal Framework for Collective Bargaining in Developing Economies." Stanford University working paper (June).

Perotti, Roberto. 1992. "Income Distribution, Politics, and Growth." *American Economic Review* (May): 311–316.

Perotti, Roberto. 1994. "Income Distribution and Investment." *European Economic Review*: 827–835.

Perotti, Roberto. 1996. "Growth, Income Distribution and Democracy: What the Data Say." *Journal of Economic Growth* 1: 149–187.

Persson, Torsten, and Guido Tabellini. 1992. "Growth, Distribution, and Politics." In Alex Cukierman, Zvi Hercowitz, and Leonardo Leiderman, eds., *Political Economy, Growth, and Business Cycles*. Cambridge and London: MIT Press.

Persson, Torsten, and Guido Tabellini. 1994. "Is Inequality Harmful for Growth?: Theory and Evidence." *American Economic Review*: 600–621.

Pestieau, Pierre. 1994. "Social Protection and Private Insurance: Reassessing the Role of Public Sector Versus Private Sector in Insurance." *Geneva Papers on Risk and Insurance* 19(2) (December).

Pigou, A. C. 1912. *Wealth and Welfare*. London: Macmillan.

Pitt, M. M., and S. R. Khandker. 1995. "The Impact of Group-Based Credit Programs on Poor Household in Bangladesh: Does the Gender of Participants Matter?" Brown University Working Paper.

Powelson, J. P., and R. Stock. 1987. *The Peasant Betrayed: Agriculture and Land Reform in the Third World*. Boston: Oelgeschlager, Gunn and Hain.

Psacharopoulos, George. 1994. "Returns to Investment in Education: A Global Update." *World Development* 22(9) (September): 1325–1343.

Psacharopoulos, George, and Jandhyala B. G. Tilak. 1991. "Schooling and Equity." In George Psacharopoulos, ed., *Essays on Poverty, Equity, and Growth*. Oxford and New York: Pergamon.

Psacharopoulos, George, Samuel Morley, Ariel Fiszbein, Haeduck Lee, and Bill Wood. 1993. *Poverty and Income Distribution in Latin America: The Story of the 1980s*. Washington: World Bank.

Putterman, L. 1989. "Agricultural Producer Cooperatives." In P. K. Bardhan, ed., *The Economic Theory of Agrarian Institutions*. Oxford: Clarendon.

Pyatt, Graham. 1989. "Social Evaluation Criteria." In C. Dagum and M. Zenga, *Income and Wealth Distribution, Inequality and Poverty*. Berlin: Springer-Verlag.

Pyatt, Graham, Chau-Nan Chen, and John Fei. 1980. "The Distribution of Income by Factor Components." *Quarterly Journal of Economics*: 451–473.

Quibria, M. G., and T. N. Srinivasan. 1994. "Introduction." In M. G. Quibria, ed., *Rural Poverty in Developing Asia*. Manila: Asian Development Bank.

Ram, Rati. 1988. "Economic Development and Income Inequality: Further Evidence on the U-Curve Hypothesis." *World Development* 16(11): 1371–1376.

Ramachandran, V. K. 1997. "On Kerala's Development Achievements." In Jean Drèze and Amartya K. Sen, eds., *Indian Development: Selected Regional Perspectives*. Delhi: Oxford University Press.

Randolph, Susan M., and William F. Lott. 1993. "Can the Kuznets Effect Be Relied on to Induce Equalizing Growth?" *World Development* 21(5): 829–840.

Randolph, Susan M., and Eileen Trzcinski. 1989. "Relative Earnings Mobility in a Third World Country." *World Development* 17(4) (April): 513–524.

Ranis, Gustav. 1974. "Taiwan." In Hollis B. Chenery et al., eds., *Redistribution with Growth*. New York: Oxford University Press.

Ranis, Gustav. 1978. "Equity with Growth in Taiwan: How Special is the 'Special Case'?" *World Development* 6(3): 397–409.

Ranis, Gustav. 1995. "Another Look at the East Asian Miracle." *The World Bank Economic Review* 9(3): 509–534.

Ravallion, Martin. 1993. "Growth, Inequality and Poverty: New Evidence on Old Questions." (March) World Bank.

Ravallion, Martin. 1994. *Poverty Comparisons*. Chur, Switzerland: Harwood Academic Publishers.

Ravallion, Martin. 1995. "Growth and Poverty: Evidence for the Developing World." *Economics Letters*: 411–417.

Ravallion, Martin. 1996. "Data in Transition: Assessing Rural Living Standards in Southern China." *China Economic Review* 7(1): 23–56.

Ravallion, Martin, and Shaohua Chen. 1997. "What Can New Survey Data Tell Us About Recent Changes in Distribution and Poverty?" *World Bank Economic Review* 11(2): 357–382.

Ravallion, Martin, and Gaurav Datt. 1995. "Is Targeting Through a Work Requirement Efficient: Some Evidence from Rural India." In Dominique van de Walle and Kimberly Nead, eds., *Public Spending and the Poor: Theory and Evidence*. Baltimore: Johns Hopkins University Press.

Ravallion, Martin, and Monica Huppi. 1991. "Measuring Changes in Poverty: A Methodological Case Study of Indonesia During an Adjustment Period." *World Bank Economic Review* 5(1) (January): 57–82.

Ravallion, Martin, Gaurav Datt, and Dominique van de Walle. 1991. "Quantifying Absolute Poverty in the Developing World." *Review of Income and Wealth*.

Ray, Debraj. 1993. "Labor Markets, Adaptive Mechanisms and Nutritional Status." In Pranab Bardhan et al., eds., *Essays in Honor of K. N. Raj*. London: Oxford University Press.

Ray, Debraj. 1998. *Development Economics*. Princeton: Princeton University Press.

Republic of China. 1999. *Statistical Yearbook of the Republic of China*.

Robinson, Sherman. 1976. "A Note on the U Hypothesis Relating Income Inequality and Economic Development." *American Economic Review* (June): 437–440.

Rodgers, Gerry, and Rolph van der Hoeven. 1995. *The Poverty Agenda: Trends and Policy Options*. Geneva: International Institute for Labour Studies.

Rodrik, Dani. 1995a. "Getting Interventions Right: How South Korea and Taiwan Got Rich." *Economic Policy* 20 (April): 55–107.

Rodrik, Dani. 1995b. "Trade and Industrial Policy Reform." Chapter 45 in Jere Behrman and T. N. Srinivasan, eds., *Handbook of Development Economics* 3. Amsterdam: Elsevier Science, North Holland.

Roemer, Michael, and Mary Kay Gugerty. 1997. "Does Economic Growth Reduce Poverty?" CAER II Discussion Paper Numbers 4 and 5 (April). Harvard Institute for International Development.

Rose-Ackerman, Susan. 1999. *Corruption and Government: Causes, Consequences, and Reform*. New York: Cambridge University Press.

Rosenzweig, Mark R., and Kenneth I. Wolpin. 1993. "Credit Market Constraints, Consumption Smoothing, and the Accumulation of Durable Production Assets in Low-Income Countries: Investment in Bullocks in India." *Journal of Political Economy* 101: 223–244.

Ruggles, Patricia. 1990. *Drawing the Line: Alternative Poverty Measures and Their Implications for Public Policy*. Washington, DC: Urban Institute Press.

Sachs, Jeffrey D. 1990. "Social Conflict and Populist Policies in Latin America." Occasional Paper No. 9, International Center for Economic Growth. San Francisco: ICS Press.

Sachs, Jeffrey D., and Andrew M. Warner. 1995. "Economic Reform and the Process of Global Integration." *Brookings Papers on Economic Activity* 1: 1–118.

Sachs, Jeffrey D., and Andrew M. Warner. 1997. "Sources of Slow Growth in African Economies." *Journal of African Economies* 6(3) (October): 335–376.

Sadoulet, Elisabeth. 1992. "Labor-Service Tenancy Contracts in a Latin American Context." *American Economic Review* 82: 1031–1042.

Sawhill, Isabel V., and Mark Condon. 1992. "Is U.S. Income Inequality Really Growing?" *Policy Bites* 13 (June).

Saith, Ashwani. 1983. "Development and Distribution: A Critique of the Cross Country U Hypothesis." *Journal of Development Economics* (December).

Sala-i-Martin, Xavier. 1997. "I Just Ran Two Million Regressions." *American Economic Review* (May): 178–183.

Samuelson, Paul A. 1947. *Foundations of Economic Analysis*. Cambridge, MA: Harvard University Press.

Saposnik, Rubin. 1981. "Rank Dominance in Income Distributions." *Public Choice*.

Schultz, T. Paul. 1988. "Education Investments and Returns." In Hollis Chenery and T. N. Srinivasan, eds., *Handbook of Development Economics*. Rotterdam: North Holland.

Schultz, T. Paul. 1998. "Inequality in the Distribution of Personal Income in the World: How Is It Changing and Why?" *Journal of Population Economics* 11(3) (June): 307–344.

Scott, Christopher D., and Julie A. Litchfield. 1994. "Inequality, Mobility and the Determinants of Income Among the Rural Poor in Chile, 1968–1986." STICERD, Working Paper No. 53 (March). London School of Economics.

Seidl, Christian. 1988. "Poverty Measurement: A Survey." In D. Bös, M. Rose, and C. Seidl, *Welfare and Efficiency in Public Economics*: 71–147. Berlin: Springer-Verlag.

Sen, Amartya K. 1966. "Peasants and Dualism With and Without Surplus Labour." *Journal of Political Economy* 74(3).

Sen, Amartya K. 1970. *Collective Choice and Social Welfare*. San Francisco: Holden Day.

Sen, Amartya K. 1973. *On Economic Inequality*. New York: Oxford.

Sen, Amartya K. 1976. "Poverty: An Ordinal Approach to Measurement." *Econometrica* 44: 219–231.

Sen, Amartya K. 1983. "Poor, Relatively Speaking." *Oxford Economic Papers* 35 (July): 153–169. Reprinted in Amartya K. Sen 1984. *Resources, Values and Development*: 325–345. Cambridge: Harvard University Press.

Sen, Amartya K. 1984. *Resources, Values and Development*. Cambridge, MA: Harvard University Press.

Sen, Amartya K. 1985. *Commodities and Capabilities*. Amsterdam: North-Holland.

Sen, Amartya K. 1992. *Inequality Reexamined*. Oxford: Clarendon Press.

Sen, Amartya K. 1997. "From Income Inequality to Economic Inequality." *Southern Economic Journal* 64(2): 384–401.

Sen, Amartya K. 1999. "The Possibility of Social Choice." *American Economic Review* 89(3) (June): 349–378.

Sheahan, John. 1987. *Patterns of Development in Latin America*. Princeton: Princeton University Press.

Sheahan, John, and Enrique Iglesias. 1998. "Kinds and Causes of Inequality in Latin America." In Nancy Birdsall, Carol Graham, and Richard Sabot, eds., *Beyond Tradeoffs: Market Reforms and Equitable Growth in Latin America*. Washington: Brookings Institution and Inter-American Development Bank.

Shorrocks, Anthony F. 1978. "The Measurement of Mobility." *Econometrica* 46: 1013–1024.

Shorrocks, Anthony F. 1983. "Ranking Income Distributions." *Economica* 50 (February): 3–17.

Shorrocks, Anthony F. 1993. "On the Hart Measure of Income Mobility." In M. Casson and J. Creedy, eds., *Industrial Concentration and Economic Inequality*. Cambridge: Edward Elgar.

Shorrocks, Anthony F. 1998. "Deprivation Profiles and Deprivation Indices." In Stephen P. Jenkins, Arie Kapteyn, and Bernard M. S. van Praag, *The Distribution of Welfare and Household Production*. Cambridge: Cambridge University Press.

Shorrocks, Anthony F., and James E. Foster. 1987. "Transfer Sensitive Inequality Measures." *Review of Economic Studies* 54: 485–497.

Soderberg, Johan. 1991. "Wage Differentials in Sweden, 1725–1950." In Y. S. Brenner, Harmut Kaelble, and Mark Thomas, *Income Distribution in Historical Perspective*. Cambridge University Press.

Squire, Lyn. 1981. *Employment Policy in Developing Countries: A Survey of Issues and Evidence*. New York: Oxford University Press.

Squire, Lyn. 1993. "Fighting Poverty." *American Economic Review* (May): 377–382.

Srinivasan, T. N., and Pranab K. Bardhan. 1974. *Poverty and Income Distribution in India*. Calcutta: Statistical Publishing Society.

Srinivasan, T. N., and Pranab K. Bardhan. 1988. "Introduction." In T. N. Srinivasan and Pranab K. Bardhan, eds., *Rural Poverty in South Asia*. New York: Columbia University Press.

Stallings, Barbara, Nancy Birdsall, and Julie Clugage. 1998. "Growth and Inequality: Do Regional Patterns Redeem Kuznets?" In Andrés Solimano, ed., *Equity, Growth and Social Policy*. Washington: Inter-American Development Bank.

Stewart, Frances. 1995. *Adjustment and Poverty: Options and Choices*. London: Routledge.

Stiglitz, Joseph E. 1993. "The Role of the State in Financial Markets." *Proceedings of the World Bank Annual Conference on Development Economics*: 19–52.

Stiglitz, Joseph E. 1996. "Some Lessons from the East Asian Miracle." *World Bank Research Observer* 11(2) (August): 151–177.

Stiglitz, Joseph E. 1997. "An Agenda for Development in the Twentieth Century." Keynote Address to the Ninth Annual Bank Conference on Development Economics, Washington (April).

Stiglitz, Joseph E. 1998a. "More Instruments and Broader Goals: Moving Toward the Post-Washington Consensus." The 1998 WIDER Annual Lecture (January).

Stiglitz, Joseph E. 1998b. "The Role of Government in the Contemporary World." In Vito Tanzi and Ke-Young Chu, eds., *Income Distribution and High-Quality Growth*. Cambridge and London: MIT Press.

Stiglitz, Joseph E., and Marilou Uy. 1996. "Financial Markets, Public Policy, and the East Asian Miracle." *World Bank Research Observer* 11(2): 249–276.

Strauss, John, and Duncan Thomas. 1995. "Human Resources: Empirical Modeling of Household and Family Decisions." Chapter 34 in Jere Behrman and T. N. Srinivasan, eds., *Handbook of Development Economics Volume III*. Amsterdam: Elsevier.

Strauss, John, and Duncan Thomas. 1998. "Health, Nutrition, and Economic Development." *Journal of Economic Literature* 36(2) (June): 766–817.

Streeten, Paul. 1981. *First Things First: Meeting Basic Human Needs in the Developing Countries*. New York: Oxford University Press.

Tan, Jee-Peng, and Alain Mingat. 1992. *Education in Asia: A Comparative Study of Cost and Financing*. Washington: World Bank.

Tanzi, Vito. 1998. "Corruption Around the World: Causes, Consequences, Scope, and Cures." *International Monetary Fund Staff Papers* 45(4) (December): 559–594.

Temple, Jonathan. 1999. "The New Growth Evidence." *Journal of Economic Literature* 37 (March): 112–156.

Thomas, Mark. 1991. "The Evolution of Inequality in Australia in the Nineteenth Century." In Y. S. Brenner, Harmut Kaelble, and Mark Thomas, *Income Distribution in Historical Perspective*. Cambridge: Cambridge University Press.

Thorbecke, Erik, and Christian Morrisson. 1989. "Institutions, Policies and Agricultural Performance." *World Development* (September).

Timmer, C. Peter. 1997. "How Well Do the Poor Connect to the Growth Process?" Harvard University (December).

Todaro, Michael. 1994. *Economic Development in the Third World*. 5th ed. New York: Longman.

Trzcinski, Eileen, and Susan Randolph. 1991. "Human Capital Investment and Relative Earnings Mobility: The Role of Education, Training, Migration, and Job Search." *Economic Development and Cultural Change*: 153–168.

Turnham, David. 1993. *Employment and Development: A New Review of Evidence*. Paris: OECD.

United Nations. n.d. *Human Development Report* (annual).

United Nations Development Programme. 1998. *Overcoming Human Poverty*. New York: United Nations.

van de Walle, Dominique. 1995. "Incidence and Targeting: An Overview of Implications for Research and Policy." In Dominque van de Walle and Kimberly Nead, eds., *Public Spending and the Poor: Theory and Evidence*. Baltimore: Johns Hopkins University Press for the World Bank.

van de Walle, Dominique. 1997. "Broad or Narrow Targeting?" World Bank.

van Zyl, Johan, Johann Kirsten, and Hans P. Binswanger, eds. 1996. *Agriculture and Land Reform in South Africa: Policies, Markets, and Mechanisms*. Cape Town: Oxford University Press.

Wade, Robert. 1990. *Governing the Market*. Princeton: Princeton University Press.

Walton, Michael, and Tamar Manuelyan Atinc. 1998. "Social Consequences of the East Asian Financial Crisis." (November) World Bank.

Watts, Harold W. 1968. "An Economic Definition of Poverty." In Daniel Patrick Moynihan, ed. *On Understanding Poverty*. New York: Basic Books.

Weisskoff, Richard. 1970. "Income Distribution of Economic Growth in Puerto Rico, Argentina, and Mexico." *Review of Income and Wealth* (December): 303–332.

Welch, Finis. 1999. "In Defense of Inequality." *American Economic Review* 89(2) (May): 1–17.

Williamson, Jeffrey G. 1985. *Did British Capitalism Breed Inequality?* Boston: Allen and Unwin.

Williamson, Jeffrey G. 1991. *Inequality, Poverty, and History*. Cambridge, MA: Basil Blackwell.

Williamson, Jeffrey G., and P. H. Lindert. 1980. *American Inequality: A Macroeconomic History*. New York: Academic Press.

Williamson, John. 1990. "What Washington Means by Policy Reform." In John Williamson, ed., *Latin American Adjustment: How Much Has Happened*. Washington, DC: Institute for International Economics.

Wolff, Edward N. 1997. *Economics of Poverty, Inequality, and Discrimination*. Cincinnati: South-Western College Publishing.

Wood, Adrian. 1997. "Openness and Wage Inequality in Developing Countries: The Latin American Challenge to East Asian Conventional Wisdom." *World Bank Economic Review* 11(1) (January): 33–57.

World Bank. 1993. *The East Asian Miracle*. Washington: World Bank.

World Bank. 1995. "Ghana: Promoting Growth, Reducing Poverty." *Findings Report* (November).

World Bank. 1997a. *Poverty Reduction and the World Bank: Progress in Fiscal 1996 and 1997*. Washington: World Bank.

World Bank. 1997b. *Poverty and Income Distribution in a High-Growth Economy [Chile]: 1987–1995*, Report No. 16377-CH.

World Bank. 1997c. *Sharing Rising Incomes*. Washington: World Bank.

World Bank. 1999. *http://www.worldbank.org/poverty/data/trends/income.htm.*

World Bank. n.d. *http://www.worldbank.org/poverty/index.htm.*

World Bank. n.d. *World Development Report* (annual). Washington: World Bank.

Xu, Kuan, and Lars Osberg. 1998. "A Distribution-Free Test for Deprivation Dominance." *Econometric Reviews* 17: 415–431.

Yaqub, Shahin. 1999. "Poverty Dynamics in Developing Countries—A Literature Review." Paper presented at the IDS/IFPRI Workshop on Economic Mobility and Poverty Dynamics in Developing Countries (April). Brighton: Institute of Development Studies.

Yotopoulos, Pan A., and Jeffrey B. Nugent. 1976. *Economics of Development: Empirical Investigations*. New York: Harper and Row.

Young, Alwyn. 1995. "The Tyranny of Numbers: Confronting the Statistical Realities of the East Asian Growth Experience." *Quarterly Journal of Economics*: 641–680.

Zhao, Renwei. 1993. "Three Features of the Distribution of Income During the Transition to Reform." In Keith Griffin and Renwei Zhao, eds., *The Distribution of Income in China*. New York: St. Martin's Press.

Zheng, Buhong. 1997. "Aggregate Poverty Measures." *Journal of Economic Surveys* 11(2): 123–162.

Index